New Yorkers

A Feisty People Who Will Unsettle, Madden, Amuse and Astonish You

Clifford Browder

New Yorkers: A Feisty People Who Will Unsettle, Madden, Amuse and Astonish You

For information about this title or to order other books and/or electronic media, contact the publisher:
BROWDERBOOKS
BROWDERBOOKS@gmail.com

ISBN: 978-1-7333782-0-8 (Print)
       978-1-7333782-1-5 (eBook)

Printed in the United States of America

Cover and Interior Design by 1106 Design

Contents

Part 5: Glories and Horrors of the Past: Cholera, the Beatles, and the Miracle of Light............ 285

Introduction

T hoUgh Born anD raiseD in the Midwest, I am a longtime
New Yorker and over the years have seen many changes.
I reside high above the Magnolia Bakery of *Sex and the City* fame
in Greenwich Village. When I first came here in 1953 to do graduate work in French at Columbia University, I had to get used to
the city's bigness, noise, and bustle, its pace and its attractions.
But get used to them I did, to the point where I needed them,
craved them, and celebrated them. For me, New York is the most
exciting city in the world. It's special, it's unique. I have even
expressed this in an equation:

$$intensity + diversity = creativity = New\ York$$

The intensity of New York is experienced immediately by
anyone coming to the city, and the city's diversity will leap out
at you wherever you may go. Which makes the city incredibly
creative; things happen here: the Gay Pride movement, Occupy
Wall Street, opera and ballet, the Empire State Building, 9/11, and
yes, the Donald and his Tower. Not everything here is admirable,
but in spite of all its faults, I love this city; I couldn't do without

it. A sign that appeared at the entrance to the Staten Island ferry once asked, **New York: Is There Anywhere Else?**

Not everyone would agree. We New Yorkers are a very special breed, tough and savvy. We challenge, we complain. And we know that New York is not for everyone, nor should it be. For quiet, for peace of mind and the illusion of stability, go elsewhere. Here are flux and change, the perennial strife of old vs. new, the turmoil and fervor of nine million strivers. We New Yorkers are great doers; we savor the charm of the old and often want to preserve it, but at the same time we forge ahead, we create, we *do*.

In this book I want to share with others what it is to be a New Yorker, who we are, how we live, what we do, our past and present glories and horrors. Ask twenty New Yorkers about these things, and you'll get twenty answers. What I'm sharing here is *my* New York. The chapters derive from posts for my blog, "No Place for Normal: New York," which is about anything and everything New York, past and present. This is the city I love; I hope you'll love it, too. Or hate it, if you must. The main thing is to know it; it's unique.

Part 1

WHO WE ARE:
800 LANGUAGES,
HUSTLERS, BASQUES,
AND CHORUS BOYS

Chapter 1
Diversity

I LoVe neW York For its diversity. If you go out on errands, you may hear Spanish, Chinese, French, German, Italian, Russian or some other Slavic language, Korean, Japanese, and who knows what else? You may see a woman in a sari, a bearded man in a turban, a bunch of giggling young girls wearing head scarves, African-American women with their hair done up in a bun on top, a woman in a burka with only her eyes visible, dark-suited Orthodox Jews with long, curly sidelocks, and women of various ethnicities wearing granny skirts or miniskirts or pantsuits or whatever is or is not in vogue.

In New York today only 51 percent of the population speak English at home, the other 49 percent speak any of a multitude of languages. Students in the public schools speak 176 languages, and in the borough of Queens alone there are 138, but some estimates for the whole city range as high as 800 languages in all. In May 2019, when I gave a book release party in my apartment for my novel *The Eye That Never Sleeps,* there were conversations going on simultaneously in three rooms. One guest came out of the living room to report, "We just realized that we've got eleven languages among us!" And when I mentioned this later to one of the guests, a young woman from Pakistan, she smiled and said, "Actually, it was twelve." At home in Pakistan, her family speaks English, Urdu, and Gujarati.

At election time instructions come to voters in English, Spanish, Chinese, and at least one other language—Japanese? Korean?—that I can't identify. My health insurance plan's monthly notice of claims filed includes phone numbers for translations into Spanish, French, French Creole, Italian, Russian, Portuguese, Polish, Arabic, Chinese, Cantonese Chinese, Tagalog, Vietnamese, Korean, Hindi, and Japanese. So it is that I now know how to say "attention"—in the sense of "pay attention"—in multiple languages, for example: *1. paunaw 2. chú 'y 3. Atansyon 4. uwaga 5. atenção.* (Can you identify these five languages? The answers are at the end of this chapter.)

But these languages, however baffling for Americans, are not uncommon. How about Vlashki, a variation of Istro-Romanian, spoken in Queens? Or Garifuna, an Arawakan language spoken today in Honduras and Belize, but also in the Bronx and Brooklyn? Or Aramaic, a Semitic Syrian language spoken long ago by Jesus and his disciples, or Chamorro from the Mariana Islands? Or Bukhari, a Jewish language with more speakers in Queens than in Uzbekistan or Tajikistan? Many of these are endangered, as their few elderly speakers die off, though in some cases there is a concerted effort to keep the language alive. New York is a refuge for lost languages, but as the children and grandchildren of immigrants learn English, it is also a graveyard.

Immigrants gravitate to the health care field. I have had ophthalmologists who were from Russia and Israel. My podiatrist is from

India, and his assistant from Guyana. My dentist is a Chinese American from Hong Kong with an assistant from Ecuador who is delighted that I remember her nationality. My partner Bob had a Norwegian doctor, a Haitian home care aide, and at one time a Cambodian nurse.

Over the years Bob and I dined in German, French, Spanish, Italian, Jewish, Indian, Mexican, Russian, Chinese, Japanese, Thai, and Burmese restaurants. The menus might be in English, but the dishes were authentic, as were the waiters and waitresses. (The Burmese restaurant offered food so highly spiced that my system was hugely roiled all the following day.) Memorable among our dining experiences have been Bengali meals of many courses served by a friend from Calcutta, and splendid Italian meals at our favorite restaurant, Gargiulo's, near the boardwalk on Coney Island. Exceptional was a sumptuous Japanese meal beginning with octopus, which our American host described as "the Japanese chewing gum," following which his Japanese wife served us dishes of sukiyaki that were a feast for both the palate and the eye.

Diversity characterized the city from the very start. Back in Dutch days New Amsterdam was inhabited by Dutch, Walloons, Norwegians, Germans, Italians, Bohemians, Africans both free and slave, Mohawks, Munsees, Montauks, and others—a population like no other on the continent. Many were refugees. There were American colonists who had fled the puritanical New England colonies, where even dancing around a maypole and drinking beer were termed "beastly practices of ye mad Bacchanalians." Sephardic Jews came later, having been expelled from Spain by their Catholic Majesties Ferdinand and Isabella. And Huguenots would follow, having fled France after his Solar Majesty Louis XIV revoked the Edict of Nantes, which had protected Protestants from persecution. In the nineteenth century large numbers of Irish would come, and Germans and Italians, and Ashkenazi Jews from Eastern Europe, all fleeing famine or poverty or oppression and hoping desperately for better.

The city's diversity is seen in its occupations as well. Some are unusual, some unique, and some just flat-out weird. Here are a few:

Structural engineer. Suppose you're buying an old house or a brownstone. How do you know if it's architecturally sound? Before closing the deal you hire a structural engineer to look it over. A walk-through inspection costs $400 to $800, but if it saves you from acquiring a nightmare, it's worth it.

Environmental consultant. Environmental regulations can be a baffling maze of requirements, and New York is fiercely regulated. In old buildings, asbestos may have been used in construction, and lead in paint; both are toxic. Waste must be disposed of properly; your building may be in a flood zone; your planned renovation may have undesirable consequences; and so on. If, as a property owner or business, you aren't sure if you're complying and you fear a fine, you hire an environmental consultant to make sure you're in compliance.

Wigmaker. If you are a celebrity or philanthropist or socialite concerned about your appearance, or a singer in an opera or a Broadway musical, you go to him (it's usually a "him") for a custom-made hairpiece or wig. This is a centuries-old trade, making wigs by hand so that the hairline blends into the skin. The cost? Three thousand dollars and up. Wigs are in great demand, but wigmakers are being supplanted by imports from China, where the painstaking work is done by thousands of factory workers. The solution, if the hairline is a challenge? Wear bangs.

Channel master. In this age of air travel it's easy to forget that ocean liners and cargo ships still come and go in the port of

New York. But the Outer Harbor, the waters beyond the Narrows but this side of Sandy Hook, is a maze of shallow channels between shifting sandbars, and risky to navigate. So who guides vessels through this labyrinth? A channel master, or pilot, who has learned the rocks, reefs, shoals, pipelines, and cables in the harbor, so he or she can board incoming and outgoing vessels and guide them through the channels.

Crematory manager. Just as cemeteries have to be managed, so do crematories, and this is the professional who does it. Order, efficiency, and tact are required, and if luxury atmosphere is desired, marble floors and stained-glass windows. The cremations are done in high-temperature retorts. The walls of the installation may be lined with niches containing the ashes of the deceased, or the ashes may be returned to the family or friends, while a smokestack conveys heavenward the fumes of the cremations in progress. Online ads offer low-cost cremations, but the total cost can be in the hundreds, if not thousands, of dollars. Often a family operation.

Tattoo artist. They're in parlors all over the five boroughs, waiting to draw on or color or stain the blank canvas of your skin with cartoons, Polynesian designs, Old Glory, crosses, monster heads, or whatever you wish, making you come off as weird, funny, patriotic, threatening, or defiant.

Photos show them to be gentle old men, or bearded machos, or spectacled Asians, or females with bold red lips and fiercely mascaraed eyes. So if you want to be so adorned, Bang Bang and Sweet Sue and Megan Massacre are waiting to serve you at a cost of $100 and up, sometimes way up.

Forensic pathologist. What happens to the body in a case of suicide or murder or any death deemed suspicious and not the result of natural causes? There's an autopsy, and that's the work of a forensic pathologist garbed in a long blue monkey suit, gloved, and wearing a white cap, with a blue mask over his or her nose and mouth. Using an array of sharp instruments, they cut into torsos, remove organs, saw into a skull so they can lift out the brain. And where is this jolly work performed? In the office of the Chief Medical Examiner, a drab building on First Avenue. When finished with a particular "subject," they make their report and perhaps—the most difficult part of their day—interview the relatives. As the last person to care for the deceased, they may feel a certain satisfaction. However unpleasant, their work is essential and well paid.

Estate liquidator. So the body has been disposed of, but what about that apartment crammed with clothing, books, utensils, furnishings, and what have you? You're the executor and you need to clear the place out before the lease expires. The job is beyond you, so what do you do? You call in an estate liquidator who will make an appraisal, and for a fee, empty the whole place out even to the point of "broom cleaning," meaning that his team will sweep up debris. Liquidators are the exterminating angels of material objects. They bestow the gift of emptiness, the purity of unoccupied space. But not for long; the next tenant will soon be moving in.

Finally, let's expand the notion of diversity even further. When I once went to a Mexican restaurant on Hudson Street, I took a table in front that gave me a good view of the front half of the restaurant. Sitting at the bar were two men, obviously partners, who were talking briskly to a woman who was clearly a close friend. At the end of the bar was a woman with long blonde hair who was hunched over her mobile device, giving no heed to anyone or anything else. At a table to my left was a Chinese-American gentleman with a Caucasian woman. And to my right, at a large table against the wall, were four men, a three-year-old girl, and an infant. One of the men was cradling the infant in his arms, while a younger man beside him looked on fondly; I gradually realized that this was a gay male couple with a child. And the other two men? One black and one white, they were sitting with their backs to me and with the three-year-old girl between them: a second gay male couple with a child.

At one point the three at the bar began talking with those at the table, with appropriate oohs and aahs over the two kids. Then a heterosexual couple came in, the man with a dark beard and the woman with long blonde hair, and sat at a table at a certain distance from the other diners, seemingly oblivious of them. On the wall I noticed two signs:

DON'T WORRY
BE HAPPY

DEAR SANTA
IS IT TOO LATE
TO BE GOOD?

Finally the two gay couples got up to leave, with all the bustle and to-do involved in preparing young children for the rigors of a wintry day: scarves, mittens, coats, and a stroller for the infant. As they left, one of the men turned to me and said with a smile, "West Village—all the gay guys," and departed. The hetero couple were still dining quietly at their table, and the woman at the end of the bar was still hunched over her mobile device. And the menu and waiter were Mexican.

Answers to language quiz:

1. Tagalog
2. Vietnamese
3. French Creole
4. Polish
5. Portuguese

Diversity is what this city and this nation are all about. Those in high places should keep this well in mind.

Chapter 2
The Heartland vs. New York

M
anY oBserVers eXpLoreD the meaning of "the heartland," when voters in that region gave the 2016 election to Donald Trump. But what exactly is the heartland? Obviously, it's a central region far from the coasts, but this is vague. I have always taken it to mean the Midwest, where I'm from. A recent survey said that residents of twelve states described them as being in the Midwest, which then includes everything from Ohio west to Nebraska, and from Minnesota south to Missouri. But if you think of it as all of the nation that is far from the coasts, you would have to include everything as far west as the Rocky Mountains and as far east as the Appalachians, as well as states like Tennessee and Arkansas that have always been considered Southern. Another definition sees the heartland as the nation's breadbasket, which then includes all states with a large percentage of farmland: the states of the Great Plains—the Dakotas, Nebraska, Kansas, and Oklahoma—plus Texas, Iowa, and parts of Illinois and Missouri. It has even been suggested that the heartland is where baseball is popular, which takes in the traditional Midwest. Given these conflicting definitions,

perhaps it is best to endorse the opinion of some historians that the heartland is above all a state of mind.

So what is this state of mind, and how does it differ from New York? I think at once of Midwestern values: a laid-back way of looking at things, as opposed to the fast pace and intensity of New York. Midwesterners think of their part of the country as the norm; for them, the rest of the country, which most definitely includes New York, is abnormal or at least a departure from that norm. "Come back to the *real* America," a Midwestern friend once said to me, and he was only half joking; he really thought his part of the country was the authentic America, and the two coasts a kind of aberration. This "authentic" America thinks of itself as quiet, sane, reasonable, not given to extremes. It believes in what it thinks are traditional American values; it is patriotic, honors the flag, and is usually—though not always—inclined to trust the government. And it goes to church, meaning one of the well-established churches, Catholic or Protestant, rather than some new sect that is noisy, self-promoting, and evangelical; here, too, it shuns extremes.

All of which may be a myth, since there are Midwesterners who are not altogether sane and reasonable, who are vastly suspicious of government, and who don't go to church. But in the 1930s and 1940s—yes, way back then—I grew up in a traditional Midwest and can certify that it did once exist, and probably still does, albeit in a modified form.

The Midwest that I grew up in—Evanston, the first suburb north of Chicago—was suburban, well educated, professional, not grievously wounded by the Great Depression, and very WASP. It flourished on the fringe of Chicago, a great, noisy, hectic metropolis that both beckoned and repelled us Evanstonians. We flocked to it for jobs and shopping and theater, while at the same time distancing ourselves from it as an utterly corrupt and Democratic city reeking of liquor, vice, and crime. As regards the first, I must explain that Evanston back then was officially bone dry, and had been ever since the founding of Northwestern University, whose 1855 charter forbade the sale of liquor within four miles of the campus—a ban that preceded the development of the town itself. Teetotaling Evanstonians looked with horror at Howard Street, the boundary between Evanston and Chicago, where liquor stores lined the south side of the street, as if eyeing Evanston with scorn and cupidity. Not that all Evanstonians eschewed alcohol. The strange fumes emanating from the discarded bottles of one neighboring house, detected by me on childhood expeditions up the alley behind our house, told me otherwise. But to get the stuff one had to drive south to Chicago or west to regions just beyond the ban, a zone sought out regularly by bibulous Northwestern students.

This heartland of my childhood was WASP to the core, and Republican. WASP, but not rabidly so. When a new family moved onto a block, one neighbor might say to another, "They're Catholic, you know," to which the other might reply with a muted "Oh." Likewise, "They're Jewish, you know," or more circumspectly, "They're of a certain religion." Yes, there were African Americans (a term then unknown), but one hardly knew them, for they lived in circumscribed enclaves and weren't allowed on the public beaches, except for one beach reserved for them. The churches were aware of these practices, disapproved, but weren't ready to campaign against them. All in all, the status quo reigned supreme, and as I grew up I accepted it as the norm, even though that vast metropolis south of Howard Street was a mix of ethic groups— Polish, Swedish, German, Italian, Irish—unknown to Evanston.

And this heartland was Republican and deplored and denounced Franklin Delano Roosevelt and his New Deal. And it was isolationist as well, thinking of itself as a sane, peace-loving heartland, immune to the warmongering of the east and west coasts, which it viewed as obsessively concerned with the doings of totalitarian states in far distant places. But when World War II came, courtesy of the Japanese attack on Pearl Harbor in December 1941, Evanston was outdone by no one in professions of patriotism, and immediately put a guard around our waterworks to prevent sabotage by the treacherous Japanese. Even the rabidly isolationist *Chicago Tribune,* a fanatical foe of the president, proclaimed:

MY COUNTRY RIGHT OR WRONG

From then on war bonds were bought, scrap metal collected, victory gardens planted, and rationing accepted. This left only one isolationist that I was aware of: my father, who declared that if the king of Sweden, a country neutral in both world wars, came over here and ran for president, he'd vote for him.

When, in 1953, I came to live in New York, as a child of the heartland I was baffled by newspapers in languages I couldn't read or identify. That my dormitory was on 114th Street, and my room on the fifteenth floor, amazed me, for I had trouble adjusting to buildings that high in a city with 114 streets and more. My forays into the wilds of Chicago had only gone so far; I had never lived in a tall building, seen an Orthodox Jew, or dined in a Chinese restaurant. I was told by a new friend not to wear "bluey blues" or "browny browns"—"Don't be one of *those.*" I learned to laugh at Jewish jokes about the mother whose son was a doctor, and to use and misuse a whole new stock of words: *schlep, chutzpah, mishegosh, kvetch, schmooze,* and by way of congratulations, *Mazel Tov!*

But this didn't make me a New Yorker—not yet, at least. That New Yorkers differed greatly from Midwesterners was borne upon me in a thousand ways. New Yorkers are intense, highly motivated, cosmopolitan, opinionated yet tolerant, skeptical, diverse. They are direct and to the point, which visitors may take for rudeness. They opine about theater and the arts the way the heartland talks about sports. And they drink. Rare is the social occasion—probably an AA meeting—where some form of alcohol isn't served. Even Union Theological Seminary welcomed students with cocktails. A friend of mine who studied there long ago told me how such occasions often prompted a fiery declaration, posted publicly the next day and addressed to students and faculty alike: *You are all going to hell!* So declared some newcomer, usually a fundamentalist from the Bible Belt, who after one short semester decamped for the dryer, less sin-prone confines of home. But not me. Eager to become an urban sophisticate, I began imbibing martinis, sometimes with deplorable results.

Nothing about New Yorkers is muted; they sign petitions, write letters, demonstrate. They think big, they talk loud, they *do.* Are there exceptions? Of course. But the New Yorkers of my acquaintance are a far cry from the Midwest of my child-hood, whose suburban confines stopped abruptly short of the vast, unruly, corrupt, and fascinating city of Chicago. Yes, the "heartland" is probably above all a state of mind and therefore subjective—a state of mind far removed from such monstrous and complex conglomerations as New York.

Today, many Midwesterners like myself have forsaken the heartland, wherever or whatever it is, for noisy, corrupt, com-plex, and exciting New York, but on occasion we also retreat to our heartland for a bit of sanity and repose. New Yorkers of my acquaintance describe the people of the heartland as decent, courteous, and kind. I see families of them walking about the West Village, their noses in a guidebook, or perched high atop double-decker tour buses, safely removed from the tumult of the streets. The subways intimidate them; they prefer to stay above-ground, where they can maybe tell uptown from downtown, east from west. They visit, but they're glad in the end to go home. The city wants their business and tries to make them feel welcome. It's hard to conceive of New York without the heartland, or the heartland without New York. They need each other intensely.

Chapter 3
Sherpas, Basques, Gypsies, Sikhs

This Chapter anD the neXt are about certain groups of immigrants, often ignored by the rest of us, who live here and contribute to the city's patchwork of diversity. Especially, these two chapters are about the most exotic, most alien groups, their customs and beliefs strikingly different from mainstream America's, and about how and why they came to New York.

Sherpas

Sherpas in New York City? That very special ethnic group in Nepal who guide climbers to the top of Mount Everest, the highest mountain in the world? Yes, Sherpas, sixteen of whom perished in a killer avalanche in 2014, causing some Sherpa guides to quit for the season and many to protest the conditions of their work. Yes, here they are, far removed from the Himalayas. A mere handful came first in the mid-1980s and more thereafter, so that there are now close to 3,000 of them, mostly in the ethnically diverse Elmhurst section of Queens, the biggest Sherpa community in the country. They are dark-skinned with Asian features, the young women often wearing their dark hair in long braids. And they are grieving for their comrades who died on the mountain.

Why are they here? Because some of them realized the risks of their traditional profession of guiding wealthy foreigners to dangerous mountaintops, so those intrepid thrill-seekers could bask in the glory of accomplishment and see their names in newspapers, followed laconically by "and six Sherpa guides." Because, if they renounced that profession, they could find no other work as lucrative in Nepal. Because a lengthy civil war in Nepal scared mountain-climbing tourists away, depriving the guides of a livelihood. Because they want to transition to another way of life. And because in New York they can make good money.

"Climbing was in my blood," said one. But after getting married and starting a family, for his own safety he stopped climbing. And what does he do for a living here? What many of them do: He drives a cab. A "good, bad, ugly job," he calls it, working twelve-hour shifts six nights a week. His chief complaint: people having sex in his car.

Are the Sherpas, good Buddhists for the most part, adapting to life here in hectic America? Perhaps it can best be summed up by two links posted on the United Sherpa Association website: "Nepal Sherpa Guide" and "Sherpa Computer Services." So it goes when one comes down from the mountains and plunges into the canyons of New York City. And back home the risks are as great as ever. In 2018, when a fierce snowstorm blew four South Korean climbers to their death, their four Sherpa guides died with them.

Basques

They first came to this country lured by the gold rush in California, taking the long trip by sea around the southern tip of South America into the Pacific and up to San Francisco, where so many dreams turned to dust, though not the dust of the goldfields. But who were they, coming such a long distance from the homeland where they had lived since prehistoric times? The Basques are a people living in north central Spain and southwestern France, straddling the Pyrenees. Their origins are a mystery, since their language is unrelated to Indo-European languages and probably predates the arrival in Europe of the Indo-European peoples. Basque tribes are mentioned by Roman writers and were probably remnants of early inhabitants of Western Europe. In recent times the Basques have been featured in the news because of their desire for greater autonomy in Spain, with the organization ETA advocating outright independence and committing acts of terrorism. But in 2010 the group declared a permanent ceasefire that is still in effect.

Today, reflecting their initial influx in the mid-nineteenth century, there are large Basque communities in the Western states. In New York City the first Basques began arriving after the completion of the transcontinental railroad in 1869. Departing from Bordeaux or Le Havre, some dockworkers came to work in the harbor, whereas others planned to move on west by railroad, but ended up staying in New York, where they found work in the ports of New York and New Jersey. For those from rural areas the city was overwhelming, but others were energized by it. The first Basque community took hold at the foot of the Brooklyn Bridge along Cherry and Water Streets in Manhattan. There were Basque groceries and restaurants, Basque delivery services, and Basque wine and beer distributors. And most of the Basques attended Mass at the nearby Catholic churches, one of which even had a Basque priest.

It was to this small but growing community that a young Basque named Valentín Aguirre came to work as a tugboat stoker in the harbor, and then on the city's boats and ferries. Then in 1917 he opened a Basque boarding house, the Casa Vizcaína on Cherry Street, that catered exclusively to Basques. He married here, and his Basque wife helped run the boarding house. When his young sons were old enough to drive, he sent them to meet incoming ships at the docks and call out, "Euskaldunak emen badira?" ("Are there any Basques here?"). Arriving Basques would shout back in relief and joy, "Bai, bai! Ni euskalduna naiz!" Of course they lodged at the boarding house, by then renamed the Santa Lucia Hotel and located at 82 Bank Street in Greenwich Village. The hotel functioned as a travel agency as well, getting train tickets and information about jobs for those bound for the West, and seeing them off with bundles of food for the long train trip ahead.

In 1913 Valentín Aquirre and other Basques formed the Centro Vasco-Americano, originally as a mutual-aid society to help members financially in need. The organization continued through the years, and in 1973 it bought a building at 307 Eckford Street in Brooklyn, where, with the name in English of New York Basque Club, they are still located today. Photos of Basque gatherings over the years show the men garbed in white with black berets, and the women with their hair tucked back in head scarves. In October 2013 they celebrated their centennial with lectures, concerts, dancing and singing, plus participation in the annual Columbus Day Parade. Among the many activities their club offers are lessons in Euskara, the language of the Basques. Euskara is the only language predating the Indo-Europeans that is still spoken in Europe today: a reminder of the mysterious origins of this persisting people.

Romani or Gypsies

In France they have been accused of shocking living standards, exploitation of children for begging, criminal acts and rioting, and prostitution, and thousands have been expelled and their illegal camps dismantled. One camp was even set on fire by a mob. Greek and Irish authorities have suspected them of abducting children. Italy has announced a "nomad problem" and initiated forced evictions. A Czech town tried to build a wall between its wealthy neighborhood and their ghetto, and some schools in Eastern Europe have posted signs that say "WHITES ONLY." Many of these dark-skinned people are unemployed, most live in poverty, and the temptation to crime is admittedly strong.

Such is the plight of the Gypsies, also called Romani or Rom or Roma, in Europe today. Little wonder that they want to come over here, where the prejudice against them, however strong, is less than in the Old World where they have lived for centuries. But just as with the Basques, one has to ask, who are they?

A people presumably of Indian origin who arrived in Europe at least a thousand years ago, the Romani are widely dispersed, many living in various parts of Europe, and since the nineteenth century, in the Americas, with a million now in the United States. The name "gypsy" derives from "Egyptian," reflecting the common medieval belief that the Romani, with their swarthy complexion, had come from Egypt. Their language, Romani, is Indo-European, but variations of it are so different that seven of them are considered separate languages.

Over the centuries the Romani have been persecuted in Europe as unassimilated, rootless nomads, allegedly ungodly, lazy, and given to petty theft and the kidnapping of children. Viewed by the Nazis as an inferior race, between 500,000 and 1.5 million died in the Holocaust. Yet in literature and art they have often been romanticized as well, with supposed powers of fortune-telling, a passionate temperament, and a love of freedom, as seen in the heroine of Bizet's opera *Carmen*.

Romani from Serbia, Austria-Hungary, and Russia began emigrating to the U.S. in the 1880s, until the outbreak of war in 1914 and the tightening of immigration restrictions in 1917 halted this early influx. Some were coppersmiths, others were fortune-tellers. Musicians and singers from Russia settled in New

York, and in 1904 a group recently arrived from England were living in a camp of wagons with curtained windows in a meadow near Broadway and 211th Street in Manhattan, and making their living as horse traders and fortune-tellers. Other Romani from Bosnia who worked as animal trainers and showmen settled in a village of homemade shacks in the Maspeth section of Queens from about 1925 to 1939, when their shacks were razed.

The collapse of Communism in Eastern Europe in 1989 led to a renewed flow of Romani emigration to the U.S. Here in New York City they often live in small communities in Brooklyn, the Bronx, and Queens that keep to themselves. They are by no means homogeneous; those from Hungary may have little in common with those from Slovakia; some may be Christian and others Muslim; some speak one dialect of the Romani language, while others speak another. In the neighborhood north of Pelham Parkway in the Bronx, some 350 families of Macedonian Romani live in a tight-knit Muslim community content to be viewed by others as Italian or Greek. Why did they come here? To find work for themselves and educational opportunities for their children that they couldn't find in Europe.

In this country the Romani have escaped the overt persecution that still plagues them in Europe, but not the stereotypical image of them as irresponsible migrants and cunning thieves. This image is reinforced by their tendency to hold themselves apart so as to avoid contamination by the larger society surrounding them. But "contamination" there is. They may speak to ghosts, but gobble hamburgers at McDonald's. They marry their daughters off in arranged marriages in their early teens, but work as car salesmen or jazz musicians, and one is an electrician who coaches soccer for Romani boys. But once they achieve a degree of success, to escape any chance of prejudice they often stop referring to themselves as Romani and identify themselves as Slovakian or Romanian or whatever their country of origin may be. Many of the most recent arrivals are undocumented, have no English, and consequently have trouble finding work.

Often preferring to be invisible, and with many cultural, linguistic, and religious differences among them, Romani communities here, unlike many immigrant groups, have failed to create statewide or nationwide organizations to promote and defend their culture. But in September and October 2013 the Ninth Annual New York Gypsy Festival was held in New York, with jazz, swing, folk, hip-hop, and funk concerts by performers from India, Turkey, Macedonia, Italy, France, the Netherlands, and the U.S. Here, finally, was a bold attempt to publicize the Romani culture through music both traditional and modern, and to break down age-old prejudices and celebrate "the Gypsy spirit." More annual festivals in New York followed.

Who, to date, has been the most famous Romani? Would you guess Charlie Chaplin? Chaplin always claimed to have been born in London but had no birth certificate to confirm it. In 2011 it was reported that a letter written to him in 1971 and only discovered subsequently states that he was born in a caravan in a gypsy community in the West Midlands that was ruled by a gypsy queen, the writer's aunt. Perhaps wanting to conceal his gypsy origins, Chaplin kept the letter locked in a writing desk in his bedroom. The desk was inherited by his daughter Victoria, who in 1991, finding this one drawer locked, hired a locksmith to force the drawer open. The family came to accept the story, and experts announced that they were "99.9 percent certain" that it was true.

Sikhs

On the evening of September 21, 2013, Columbia University Professor Dr. Prabhjot Singh, a practicing physician, was attacked by a gang of twenty-five to thirty black youths near 110th Street and Lenox Avenue. They yelled "Get him!" and "Osama!" and

"Terrorist!" and grabbed his beard and punched his face repeatedly, knocking him to the ground. Before bystanders could come to his aid, he sustained injuries that required hospitalization. His offense: wearing a turban; he is a Sikh. In a press conference later Dr. Singh expressed no anger or desire for revenge, but the hope that his assailants would engage in some other way and learn. He had no intention of leaving Harlem, where he lived with his wife and infant son, and planned to return at once to treating his patients. A gentle man practicing a gentle religion.

Sikhs are believers in Sikhism, a monotheistic religion founded in the Punjab region of India in the fifteenth century. Early in the twentieth century many Sikhs emigrated to the U.S. and found jobs on farms in California, in lumber mills in Oregon, and in railroad construction throughout the West. Their presence reinforced the racism already prevalent in the area, which was directed especially at the Chinese. As a result, Congress passed the Immigration Act of 1917, which banned immigration from India and other regions, thus halting Sikh immigration for the next thirty years. Immigration quotas were established by legislation in 1946, but it was the Immigration Act of 1965 that made a difference, giving visa preference to applicants whose skills were needed. After its passage more Sikhs entered the country, most of them highly educated professionals who gravitated toward cities like New York, and many became citizens. Prominent Sikhs today include writers and lecturers, physicians like Dr. Prabhjot Singh, businessmen, scientists, and politicians. New York's largest Sikh community is in the Richmond Hill section of Queens, where a gurdwara, or Sikh temple, opened in 1972.

Sikhs are required to wear a kirpan, or short sword, and when one of them was arrested for doing so on a New York subway in 1987, the case was dismissed when it was learned that this was a religious custom. April of the following year saw the first Sikh Day Parade in New York, with thousands of initiated males wearing their long hair and beards unshorn, topped by the mandatory turban, and Sikh women wearing head scarves, some of them in brightly colored saris. The parade is still held annually in Manhattan, with free vegetarian food and nonalcoholic drinks available to everyone. At the 2017 celebration, Times Square became a rainbow of colors, as Sikhs and non-Sikhs alike had their heads wrapped in pink, green, blue, red, and black turbans in what was now christened Turban Day.

After the 9/11 attacks, people often took the turban-wearing Sikh men for Arabs or Muslims, blamed them for the attacks, and committed hate crimes against them. That an assault like the one on Dr. Prabhjot Singh could occur in supposedly liberal and enlightened New York alarmed many, myself included. Such attacks are all the more reprehensible, given the very nature of Sikhism. Just consider these aspects of it:

+ It makes no claim of exclusivity, but respects all monotheistic faiths.

+ It believes in the equality of all humans, including equality of the sexes, and abhors the Hindu caste system.

+ It shuns not just alcohol, smoking, and drugs, but also superstition, ritual, fasting, pilgrimages, and idolatry, and has no priests.

+ It honors honest work and charitable actions and sharing.

+ It has no quarrel with science.

+ It advocates a simple vegetarian diet.

Obviously, this is not a religion for bigots, male chauvinists, or playboys and the idle rich, and carnivores might have a problem, too.

That such a religion, now the fifth largest in the world, suffers from the ignorance and intolerance of other Americans is a scandal, and even more so, given Sikhism's commitment to tolerance and love. We should be honored to have Sikhs among us.

Chapter 4
Tibetans, Afghans, Mohawks

Here noW are some more interesting ethnic groups to be found in and around New York. But for an unusual twist, I'll begin by mentioning Gamal, who used to deliver takeout to us from a nearby restaurant. Though his English was quite good, I knew he was from Uzbekistan; but when I questioned him further, he explained that he was not an Uzbek but a Tatar, and graduated from the University of Tashkent. Tashkent … Uzbekistan … Tatar … For my uninformed Western mind, these names conjure up visions of long westbound caravans on the Silk Road, the endless steppes of Central Asia, mysterious nomadic peoples, Genghis Khan and the Golden Horde. But Gamal presented a modern-day reality. He and his family came here for better opportunities, and to get free of the corruption prevalent in Uzbekistan. Here they launched a business supplying provisions to restaurants, and it was now expanding across several boroughs. Gamal delivered takeout in his spare time simply to earn a little extra cash. When he came to us he invariably flashed the warmest smile and gave us the heartiest of greetings. But in time we lost him, for he and his family planned to move to Boston to take advantage of that city's lower rents and shorter commutes. But for a while we were fortunate to enjoy the services of a friendly Tatar from Uzbekistan, the embodiment of the city's ethnic diversity.

Tibetans

The Jackson Heights section of Queens is one of the most ethnically diverse neighborhoods in New York. Seventy-Fourth Street between Roosevelt Avenue and 37th Avenue is the heart of Little India, where Indians and other South Asians have predominated, though more recently Latin Americans have settled there, too. Women in saris are seen on the streets with their children, retailers offer Indian music and Bollywood films, and Indian restaurants abound. But among the Indian jewelry and sari shops and Ecuadorean bakeries, one often sees strings of brightly colored cloth rectangles fluttering in the breeze, and pictures of some revered figure. The rectangles are the prayer flags inscribed with symbols, mantras, and prayers that Tibetans install in front of their residence or place of spiritual practice so that, fluttering in the breeze, they can bring happiness, long life, and prosperity to the residents and neighbors. And the pictures are of His Holiness, the Fourteenth Dalai Lama. For here in the midst of Little India is what amounts to a Little Tibet.

Tibet: a remote and mysterious land that Westerners have always thought of as the rooftop of the world, bordered by the towering snowcapped Himalayas, with Buddhist monasteries, shaggy beasts called yaks, a vast hilltop palace in Lhasa, the capital, and a culture going back thousands of years. The spiritual leader of Tibet, the much revered Dalai Lama, is believed to be the reincarnation of the previous Dalai Lama. When a Dalai Lama dies, his successor is found only when the high lamas seeking him receive a vision in a sacred lake. The vision guides them to one or several boys who must then pass a series of tests until the future Dalai Lama is found. This can take years—four in the case of the present Dalai Lama.

Our view of this legendary land changed forever once the Communist Chinese took control of the country in 1950, and in 1959 crushed a Tibetan uprising. The Dalai Lama then fled over the towering Himalayas to India, soon followed by some 80,000 Tibetans. Granted sanctuary by the Indian government, the Dalai Lama established a government in exile, and every year more Tibetans emigrated to India, Nepal, or Bhutan, and small numbers of them began migrating from these countries to the West. By 1985 there were 524 Tibetans in the United States. Then a section of the Immigration Act of 1990 authorized the issuing of a thousand immigrant visas to Tibetans living in Nepal and India, following which there has been a steady immigration to these shores.

There are now at least 10,000 Tibetans here, probably more, with about 4,000 in New York City, the largest Tibetan community in the U.S., mostly concentrated in Queens. Some came from India, Nepal, or Bhutan, but others were born here and have never set foot on their family's mysterious native land. They feel welcome here, where the plight of Chinese-dominated Tibet arouses much sympathy. And they can become citizens, whereas in India and Nepal they have only refugee status, with few rights as citizens. But many hope to earn enough money here so they can move on to Minnesota or Wisconsin, where there are large Tibetan communities and a less stressful environment for raising a family.

Many Tibetans here are undocumented, so the women work as nannies, housekeepers, and caregivers for the elderly, and are much in demand, having a reputation for being patient, diligent, soft-spoken, and caring. The men find work as interpreters or translators, or drive cabs or sell produce in greenmarkets or become construction workers, but some work in (O irony!)

Chinese restaurants. I have encountered them manning the organic bread stands that I patronize in the Abingdon Square and Union Square greenmarkets. Inevitably, many older Tibetans don't know English and find it hard to adjust to American life. They may ride the subway a short distance to attend a Tibetan prayer session, but otherwise they depend on family for social life. If that is limited because their relatives are away at work, their life here can be bleak: prayers at home and maybe a very short walk to a park.

Since many Tibetans came here from India, they feel comfortable in the Little India section of Jackson Heights, where restaurants offer authentic Tibetan and Nepalese food, including the Tibetan dumplings known as momos and a Tibetan tea with yak butter and salt. The yak meat offered in these restaurants is said to be juicier than beef and so delicious that one taste of it may lead to addiction. But until recently yaks existed in this country only in crossword puzzles, so where does yak meat come from? From Colorado and Wyoming and Idaho, where yaks are now being raised by American ranchers eager to accommodate a profitable and growing niche market.

Unlike many immigrant ethnic groups here, Tibetans are highly political. If you are visiting New York while there is unrest or riots in Tibet, don't be surprised if you see a bunch of young Tibetans picketing the Chinese consulate on 12th Avenue, or staging a hunger strike outside the U.N. building to demand a fact-finding delegation to assess the situation in Tibet. Founded here in New York in 1994, Students for a Free Tibet are dedicated to campaigning for human rights and independence for Tibet.

The Dalai Lama has often come to New York to give teachings on various aspects of Buddhism and to address huge gatherings of the general public. But His Holiness is aging. After he is gone, the worldwide Free Tibet movement, given the intransigence of the Chinese Communists, may find it hard to remain nonviolent. Nor is it clear how the next Dalai Lama will be chosen. The Chinese authorities are bound to try to manipulate the process to their own advantage. Be that as it may, even Tibetans born here feel a loyalty to the homeland they have never seen. Most become U.S. citizens, but deep inside they remain Tibetan. Some keep an altar in their apartment where they light incense and offer water daily to statues or pictures of various Buddhas and gurus, but others insist that spirituality is cultivated internally and requires no outward observances. Being greatly concerned lest their children growing up here become too Americanized, they take pains to instruct them in Tibetan culture and have them learn the Tibetan language.

Afghans

One woman in Flushing, Queens, whose grandson is a doctoral candidate at the New School, has told how the FBI raided her home, rummaging through her closets while ignoring her protests that she had lived here for twenty-five years. Who called the FBI in? The intruders wouldn't say, but she was sure it was a downstairs neighbor. And the owner of a restaurant claims that he can spot the FBI on sight, and they him. "Yeah, we all know each other." All this after 9/11. Such is the troubled life of the Afghan community in New York.

Afghanistan is a landlocked, mountainous country in Central Asia, historically almost as remote as Tibet, with towering snow-covered peaks, arid plains, and sandy or stony deserts. It is an impoverished and underdeveloped country with a hodgepodge of peoples and languages, and a harsh climate: a land ravaged in recent times by war and civil strife, terrorism, and a flourishing opium trade that defies all efforts to eradicate it. Clearly, a land that many might want to leave. Afghans may have started coming here as early as the 1920s. More came in the 1930s and 1940s, most of them educated and some with scholarships to study in American universities. Afghan immigration increased after the 1979 Soviet invasion, when asylum passports were granted freely by the U.S. government. And that immigration increased again after the Taliban took control of Afghanistan in 1996, and yet again after the U.S. bombing began in 2001.

Unlike their predecessors, these later immigrants came not enamored of the dream of America, but out of sheer necessity, with little knowledge of English or of American society, and sometimes even illiterate in their own language. Though glad to be here, they were—and are—strangers in an alien land, with the largest communities in California and the Northeast. Most are Sunni Muslims, but ethnically they may be Pashtun (the majority), Tajik, Uzbek, Hazara, Aimaq, Turkmen, Baloch, or various other ethnicities, including even a few Jews.

Today there are at least 9,000 Afghans—some sources say as many as 20,000—in the New York City area, most of them in various locations in Queens, with the biggest concentration in Flushing. Here in Manhattan, without knowing them as Afghans, we encounter the men as cab drivers, restaurant workers, and coffee and bagel cart vendors. Many of the women are stay-at-home mothers with little exposure to American society, but others take jobs below their former status in Afghanistan and work as housekeepers or babysitters.

When the United States intervened militarily in Afghanistan, some local Afghans were angry, feeling that Saudi Arabia, not Afghanistan, should be blamed for 9/11, since most of the hijackers were Saudis. But others celebrated the intervention, convinced that a defeat of the Taliban would be a blessing. Yet all of them are leery of FBI surveillance and aware of being suspect in the eyes of fellow New Yorkers, who have shouted "Terrorist!" at them only too frequently and called them a wild, barbaric people. Even as they adjust to American ways, Afghan New Yorkers continue to feel alien and besieged.

But change is coming. In traditional Afghan society, where family and tribal bonds are strong, and the sense of family honor fierce, most women wear head scarves and show no flesh below the neck, and must not make eye contact with a man in public. As for education, they have little or none, marry early as the family dictates, and are subservient to their husband for the rest of their life. These restrictions have been loosened to some extent in recent years, but still prevail.

Imagine, then, the shock when a traditionally raised Afghan woman finds herself planted in American society, where no such rules apply. Yes, she is in a tight-knit Afghan community, but circumstances may force her to take a job outside. The contrast between the traditional life she has known and what she sees all around her is overwhelming. And yet, Afghan women are said to adjust even better than the men. They do find jobs outside the home, and they do want education.

Answering that need locally is Women for Afghan Women (WAW), a Queens-based human rights organization founded in April 2001, six months before 9/11, that advocates both here and in Kabul for the rights of Afghan women. Funded by government and nongovernment agencies and private donations, it helps women here with immigration issues, parenting, family matters, and domestic violence. A Women's Circle holds popular monthly meetings with lectures and discussions, and a chance for women to share experiences and provide mutual support. There is also a girls' leadership program, and free classes in English, computer skills, driving, and applying for U.S. citizenship.

Against the background of Afghan history and the role of women in traditional Muslim societies, the program of Women for Afghan Women is nothing short of revolutionary. Even today, in regions where Muslim extremists prevail, a girl or young woman who wants education risks kidnapping, acid in the face, or death. What do the extremists most fear? Drone strikes? No. Boots on the ground? No again. Free elections? Not even this. It's the education of women. An educated woman, even if she remains a good Muslim, is lost to them; she will begin to think and act for herself. The extremists must eliminate her, or their own cause will in the long run be doomed.

Even here in New York there are risks for the educated Afghan woman. Sometimes these young women seem too Westernized to be suitable mates for Afghan men, who prefer to find wives among communities still living in Afghanistan or Pakistan. Progress is slow and uneven; often it is three steps forward, two steps back. But it doesn't stop, it continues. And it continues right here in New York.

Mohawks

There are many other immigrant groups in and around New York City: Turks, Armenians, Ukrainians, Koreans, Croatians, Thai—the list is endless. But there is a very special group who have contributed hugely to the city's skyline, helping make it what it is today: the Mohawks. They aren't immigrants at all, of course, since they were here long before the rest of us; by comparison, *we* are the immigrants.

Some of the Mohawks once lived with their families in Brooklyn, but most of the two hundred working here now live during the week in boarding houses or apartments or motels scattered across the metropolitan region. Then, on Friday afternoon, they begin the six-hour drive 400 miles north to the Kahnawake reserve on the south bank of the St. Lawrence River about twenty miles from Montreal, to spend the weekend with their families. But on Sunday night they begin the long trip back to New York, arriving at the jobsite just in time for work.

It all began in 1886, when the Canadian Pacific Railroad wanted to build a bridge over the St. Lawrence River, one end of which would be on Mohawk property, and agreed to hire tribesmen. The railroad meant to use them simply to unload supplies, but at every chance they got, the young Mohawks would go out on the bridge and climb up high. Seeing that the Mohawks seemed to have no fear of heights, and needing riveters for dangerous work high up, the railroad began training them, and they worked on many jobs in Canada. Then in 1907, when the collapse of another bridge under construction killed thirty-three Mohawks, the Mohawk women insisted that, rather than all working on the same site, their men work in smaller groups on a variety of projects. So they began coming to New York, where such projects were plentiful. And thus a people with age-old traditions centered in the earth left that earth far behind to work here in high steel.

The Mohawks weren't the only workers in high steel; many European immigrants worked there, too. But the fathers, grand-fathers, and even great-grandfathers of today's Mohawk workers guided bars of steel into the skeletons of the city's skyscrapers and bridges, and then a fourth generation helped rebuild the World Trade Center site. On 9/11 Mohawks working on other projects flocked to the Twin Towers to help people escape from the flaming buildings. When the towers came crashing down, they helped look for victims, and over the months that followed, worked in the cleanup of what some of them had helped build years before. Later they worked frantically to make One World Trade Center, also known as the Freedom Tower, rise by one floor every week so it could open on schedule in 2014. The 104-story structure is the tallest in the Western Hemisphere, and the fourth tallest in the world. I see it from my kitchen window, lit up at night and crowned by an antenna topped with a flashing red light. I call it my Tower of Light.

How do the Mohawks feel, working twenty-five or thirty or fifty stories up over Manhattan? One says it's like you're on top of the world, you feel like an eagle. Another, a fourth-generation Mohawk hard hat, says you have to like what you do, it's fun. Do they ever fall to their death? Yes, occasionally. Many graves on the reserve are marked with crosses made of steel girders.

But the Mohawk "skywalkers" love what they do. And what have they and others done in the past? Rockefeller Center, the Empire State Building, the Chrysler Building, Madison Square Garden, the U.N. building, the World Trade Center—you name it. And most of the city's bridges as well. It's a long six-hour commute from Canada, but it pays well and the benefits are good. But if there are 200 Mohawk ironworkers here now, in the 1950s there were 800. It's hard work, and dangerous; now more young Mohawks are working in a tobacco industry flourishing on the reserve. And some ironworkers urge their sons to find other, less dangerous jobs. So maybe the tradition is dying, dying slowly, but dying. Time will tell.

Chapter 5
Scavengers

S CaVenging—FinDing anD appropriating something discarded on the street—is an old New York tradition. In a densely populated city where people are constantly moving in or out, discarded items like books, furniture, appliances, luggage, and even paintings are all fair game for scavengers. According to the city's administrative code, discarded items on the street should be left for the Sanitation Department and other professional trash carters to collect, but just try telling that to New Yorkers, who routinely, out of need or curiosity or the sheer fun of it, grab stuff left on the street.

So what do New Yorkers scavenge? Maybe a Persian lamb jacket or a cat-scratching post. Or discarded computers that a maintenance worker delights to find, since he can repair them and restore them to use. Clearly, one person's junk is another's treasure. Some New Yorkers even boast of completely furnishing a small apartment with the spoils reclaimed in a day or two of strenuous scavenging on the first of the month, when people move out or move in, and discarded furniture can be found on the street.

I confess to having, in my time, scavenged. Once, en route to a restaurant on Seventh Avenue, I saw a small piece of nicely finished blond wood lying on the curb. Picking it up, I detected a slight crack that probably explains why it had been thrown out, but the crack was barely noticeable, blending in with the grain of the wood. So I grabbed it and took it with me to the restaurant, having not the slightest idea what I would do with it. It now sits on the windowsill near my desk, where I can simply enjoy the sight of it. Recently I placed a potted cactus on top of it, but I really prefer leaving it bare, so I can see it unadorned. And this at a time when I am trying to get rid of things, not acquire more.

Yes, New Yorkers don't just scavenge; they also put things out on the street, hoping a passerby will take them. When I convinced my partner Bob that we had to get rid of some things accumulated over the years, he agreed. Finding whole shelves of unused glassware in the kitchen cabinets, I showed them to him item by item, and he, being the presumed owner (we didn't even know where they came from), decided which should be kept and which discarded. I then put a few downstairs beside the steps at the entrance to our building, with a sign urging passersby to help themselves, and in every instance they disappeared within a day, often sooner. Someone somewhere—or more likely several someones—can now enjoy a shelf of glistening glasses and goblets that cost them not a cent. And when, recently, having insisted that Bob get rid of books hidden behind other books on his bookshelves, I found some hidden books of my own in a bookcase beside my desk—French and Spanish textbooks that I had no need of—out they went downstairs. Within hours, they too were gone. Hopefully, someone somewhere is now exercising their mouth muscles in an attempt to pronounce French, or puzzling over the difference between the prepositions *para* and *por* in Spanish. I wish them well.

I'm more of a scavenger than Bob was, but years ago he came home lugging a small bookcase that we could clearly use. Why would anyone discard a perfectly fine little bookcase? The explanation was soon forthcoming, when roaches began to emerge from tiny gaps between the shelves and the case. Quickly I deposited the bookcase in the bathroom, shut the door, grabbed a can of insecticide spray, and began spraying the intruders as they came out of their hiding places. This went on for at least twenty minutes, until forty little corpses lay in a heap on the floor. I then flushed the corpses away, scrubbed the bookcase clean, and announced to Bob that we had a new, very serviceable bookcase. It filled up quickly and stands in our hall to this day.

What else have I scavenged over the years? All kinds of thing, for instance:

+ Books, always on an impulse and never in numbers, since we lack space for them.

+ Folders that a law student had discarded, each labeled with the name of a course; from then on, instead of his vanished class notes, they housed some manuscripts of mine.

+ A small rainbow flag that I found in a trash can the day after a Gay Pride parade, its splintered shaft easily repaired.

+ Two very usable wineglasses that someone had left in our trash area downstairs.

+ Two plump little throw pillows abandoned in a neighbor's apartment when he moved out and invited other tenants to enter and help themselves.

It can even happen that an item doesn't just sit on the curb, awaiting a new owner, but goes in search of one. Once, on a very windy day, a huge black umbrella came flying toward me, carried along by gusts of wind. I grabbed it, found it intact except for a missing handle, and waited for the owner, handle in hand, to come chasing after it. When no one appeared, I took it home, and it has served us as a spare umbrella ever since.

But my specialty is pens: push-point pens or ordinary pens, blue-ink pens or black-ink pens, fine-point pens or medium-point pens—any kind of pen. Over the years I have found them on the sidewalk while doing errands in my neighborhood, or in parks, or even along trails in upstate wilderness areas where I used to hike alone on weekdays. And if half of them didn't work, the other half did. Result: for years I never had to buy a new pen. Only recently, in the throes of advancing maturity, have I hesitated to claim them, since they are way down there, and I am way up here. But if the item looks interesting, I'll make the effort. My presumed epitaph:

THE GUY WHO FOUND PENS

A stellar claim to fame.

Of course nothing is simple in New York. Lone scavengers and organized teams of scavengers are compromising the city's efforts at recycling. How so? Before the sanitation workers can get to the discarded items separated out for recycling—paper, plastic, glass, and metal—the scavengers get them and tote them off to be recycled. That rusty old air conditioner can be sold for scrap metal; those cans from last night's boozing can be turned in for a nickel apiece. Some homeless people depend on what they get from scavenging to buy a little food. And why does the city object, if the stuff still gets recycled? Because it makes it difficult for the city to meet its recycling goals. The city, not the scavengers, must get the credit for recycling. What the scavengers are doing, says the city, is just plain theft. To which the homeless reply indignantly that they are simply trying to get by, while at the same time helping clean up the city.

Am I myself a thief? No, because I have never taken stuff meant for recycling. My spoils are simply stray items found here or there, often put out in hopes that someone will take them. To grab a pen on the sidewalk, or a rainbow flag in a trash can, or an escaped umbrella flying by on a windy day, is not to compromise the city's recycling campaign; it simply reduces the clutter on the streets.

Having researched nineteenth-century New York, I have a better idea of the scavengers of that era than I do of the ones today. Back then they were above all women, usually German, Irish, and Italian immigrants who trudged the streets in all kinds of weather, dodging the rushing carts and stages not yet impeded by stop signs and red lights. Often they had a district where they claimed priority, fighting off any intruders who dared to invade their territory. Nasty hair-pulling and face-scratching fights resulted, with other women cheering on one or both participants.

These ragpickers scavenged all kinds of clothing and rags, bits of metal, discarded clocks, busted parasols, cracked chamber pots, lumps of coal, buckles, hatpins, and bones. Sometimes they even crouched at the mouths of sewers and reached past odiferous wastes, or even the remains of an aborted embryo, for anything that glinted. Usually they hoped for rings, got spoons. Having sorted out their spoils and washed their rags in their tenement quarters, they then sold them to the ragman, the bone man, or the junkman, earning a few pennies that might get them two days' rent in their room crammed in with other women, and some boiled beans and a penny of rum.

And today? The supermarkets grudgingly receive recyclable cans and bottles, but restrict the hours when they will take them, and the amounts they will receive. One often sees the scavengers with their bulging plastic bags of recyclables gathering near the entrance at the appointed time. But there are redemption centers as well, and scavengers flock to them with their spoils, even though raiding trash cans for recyclables is against the law. And not all the scavengers are trudging on foot with pushcarts. Some arrive in automobiles laden with cans, bottles, appliances, and bits of metal.

A year or two ago I encountered a scavenging mystery. At the curb next to the little park across the street from my building, there suddenly appeared a huge heap of plastic bags jammed with recyclables, a heap some ten feet high and piled on top of a cart that was hidden beneath it. Next to the heap was a man in a brown jacket with a hood, sorting items in a steady rain. In addition to the big heap, he had three small carts or bundles that he was also looking after. I had never seen him there before.

The next morning, when I went out on an errand on the second day of rain, his stuff was still there, and on one of the park benches there was another heap under a big white blanket: presumably, the scavenger, homeless and trying to get some sleep in the rain. But how one man by himself could manage all those bundles baffled me.

On the third day, when it was still drizzling, I went out to get a paper and saw an older, bearded African American man sitting in a shop doorway out of the rain, with a few small bundles beside him, staring sullenly out from under his brown hood. This was surely the scavenger. Coming back with the paper, on

an impulse I flashed the friendliest of smiles and asked cheerily, with a gesture toward the heap across the street, "Is all that
stuff yours?" "Get away from me!" he screamed. So savage was
his look that I did exactly that. Probably many rejections and
orders from the police to "Move on!" had rendered him aggressively defensive and leery of any stranger who approached him.
His was not a happy life, least of all in the rain.

The next day I saw him sleeping again under the big white
blanket on a bench, though the rain had finally stopped. Why
he lingered there with all his accumulated booty I still couldn't
figure out. Then, the following day, he and all his stuff had
vanished, either by his own choice, somehow transporting all
those bundles to another location, or because the police had
ordered him away.

I thought the story had ended, but I was wrong. Three
days later he and his mountain of spoils reappeared in the
park in exactly the same spot as before, his stuff sticking out
and blocking the bike lane in the street. And there he was in
his hooded brown coat, sometimes sorting things out, and
sometimes slumbering under the white blanket on a nearby
bench. Why couldn't he get rid of his stuff and maybe even
realize a modest profit? Why did he linger there day after day,
married—or maybe chained—to his gleanings? After that I saw
him once again, with all his stuff, on West 11th Street, not far
from my building, but then he vanished.

But not forever. A year later he popped up yet again, squatting
on the sidewalk in the same little park across the street from my
building. This time I couldn't lay eyes on him, because he was
lying under a pile of blankets pulled over his head. In the bike
lane next to his blankets there were now four big carts, each piled
high with gleanings, most of them in a rainbow of bulging plastic
bags, scores of them, if not hundreds, presumably packed with
recyclables. Crammed in among the bags were pots and pans, a

small air conditioner, a patterned blanket or fabric of some kind, scraps of clothing, parts of a vacuum cleaner, other hulking strange objects, and poles that poked out at odd angles, suggesting mops or brooms or maybe legs of some unidentified object.

Again I wondered why he hadn't recycled his loot. Instead, he seemed to be amassing and amassing, and now, with his carts heaped high, through rain or snow or sleet he was snoozing under blankets in the cold. One day later I saw a squad car at the curb, and officers looking him and his stuff over. He must have seemed harmless, since they left him alone. Then a green Parks Department truck showed up, but they didn't interfere either. After that I saw him daily sitting on the sidewalk by his carts, or lying next to them, covered with a thick white blanket that was even wrapped over his head. Sitting up, he looked like a sheik of Araby, or a guru in his ashram. There he remained for days, then once again vanished. What wisdom could he impart, if he didn't hold himself so fiercely aloof? I will never know.

Chapter 6

Hustlers

The WorD "hUstLer" has many meanings. It can mean a male prostitute, but publisher Larry Flynt's *Hustler* magazine is a monthly porn sheet that is blatantly heterosexual. Here I take "hustlers" to mean people who promote themselves or something else aggressively. Hustlers of this variety are endemic in New York City and always have been. This city is a mecca for hustlers of every kind, from the Wall Street sharper to the sorriest, most down-and-out panhandler.

Have I ever been hustled? (And I don't mean by male prostitutes, though there's an exception.) Yes. Long ago, while dining in a New York restaurant with friends on Halloween, our table was approached by a black kid who wanted money—a twisted variation of "trick or treat," since he wore no costume and just wanted cash. How he even got in there I can't imagine. In any case, we gave him nothing.

And once, returning from vacation, I was approached at Grand Central Station by another black kid who opened a taxi door for me and for this needless act wanted a tip. The taxi driver told him to clear out, but being in a good mood, I gave him a quarter.

On another occasion I saw a woman in a floor-length nun-like gown stride brazenly into a bar and get, from an obliging bartender, a dollar or two, and then immediately leave, bound, no doubt, for other bars. She was, of course, a hustler, for no authentic nun would walk into a bar in quest of donations. In my experience a nun may sit quietly in a public place, eyes down, with a dish for donations, but she never solicits and rarely even makes eye contact with others.

A few years ago, I had a curious adventure. It was the night of my eye surgery, and with a big patch over my right eye I had gone to bed early. An hour later I heard the hall door, which at that time could not be closed tight, creak and squeak a bit, which told me someone had entered the apartment. Flashlight in hand and still half asleep, I went to investigate and found a young man in his mid- to late twenties just inside the door.

"I saw your door was open," he explained. "I'm waiting for a friend. Would you mind if I used your bathroom?"

Being barely awake and not knowing everyone in the building, much less their friends, I said yes. Minutes later he called me into the bathroom, said that his belt was broken and asked if I could give him some rubber bands to fix it.

"Rubber bands?" I asked incredulously.

"Or some string," he added.

Eager by now to get rid of him, I fetched both rubber bands and string. But when I returned to the bathroom he had dropped his pants enough to display his private parts, a sight I could barely believe. My look of total disinterest must have registered, for he then announced, "I can do this in the hall," and departed with the string. Anxious to prevent his return, I put a heavy wooden card table against the slightly open door, so if the door budged even a little, the table would fall with a crash. The night passed peacefully, and now it all seems like a dream.

Was my visitor a hustler in the broadest sense? Absolutely. And in the narrower sense, meaning a male prostitute? I assume so, but certainly not a professional. A real pro wouldn't have wasted time on me, least of all with a bandaged eye, when he could have been hanging out wherever hustlers hang out and their patrons know to find them. This incident will not be repeated, for our super has now fixed the door so it can be closed and locked every night.

For real hustlers you can't beat Times Square. It has long been populated by costumed characters, many of them inspired by TV shows and comic book superheroes. There are Elmos, shaggy red-suited monsters with black dots of eyes and an orange nose; armored, helmet-faced Iron Men; Spider-Men in torso-hugging red-and-blue outfits adorned with a spiderweb; big-eared Minnie Mouses (or Mice?); and brazen bare-breasted *desnudas* with wild feathered headdresses. Also on the scene are the Cookie Monster, SpongeBob SquarePants, Batman, Superman, and the Statue of Liberty.

So who are these hustlers? For the most part, Latino immigrants willing to parade about in cartoon-character costumes that are stiflingly hot in the sticky summer heat, so they can stand beside children while their parents take photos, following which Elmo or Minnie wants a tip. Or topless Latinas with feathered headdresses, painted breasts, and thongs who pose with male tourists for photos and hope to extract twenty dollars or more. Costumed or near naked, Times Square hustlers usually speak little English, fear deportation if arrested, and would do something else if they could. Interviewed, a nineteen-year-old Nicaraguan Spider-Man said he averaged nine dollars an hour, better than he would do with a job, if he could get one.

In fairness, it should be noted that tourists with children often initiate contact with Spider-Man or Elmo, and some *desnudas* insist that they don't bother anyone, that being topless in New York isn't illegal (true enough), and that only a few of them harass tourists and give them all a bad name. And let's face it, these antics are a part of New York, they're what bring tourists here eager to see something in the deliciously wicked city that you can't find in Topeka or Des Moines. (No offense intended to Topeka or Des Moines, which are probably delighted not to be so graced.)

Let's have a look at some other types of New York hustlers. In Brooklyn a few years ago young black gang members would jam the dollar-bill slot in MetroCard machines, so commuters couldn't buy cards. Then the hustlers would offer to get them through the turnstile by selling them an illegal swipe for a dollar or two, or for the same fee let them through a service gate. This being clearly illegal, arrests followed.

More controversial are the young black hip-hop artists who peddle their compact disks to passersby in Times Square. Often arrested for disorderly conduct and aggressive begging, the rappers claim that they aren't breaking the law, that the police have it in for them, treat them differently from other vendors, and violate their First Amendment rights. The police insist that the rappers shove CDs at pedestrians, block the sidewalk, and follow potential customers down the street, allegations that the rappers deny; in time, their cases are usually dismissed. Some of the rappers have been arrested thirty times, and in 2014 their exasperation reached the point where eight of them filed joint lawsuits in Manhattan Federal Court against the city and seventeen policemen. How their lawsuit played out I don't know, but these guys are spunky and innovative, tailoring their sales pitch to what people are wearing and how they look. They remind me of the squeegee men who used to clean the windshields of cars stopped for a red light, for which unsolicited service they hoped to get a tip.

Another species of hustlers are the Buddhist monks with shaved heads, benign smiles, and flowing orange robes who haunt the High Line, Bryant Park, and Times Square, pushing cheap amulets at passersby and expecting, even demanding, a tip. I saw one once on Sixth Avenue offering his trinkets right and left, but now they're all over the city. When one on the High Line got five dollars from a visitor, the holy man protested, wanting twenty. Of course they are fakes, just like the nun I saw in the bar. Usually they are Chinese immigrants who return to flophouses in Flushing, Queens, with their day's earnings, some of them doffing their robes en route on the subway, before setting out in khakis and Nike sneakers for a meal spiced with liquor in a local restaurant. Some have also been seen sneaking a smoke on the sly, or napping on ledges of the Fifth Avenue public library. Real Buddhist monks might carry a beggar's bowl to receive gifts of money or food, but they would never aggressively solicit cash, and would shun cigarettes and alcohol. Authentic New York Buddhists are offended by these fakers, who disrespect the faith.

Other hustlers haunting Times Square have included these:

✦ Ticket hustlers who try to sell you tickets for comedy clubs.

✦ Coupon hustlers who thrust at you coupons for sandwiches, massages, and strip clubs.

✦ The Naked Cowboy playing his guitar in his undershorts, sometimes joined by scantly clad Naked Cowgirls likewise strumming guitars.

- ✦ Statue people who stand stock still, spray-painted gold or silver or purple, including one or several Lady Liberties, sea-foam green replicas of the Statue of Liberty.

- ✦ Religious hucksters parading about with signs urging **REPENT! FOLLOW JESUS** and similar messages, and buttonholing passersby to ask if they can tell them about their Savior.

And some of them get into fights with one another, which should vastly entertain the tourists, as long as they keep to one side.

Another species of hustler is the man who, combining a distaste for regular employment with a gift of gab, stakes out a neighborhood where he gets to know the locals and makes himself useful to them. He helps shoppers unload purchases from handcarts and put them in their car, maybe offering a bit of gossip as well, as for instance who's in jail or out of it, and whose wife or girlfriend just left him. Or he holds a parking space for a motorist, feeding the meter until the motorist returns from shopping. For these and similar services he either charges a fee or hopes for a generous tip. But if a hunk of money ever came to him, he'd probably blow it all on liquor or cocaine. He has joy and exuberance, energy and initiative, independence, and a love of the life of the streets. Living for the moment, he shuns the bourgeois virtues of order, prudence, and responsibility. In the end he pays a price.

A brilliant nineteenth-century hustler was Vermont-born James Fisk Jr., who hustled his way from peddling in New England to wartime cotton smuggling to control of the Erie Railway and an attempt to corner gold on Wall Street. Meanwhile he was staging a flashy musical with one hundred chorus girls kicking high in a cancan, but also ran a steamboat line and strutted in a gold-laced uniform as colonel of the Ninth Regiment of the New York State National Guard. Whatever his endeavor, always he was promoting himself. Only an assassin's bullet stopped him, the result of an affair of the heart. Even then he went out in a splash, with his coffin paraded through the streets, led by six colonels and a general in black-draped solemn pomp.

A hustler of a different stripe is Martin Shkreli, a Brooklyn-born millennial Wunderkind who concocted a series of financial and pharmaceutical enterprises that he got investors for, each one losing money and failing as he went on to the next. Failure never dimmed his enthusiasm and self-confidence, for he could take the funds from his latest creation to repay the investors in its predecessor. He had the hustler's promotional and self-promotional skills, reinforced by total self-confidence, utter self-absorption, and arrogance. In 2015 his raising the price of the drug Daraprim from $13.50 a pill to $750 vaulted him to the status of the most hated CEO in America, which, he claimed, so enhanced his image that women found him irresistible. He was, in fact, quite good-looking, with several dark curls dangling down on his forehead so as to enhance his boyish charm.

When not dabbling in dubious financial and pharmaceutical adventures, Mr. Shkreli tweeted brazenly and live-streamed for hours on YouTube, always promoting himself. Finally, in December 2015, at the tender age of thirty-two, he was indicted by the government for fraud related to his financial escapades. Throughout the trial he rolled his eyes or showed an insolent smirk, until the jury convicted him on five of eight counts. Out on bail, online he offered $5,000 per hair to anyone who grabbed a hair from Hillary Clinton, who was then on a book tour. He claimed this was only a prank, but the judge deemed him a threat to society, revoked his bail, and confined him to durance vile in Brooklyn. Convicted on several counts of fraud, in 2018 he was sentenced to seven years in prison, plus fines. He was committed to the federal prison at Fort Dix, New Jersey; but in March 2019, after claims that he was running one of his pharmaceutical firms with the help of a contraband cell phone, he transferred to another facility in Allenwood, Pennsylvania. Which did not keep him from suing three former colleagues for $30 million, alleging that they had illegally ousted him from one of his pharmaceutical companies.

That Mr. Shkreli is Donald Trump writ small should be obvious: the same arrogance, the same self-promotion, the same flamboyance, the same distaste for the truth, the same tweet-inspiring impulsiveness. And in the Donald himself one sees the ultimate in hustling, for it took this other native son of New York from real estate deals and a series of casino bankruptcies (from which he himself always emerged unscathed) all the way to the White House. Martin Shkreli and the Donald are homegrown, stellar specimens of the New York hustler.

Have I myself ever hustled? In the sense of self-promotion, that is. The honest answer is no, not really. I'm too middle class, too bourgeois, too genteel, maybe too Midwestern, too timid, too polite. I've been known to compliment a stranger on his shirt, or in a restaurant once, a diner on her handsome blouse, but that's rare and hardly a hustle. The closest I've come is hawking my wares at a book festival, but there it's appropriate and not too brazen, since people who attend fairs are looking for books. I'm a dedicated New Yorker who loves and celebrates his city, but a hustler I am not.

The New York hustlers of today are desperate but resourceful, and too full of energy to give up. They are driven, they have to *do,* they can't stand still. And why do they hustle? For money, for excitement, for power, and for glory. They insist that they aren't panhandlers or beggars. They indeed offer a service or product, and they entertain. Whatever you think of them, New York wouldn't be New York without them. But if you encounter them, hang on to your wallet and your wits.

Chapter 7
The Rich

I see them passing in elongated limousines with blinded windows. I see the high-rises where they luxuriously nest, and read about their gilded doings, but I don't know the rich. And I'm talking not millions but billions: the 1 percent of the 1 percent. So who are they and how do they live?

For who they are, *Forbes* magazine's annual list of the 400 richest Americans is a good place to start. Among the top 100 names listed in 2015, for instance, were sixteen New Yorkers, with the source of their income as finance, real estate, media, cosmetics, luxury clothing and housewares, and television and real estate. Conspicuous by its absence was technology, more of a West Coast phenomenon.

Finance and real estate were biggies in the nineteenth century also, but the Wall Street of today is not the Wall Street of then, for hedge funds and leveraged buyouts are recent creations, and very different creatures indeed. How many of us even know what a leveraged buyout is, or what a hedge fund or private equity firm does? In the nineteenth century the public was surely baffled by short sales, puts and calls, and straddles, but those strategies never by themselves precipitated a worldwide financial crisis, which is more than can be said for the financial gimmicks of today. How reassuring it is to find cosmetics and luxury clothing included in the first 100—real stuff that you can see and smell and touch. Even if you can't afford them, you can understand such products and wish their creators well.

Who in 2015 was the richest New Yorker? According to *Forbes*, Michael Bloomberg, whose fortune derives from Bloomberg LP, a leading financial services and news provider. A business magnate credited by *Forbes* with $38.6 billion, he was also the eighth richest man in America. (As of 2015, that is. These things can change from year to year, as we will see.) And yes, he was the 108th mayor of our fair city, serving no less than three consecutive terms. A successful business magnate, independent politician, and philanthropist, he is not to be dismissed lightly. By serving as mayor he continued a tradition of New York businessmen. In the first half of the nineteenth century, before the advent of the professional politician and the dominance of Tammany Hall, prominent merchants took two years or more out of their business career to govern, or try to govern, the city of New York. For them, it was a matter of public service, even though their heart was in their business.

For Michael Bloomberg, a phenomenally successful businessman, politics was probably the only place to go for the thrill of further achievement. The results? Both negatives and positives. The negatives included pervasive homelessness, a stop-and-frisk police policy that abused minority communities, and cozy relations with banks and real estate. The positives: restrictions on smoking in public, pedestrian plazas, 850 more acres of parkland, 470 miles of bike lanes, and a safer, cleaner city. These,

at least, are things most people can understand. That he had a
lady friend on the side bothered New Yorkers not at all, since she
didn't meddle in politics. His appearance? Dignified, mayoral,
but with a winsome smile.

The next richest New Yorker in 2015, according to *Forbes,*
was Carl Icahn, a Far Rockaway native and Princeton graduate
turned hedge fund manager and activist shareholder whose
wealth was pegged at $20.5 billion. His involvement in risk
arbitrage and options trading is enough to baffle the uninitiated
(of which I am one), and his reputation as a ruthless corporate
raider is not likely to endear him to multitudes. In 1985 he staged
a hostile takeover of TWA, then sold TWA's assets to repay the
debt he used to acquire the company, a procedure known as
asset stripping. Finally, in 1988 he took TWA private, reaping a
profit of $469 million, while leaving the company saddled with
$540 million in debt. So if Bloomberg is the big fish in the pond,
Icahn is a shark. Labeled a financial parasite by some, he insists
that he is always acting in the company's best interest by ousting
incompetent management. Also, he tends to hold stock for over
three years, which makes him something of an investor. Hostile
takeovers, proxy fights, stock buybacks, chairman of this and
acquirer of that—no layman could follow his career or grasp his
motivation, but it all explains why in 2015 he had the second
biggest New York fortune. A sober-looking, well-dressed business
type whose features have graced the cover of *Forbes* and *Time,*
he manages to work in some philanthropy, too.

The third richest New Yorker, with $12.5 billion, was inves-
tor and philanthropist Ronald Perelman, whom I confess I had
not heard of, but whose photos show a chubby, balding fellow,
rather jolly-looking with a hearty smile. *Forbes* described the
source of his wealth as "leveraged buyouts," so I'm baffled already.
His modus operandi is to buy a company, strip it of superfluous
divisions so as to reduce debt and generate profit, then focus on

the company's core business and either sell it or hang on to it for its cash flow. So is all this good or bad? I haven't the slightest idea, but I gather that Perelman, like Icahn, is a corporate raider, which makes him shark no. 2. One of his favorite operations is greenmail. He buys a big chunk of a company's stock, then threatens a takeover unless they buy his stock back at a much higher price; if they do, he reaps a phenomenal profit. The mere acquisition of shares by such a raider precipitates panic in management and a buying frenzy in the public. But like Icahn, he finds time for philanthropy, and for five marriages as well. He does get around.

Compared to these other richies, not to mention Donald Trump—no. 121 on the 2015 *Forbes* list, with $4.5 billion—Michael Bloomberg comes off looking good. He isn't a pirate or an egomaniac, gave us bike lanes and greenery, made it possible for us to stroll in Times Square, and cleansed our indoor public spaces of nicotine. Not bad, Mike, not bad.

Now, for comparison, let's have a quick look at the *Forbes* 400 list for 2018. What strikes one first is the prevalence of techies—Jeff Bezos of Amazon (a new no. 1), Bill Gates of Microsoft, and Mark Zuckerberg of Facebook—whose names are known to all, and who are most definitely not from New York. The first New Yorker is David Koch (pronounced *coke*), no. 7, who with his brother Charles has long dominated Koch Industries, a multinational corporation based in Wichita, Kansas, with David running their office in New York. And what does Koch Industries do? Just about everything: petroleum, chemicals, fiber, fertilizers, finance, commodities trading, and investing.

But it isn't these multiple activities, employing some 120,000 people in sixty countries, that most impress the American public, myself included. David is one half of the Koch brothers, a notorious duo denounced, decried, and defamed by liberal circles for their political activities, which almost always serve the Republican Far Right. As the Libertarian Party vice-presidential candidate in 1980, he wanted to abolish Social Security, the Federal Reserve, welfare, any number of federal agencies, minimum wage laws, corporate taxes, and limits on campaign spending. The party got only 1 percent of the vote. Today he just calls himself a Republican, and gives generously to worthy causes. Photos show a rather handsome man with graying hair and a genial smile. Who wouldn't smile, with a net worth of $53.5 billion? But he has long battled prostate cancer, and for health reasons has retired from Koch Industries.

A true New Yorker, though hardly a typical one, he lives in an eighteen-room duplex on the fourth and fifth floors of 740 Park Avenue, a luxury coop apartment building between East 71st and 72nd Streets in the Lenox Hill neighborhood of Manhattan, a building that has been hailed as a legendary address and arguably the most luxurious residential building in the city. Other famous residents have included Jacqueline Kennedy Onassis as a child, John D. Rockefeller, Jr., and assorted heirs and heiresses, CEOs, hedge fund managers, and philanthropists.

The next New Yorker on the 2018 *Forbes* list is Michael Bloomberg, no. 10, with $51.8 billion, who keeps turning up like a bad penny. After that, to find a New Yorker one has to drop down to no. 23, Jim Simmons, a hedge fund manager with a mere $20 billion.

So what do these folks do in their spare time, if they have any? For one thing, they give. New York is full of big-name cultural institutions that gobble up big money so as to realize big dreams, and big donors are in their sights. In 2008 Leonard Lauder, the cosmetics magnate, gave $131 million to the Whitney Museum of American Art, the biggest gift the Whitney had ever received. And in 2013 he gave the Metropolitan Museum of Art seventy-nine Cubist works, a collection of Picassos, Braques, and Légers valued at more than $1 billion, to be housed in a projected new wing for contemporary art. Lauder embodies an old money model of largesse, concentrating on one or two institutions and in so doing making a big splash.

But today's moneybags don't give just to the arts; they give big money to the candidates of their choice. Mostly Republicans, of course. And who are these donors? White, wealthy, older males clustered in a handful of communities throughout the nation, the biggest of these being New York. So right away I smell one half of the Koch brothers, plus hedge fund managers and the manipulators of leveraged buyouts and private equity. These donors aren't from old big money, haven't inherited their wealth. They're newbies who launched their own businesses, took risks, and reaped huge gains, prominent among them the hedge fund managers of New York. And they support Republican wannabes who promise lower taxes, fewer regulations, stingier entitlements. Not that it's easy to sniff these donors out. They hide behind business addresses, post office boxes, and limited liability corporations and trusts.

For Halloween, hedge fund billionaires leave their mark on Manhattan, bedecking their townhouses with goblins, crones, witches, zombies, skeletons, ghouls, ghosts, spiders, and bats leering from balconies, peering through railings, or guarding entrances. Outside the East 74th Street residence of Marc Lasry, a cofounder of Avenue Capital, bloody life-size dummies have dangled from a balcony, while a chaste neoclassical entrance on East 67th Street has featured an effigy of a two-headed girl standing in a multitude of rats. But it could have been worse. The façade of hedge-fund billionaire Philip Falcone's residence on East 67th Street, a street that seems to lure spooks, was once graced with a crone cradling a dead infant, while inside a hearse parked at the curb the Grim Reaper was seen beheading a corpse—a display spooky enough to provoke protests by the neighbors. All of which shows where some of the millions reaped by fat cats goes.

The spending of another fat cat is colorful indeed. In 2005 Dennis Kozlowski, CEO of Tyco International, a security systems company, was found guilty of stealing more than $150 million from the firm. What had he done with these ill-gotten funds? Here's a sampling that came to light at his trial:

✦ A $30 million Fifth Avenue apartment

✦ A $6,000 gold-and-burgundy shower curtain

✦ A $15,000 dog umbrella stand

✦ Paintings by Renoir and Monet worth millions

✦ A multimillion-dollar oceanfront estate on Nantucket

In addition he dished out one million in 2001 to pay half the cost of the fortieth birthday party of the second Mrs. Kozlowski on the island of Sardinia. Gracing the occasion were helmeted gladiators to welcome arriving guests, toga-clad waiters crowned with fig wreaths, wine served in chalices, and an ice statue of Michelangelo's *David* pissing vodka. (Mrs. Kozlowski later filed for divorce.)

Photos of Mr. Kozlowski show a man in his sixties with an oval-shaped head, quite bald, and a hearty grin: a happy little porker. His lavish lifestyle came to symbolize the decadent luxury of high-living Wall Street and hastened his downfall, since videos of his Roman orgy were shown to jurors, who saw dancing women and near-naked male models cavorting with guests, and a beaming Kozlowski promising guests a "fun week" with "eating, drinking, whatever. All the things we're best known for." After serving eight years, he was paroled in January 2014 and now lives modestly in a two-bedroom rental overlooking the East River with a nondescript white shower curtain and wife number three.

It must mean something when the ultrarich get ribbed in advertising. The New York Lottery once launched a humorous ad campaign showing richies wasting their money in oddball ways. In one TV commercial a man was soaking in a bathtub of pinot noir; when his butler let a bit of cork fall in the tub, he was furious. The viewer, suggested the ad, would make a much better rich person than this fool in a tub, and Lotto is the way to do it. Advertisers know you can't make fun of the poor, but the wealthy are fair game. So the Lottery satirizes the truly rich so as to encourage the not-so-rich to get a little less rich.

Television shows like to feature the ultrarich and want to do it with accuracy. But how do billionaires live? In luxury, of course, but how about some details. Those worth billions don't have to prove anything through conspicuous consumption and often shun publicity. So the TV shows hire wealth consultants, some of them billionaires themselves, and some of them are vendors who sell to billionaires. There is great attention to clothing, furnishings, accessories. And occasionally the billionaires themselves chime in, as when one emailed a TV show to complain about one TV character's private jet, declaring that he wouldn't be caught dead in a sardine can like that.

So what do the shows come up with by way of residences for their billionaires? Comfy and cozy are out. They must intimidate, amaze, overwhelm. Double-height living rooms, with wraparound terraces affording breathtaking views. Not frilly and feminine; masculine and stark, tasteful but subdued. Which may explain why furnishings shown in ads for luxury high-rises strike me as unlivable and cold. But then, I'm not even a multimillionaire.

Chapter 8
Freelance Editor

B etWeen the VerY riCh and the very poor in New York there
is a host of middle-class professionals, neither rich nor poor,
who help make the city work. This chapter and the next will have
a look at two of them, starting humbly with myself.

In the *New Yorker* in 2015, veteran editor Mary Norris told how
she had, almost by chance, become a "comma queen" at the
prestigious magazine, thus introducing the term and notion of
a "comma queen" to the general public. That being the case, as a
longtime freelance editor, now retired, I can present myself as a
onetime "comma king," though not one so prestigious as a *New
Yorker* practitioner of the trade.

To start with, why do manuscripts need editors? Because
authors screw up. If you ever read a book that was lightly edited,
or even not edited at all, you'll find yourself entangled in confusing sentences, needless repetitions, misspellings, puzzling

omissions, and other annoyances that keep you from focusing on the book's content. So editors exist for a reason.

And what is a freelance editor? An editor whose lance—meaning his or her sharpened pencil—is for hire. An editor who operates independently, probably wanting more free time and a more flexible schedule than a regular job would allow. The profession is a refuge for would-be novelists and playwrights and other literary ne'er-do-wells at the outset of their hopefully brilliant careers, when they must focus on the manuscripts of others, and not on their own presumed masterpieces. And it has always been peculiar to New York, since that is where big publishers cluster, though today there are freelance editors all over, thanks to the Internet.

As a profession, editing requires good knowledge of grammar, punctuation, and spelling—stuff once taught in schools but now generally neglected. Also, a fiendish attention to detail. Should one put a comma here, a semicolon there? And what the hell is this sentence trying to say? A good editor feels horror at a dangling participle, disgust at a puffy paragraph, a tangled sentence. Order, clarity, concision! Editors are fusspots.

And how do these fusspots get manuscripts to work on? By networking, by telling friends in publishing what they're up to, by advertising or sending out letters to publishers (rarely successful, in my case), by getting to know editors who will then recommend them to other editors. And today, of course, by advertising online. Once you get your foot in the door, résumés and interviews are rarely necessary; personal recommendations are all that matters. And why do publishers hire freelancers? To save money. They hire them when they need them, and not when they don't. And they don't have to give them pensions or other benefits. Freelancers are on their own.

What is a freelancer's equipment, aside from sharpened pencils and an eye for detail? When I was a freelancer back before the Internet, three books:

1. *Merriam-Webster's New International Dictionary of the English Language, Unabridged,* 2nd edition, 1934. A huge hunk of a dictionary that sits on my desk today, but is rarely used, since now it's easier to consult the Internet. This was the bible of freelancers, much preferred to the 3rd edition of 1961, since it indicated preferred usage; it was the schoolmarm of dictionaries.

2. *The Chicago Manual of Style,* 13th Edition, Revised and Expanded, The University of Chicago Press, 1969. A second bible. No graduate student writing a dissertation could be without it.

3. *The Elements of Style,* William Strunk, Jr., with additions by E.B. White, 2nd edition, Macmillan, 1972. Affectionately referred to as "Strunk" and known to the knowing few.

From Strunk one learned to use serial commas and commas with nonrestrictive relative clauses; to delete "the fact that" as superfluous; to express coordinate ideas in similar form; and to distinguish between "comprise" and "constitute." ("A zoo comprises many species of animals," but "Many species of animals constitute a zoo.") If the very thought of all this baffles or exasperates you, you'll understand why editors exist.

But there are different kinds of editing, requiring different skills. I often worked on textbooks from several major publishers—Holt, HarperCollins, Harcourt Brace Jovanovich—with a scattering of novels and nonfiction titles from Viking, and scholarly works from the New York branch of Oxford University Press. Proofreading involved reading the galleys of a manuscript and making finicky corrections in the margin, using proofreading symbols. Copyediting involved reading the manuscript at an earlier stage and, depending on the needs of the publisher, doing light or heavy editing. Light editing meant the manuscript was already in good condition, or more likely, the author was resentful of changes. "She doesn't like her words being monkeyed with," one editor warned me about an author, "and some of her words are just begging to be monkeyed with." So, against my better instincts, I didn't monkey.

Finally, there is manuscript editing, where the manuscript may be in need of changes, in which case the editor, often working with the author, is expected to intervene. This was common with textbooks, rare otherwise. I edited manuscripts requiring a knowledge of Spanish, French, or German, and once or twice even some knowledge of Latin. Ah, how I loved to strut my high school Latin among the hoi polloi! (Oops—that's Greek.)

When editing textbooks, I often got to know the authors, either by phone or in person, and a rum bunch they were. Some of them, at least. My least favorite one was the coauthor of a very successful English college reader. A former salesman, he knew the market and knew how to present his book to the instructors who might adopt it. Which evidently entitled him to be nasty. Me he spared, but everyone else involved in the project he dismissed with scorn. The top editor of the department hiring me was lazy, he insisted, and had to be prodded to give his manuscript the attention it required. Not true, of course. The editor was diligent, but in charge of some fifteen or twenty manuscripts, each of them requiring his attention. And the manuscript's production editor, he announced, was "just your or anyone's Polish grandmother," though she was likable and totally competent. I was glad to be done with him and came away unscarred.

The French author of a second-year reader was described to me as "quite dashing and continental. When he's due to drop in, all the girls are aflutter with anticipation." When I met him, I found him to be continental indeed and very sophisticated, but a rather homely forty-year-old. His French sophistication had dazzled them all, more than making up for his lackluster looks. A German textbook author based in Salt Lake City had amusing stories to tell about the Mormons. But the best story of all, relayed to me by an editor who had visited him there, concerned the noted Argentine author Jorge Luis Borges, whose unique and challenging stories I have read in translation. Borges had visited the author, who asked the blind writer what he would like to do. "Take me to the mountains," said Borges, and to the mountains they went. It was spring and the birds were singing, and Borges listened intently with great pleasure—a revelation for his host, fascinated to see how a blind man could richly appreciate the unseen spectacle of spring.

For a while I had a job as researcher for William Jovanovich, CEO of Harcourt Brace Jovanovich, who in my one brief meeting with him explained that he had departments in distant locations all over the country, and therefore needed someone constantly available to do research. For this work I would get a monthly stipend, whether I had any assignments or not. This made for financial stability, but I never knew when one of his underlings would phone me with an assignment needing immediate attention.

One such summons was almost comically bewildering. I was summoned to the Harcourt office of a vice-president of something-or-other, where he introduced me to a young woman on the Harcourt staff.

"This is Monica. You of course know of her very successful book *Instructor.*"

"Oh yes," I said, having never heard of her or her book.

"You'll be working with her," he announced. "And now I have a plane to catch."

With that, he grabbed his hat and left, leaving me totally ignorant of the project in question. Fortunately, Monica took me to her desk and explained what was wanted: a quick survey of some articles on computers, so Harcourt could publish a bunch of them in a magazine and beat out other possible competitors. The magazine would be devoted to a small new computer about to be introduced by IBM and already nicknamed the "Peanut," which would also be the catchy name of the magazine. I got them the articles, but have no idea if the computer or the magazine materialized.

Especially challenging was one of the last manuscripts I worked on before retirement: *The HarperCollins World Reader,* an ambitious anthology of world literature in translation, with an American editor whose enthusiasm recruited contributors, and an English editor who was hired to do the nuts-and-bolts work of editing. I worked with them both. My job was not to edit the manuscript, but to be in touch with the twenty or more contributors, each a specialist in his or her field, and to encourage them to get their contributions in on time. The schedule was tight, so the pressure mounted.

Some of the contributors were a delight to work with, others were cranky and opinionated, supreme examples of the academic mind at its worst. "You keep changing your mind!" complained the Korean contributor, when I told him HarperCollins had decided to present the book in two volumes, so he would have to do two introductions, instead of one. I explained tactfully that for the publisher this was an undertaking without precedent, a truly ambitious project, and we were of necessity feeling our way.

"All right," he said, "but you do the second introduction!" So I did it, knowing nothing of Korean literature, culture, or history, but focusing on the postwar division of Korea and the onset of the Korean War. By way of contrast, when I informed another specialist of the need for two introductions—a woman who was busy moving from one university to another, having just been made department head at the second school—she answered "Got it!" and soon delivered what we needed.

An unforeseen dilemma arose when one of the contributors, a respected specialist in African literature, suddenly died. A dilemma and near panic ensued, until another distinguished scholar was found to replace him. But we weren't always so lucky. The Australian who was supposed to work with another specialist to present the literature of Polynesia and other regions of the Pacific kept putting me off: "Yes, yes, I'll get to it soon." Then he announced that he would be disappearing into Tahiti for the summer and would be incommunicado, but of course he would be sending his material. Incommunicado in Tahiti, that storied paradise of grass-skirted dancers, its enticing young females immortalized by Gauguin? Kindled long since, my suspicions roared up in a blaze. And sure enough, HarperCollins got a brief note soon thereafter, announcing that he was resigning from the project, no reason given. It was too late to find a replacement, so the Pacific region had only half the material intended. Vanishing into the tropical never-never land of Tahiti, he shortchanged both the publisher and the book's future readers.

Always hanging over us was the schedule, forcing us to constantly hurry the contributors along. When the in-house editor informed me that, because of budget considerations, they would have to terminate me, I was relieved. I wished them and the project well, but I was free at last from the constant pressure. The anthology appeared in 1994 in two volumes with the thinnest of pages—2,796 in all. Given a copy, I skimmed those pages often, lingering over the Chinese poetry, and tasted an excerpt of Lady Murasaki's eleventh-century *Tale of Genji*, considered by many to be the world's first novel, a Japanese epic relating the amorous adventures of Prince Genji, an emperor's son by a concubine. Intrigued by the excerpt, I obtained a copy of the novel in modern translation and read through its hundreds of pages to the very end.

The in-house editors I worked with, more often than not women, were competent and committed to their work. Coming from college teaching, where some of my colleagues were dedicated to their work and others were just coasting along, this was a pleasant change. But their remote top bosses, sometimes a new team brought in through a merger or acquisition and invariably male, had little knowledge of, or respect for, these underlings and their daily operations, and the relationships that developed among them over the years. All too often those distant potentates decreed purges where a dismissed employee was suddenly told to leave immediately without speaking to anyone. Or they might order a whole department's removal to another state, thus severing the longstanding bonds between professionals, some of whom would stay while others quit. In such cases, morale plummeted. As a freelancer, I was affected primarily if the editors I worked with were dismissed or chose to quit. "The only security," I told my in-house friends, "is insecurity." Knowing that no pension would await me at retirement, I worked to assure my future on my own.

In the same year that saw the publication of the *World Reader*, I retired from freelance editing. At least, from *paid* editing. Since then I have helped several friends write their memoir: a gay prison inmate who recounts his arrest and imprisonment;

a lady from Calcutta whose memoir/cookbook combines accounts of an idyllic childhood with Indian recipes related to each of her reminiscences; and a Sister of Mercy who tells of her bout with a life-threatening brain tumor and the recovered memory of being molested in her childhood. The latter two have now been published, and I'm hoping that the inmate's memoir, which reads like a novel, will likewise appear in time. And even as I write this, I find myself involved with another aspiring writer in a novel that looks promising. Once an editor, always an editor, even if you're retired. Such is the fate of fusspots.

Chapter 9

Broadway Chorus Boy

Ted Was a BroaDWaY chorus boy, young, short, and blond, more "cute" than stunningly good-looking, whom I knew in the 1950s and 1960s, when I was a graduate student at Columbia and began teaching French. We met in Ogunquit, Maine, where he was appearing in the musical *Pajama Game.* I went to the show with friends, found myself sitting in the front row but a few feet from the stage. During one of the dance numbers a young blond dancer appeared on the stage right in front of me, and for an instant our eyes connected. I thought no more about it, but later that evening I was at a table with a friend in a seaside bar nearby, when several of the chorus kids came in, including the short blond. They knew my friend and joined us, and the blond looked straight at me.

"You're the one who wasn't applauding," he said with a laugh.

Surprised, I insisted that I had indeed applauded, though maybe less vigorously than some others. Random chitchat followed, and later my friend, who had a car, offered to drive me and Ted back to our hotels. En route, fortified by a few beers, I gently stroked Ted's neck in the car, without the driver noticing. He dropped Ted off at his hotel and then drove me on to mine. When he drove off, some strange impulse made me walk back toward Ted's hotel, savoring the quiet of the warm summer night, and out of the shadows came Ted, impelled by the same strange urge. Exchanging a few words, we walked back to his hotel, a palatial one where no one was at the front desk or in the lobby. A strange midnight silence pervaded the place as we went up to Ted's room. Of course we had sex, and hours later we looked out a window and saw the milk-white dawn yielding to a fiery sunrise. I went back to my hotel dazed and sleepy; it had all been like a dream, and I was sure I was in love.

Ted and I reconnected in New York, where he gently eased my fervor into a milder, more manageable relationship. Through him and his friends, I got a glimpse into the life of Broadway chorus boys, a world within a world, small, exciting, self-contained. Ted lived in a cold-water flat in the West 40s, near the theaters, his agent, and the bars that the chorus kids frequented. Cold-water flats were low-rent apartments, and as such got passed along from one struggling young actor or dancer to another. Ted's had once been the home of the veteran stage and film actress Jo Van Fleet, whom I especially remember from her role in the movie *East of Eden.* Ted's apartment, as I dimly recall, was small and sparsely furnished, probably with running cold water in a sink. For baths and other bodily needs, he had to go down the hall to a communal facility. But this was how the chorus kids lived; they were glad to get such a place and thought no more about it. It was less a home than a base of operations, for their real life was on the stage, whether in the city or on tour, and in the bars.

Ted had been in a number of big-time Broadway musicals, including *Guys and Dolls,* as commemorated by a number of photos on his wall. Also on the wall was a photo showing him in a classical ballet pose with a ballerina, but it seemed all wrong for him, whereas *Guys and Dolls* and *Pajama Game* seemed right, and he knew it. His life was a matter of waiting for phone calls from his agent about a possible part in a musical. He had strange and hilarious stories to tell about tryouts and casting. On one occasion he was told, "Sorry, Ted. You're just what we need, but we don't want another blond in the chorus." So he went out and got a dark-haired wig, hurried back, and tried out again. They laughed and said, "Okay, okay, you're hired. But don't wear that lousy wig. Dye your hair." He did. "Sometimes," he told me, "you have to do their thinking for them."

"Don't you ever just walk into a part and get hired immediately?" I asked.

"Just once. The male chorus in *The Boyfriend* is supposed to be English, but there's one American. When they saw me, they said, 'We hope you can sing and dance. You're short and blond, just what we want for the American.'" Ted could sing and dance; he got the role.

Ted had tales to tell about rehearsals as well. Once they had the heaviest of the women dancers paired off with him, the smallest of the males. When, at one point, the girls were supposed to leap up on their partner's shoulders, Ted's partner slid right down to the floor, taking his pants with her. "Embarrassing," he told me. "There I was only in my dance belt," meaning the jock worn by male dancers. But he was laughing as he told me.

At Ogunquit, on the last night of the performance there, he had invited me into his dressing room, where I saw him and two other dancers sitting in their underwear, busily applying makeup. It was the last night of the tour, always a time of joyous celebration and high jinks, with jokes and banter flying about. Ted planned to black out some of his teeth and then, during the performance, flash a gap-toothed smile at another dancer, a friend, hoping to break him up. But one of the company's staff, wise to the ways of dancers, made an announcement warning against such shenanigans. "Remember," he said, "you may want to work for these folks again." So Ted didn't blacken his teeth.

When there were few shows in the offing, dancers had a recourse to industrials, lavish spectacles with dancers used by big corporations, especially automakers, to introduce a new product. Industrials went all over the country and they paid well, so dancers took them to bring in some cash, but their heart was in the theater. I recall seeing an industrial on a friend's TV set, with dancers dancing around glistening new limousines lit with bright lights. Said my friend, who was in advertising, "You wouldn't believe what all of that costs!" Why dancers were needed to introduce a new model of car, I never quite grasped, but the automakers presumably knew what they were doing.

The social life of chorus boys was centered in a handful of more-or-less gay bars in the West 40s. I went to one once with Ted. The emphasis was less on cruising than socializing, and everybody seemed to know everybody. The latest bit of gossip was about a young dancer who had just broken up with his lover, the show's dance captain. The dance captain then got his ex-lover fired. When the kid just fired showed up, all the others flocked around him to sympathize; the dance captain was vilified by one and all. As Ted observed to me, mixing your private life with your career was risky; he never did.

On another occasion a friend of Ted's told him and some other dancers how he had gotten a part given up by a strikingly good-looking dancer. "I knew I couldn't match him in looks, so I decided to strut like a stud, as if to say, 'Honeys, what I've got going for me is right down there between my legs.'" All the other chorus kids agreed that, under the circumstances, this was the only thing to do.

Yes, Ted had had sex with women. "It's work," he said. "You have to pump."

Dancers were always socializing; they weren't ones for quiet times at home with a book, or for reflection. And when they went on tour, the socializing wasn't diminished, for they were constantly being partied. Once Ted met Tennessee Williams, who had invited the chorus boys to a private party. Williams scanned each as he arrived, and said to Ted, "Hmm, yes, you can stay." *Thanks a lot,* Ted thought to himself, *I thought I'd already been invited.* But in Denver a wealthy young businessman was so taken with Ted that he offered to keep him in style. Ted politely declined the offer, which his admirer pressed repeatedly, sure that he could wear down Ted's resistance. But Ted knew that in the long run such a relationship led nowhere; he stuck to his guns, said no.

Ted's family had come to this country from Poland before the war; that was all he ever said about them. He had been raised a Catholic, and once, when he went back home, a priest had urged him to leave the gay life. He tried, but the moment he was back in New York, he slipped back into it. Far from seeming troubled by this, he shrugged it off.

Ted and I weren't steady lovers, just on-and-off-again part-ners. Weeks, even months might pass, and then, on the spur of the moment, I would phone him and we would get together. We were of different worlds—me in Academia, a teacher, and him a dancer steeped in the small, rich world of Broadway chorus boys. But at times he needed to come out of that world, even though he always went back into it. "It's always good to see you," he told me more than once. "Theater kids aren't in the real world, they're off in some fantasy world of their own." At first I shrugged off his remark, but when he repeated it several times, I realized that it was for real. Being in that world but not altogether of it, he needed to come out and get a breath of fresh air. Seeing me was that breath of fresh air, and at the same time I could escape from my own world, the tight, small world of academics.

Ted knew that you can't be a chorus boy forever—a problem explored decades later in the musical *A Chorus Line.* Some dancers end up teaching dance or becoming choreographers, but only a very few. Ted's plan was to transition into acting. His acting teacher encouraged him, but his agent and others resisted. "Ted," they said, "you're a dancer." Which didn't leave much room for transitioning. Like all young actors in search of credits and experience, he took parts in what veteran actors laugh at and deride: children's theater. In one, I recall, he played a mad physicist. I never saw him perform, but an actor acquaintance of mine did. "It's fascinating how dancers get into a role," he told me. "When I do it, I'm exploring the character's emotions, finding out what the character *feels.* But dancers do it through movements. They *dance* themselves into the role."

But what chance did a dancer have of getting into acting in New York, where he was competing with hundreds of young actors doing the same? Often as not, an aging dancer—and in that profession aging comes fast—goes back to his hometown, Pittsburgh or Cleveland or Denver, where family and friends are waiting, and a job in some mundane profession offers the security that theater can never provide. More than once Ted told me, "You may get a phone call that can change your life." Now he was waiting, not for a call offering yet another job as a dancer, but for a call offering a serious role as an actor. But as long as I knew him, that call never came.

One day I finally suggested to Ted that we continue as friends minus sex, prompting his wistful reply, "I hate for things to change." Soon after that I met my partner Bob, and from then on Ted was out of my life. With hindsight, I now regret this; it wasn't necessary. For years I assumed that Ted finally went back to Pittsburgh, or wherever he was from, and the inevitable mundane job.

The story of Ted has a surprise ending. Years passed, then decades. Finally, on the spur of the moment I Googled Ted by both his real name and his stage name. I expected nothing, since he was only one of hundreds of young male dancers who have their moment of glory on Broadway, then disappear. But to my astonishment, several obits in New Jersey newspapers came up, announcing the death in 2015 of an eighty-eight-year-old man with the same two names, a resident of Bayonne. A coincidence, I told myself, but soon became convinced that this was, indeed *had* to be, the Ted I had known. This Ted in the obits was a Broadway chorus boy who, when the he retired from dancing, began working in wardrobe, and years later retired with honors after forty-five years on Broadway. So Ted found a way to stay in Broadway theater after he left dancing, and it wasn't acting. And to get into wardrobe, I'm sure, you had to have connections.

The obits told me other things that I didn't know:

+ He was born in the small town of Eynon, Pennsylvania, the son of a coal miner, and the youngest of three children. So his leap into a career in dancing anticipated the story of the Broadway musical *Billy Elliot*.

+ He was a year older than me, whereas I had always thought he was two or three years younger.

+ He had been briefly in the military at the end of World War II.

+ After I knew him he married a dancer and by her had a daughter.

+ He had a Catholic funeral and is buried in Holy Name Cemetery in Jersey City.

One obit quoted him memorably: "I had a wonderful life. I have no regrets. Always follow your dreams."

My reaction to this news was astonishment, then sadness, then joy. Astonishment for obvious reasons. Sadness because I just missed discovering him in time to reconnect, talk old times, say hello and good-bye. And joy because he solved the problem of what to do when he quit dancing: He followed his dream and stayed in the world of theater that he knew and loved. To be backstage in wardrobe, and not out there performing, must have been an adjustment, but he managed. He had a rich, full life. I wish I could have shared a little of it in the years after I knew him a half century ago on Broadway. Good-bye, Ted, and good luck! Have a dance with the angels.

Part 2

HOW WE LIVE:
BOOZE, BAGELS,
GAY BARS, AND GRAFFITI

Chapter 10
Fun

New York is, and always has been, Fun City, a place where people come to have a good time, maybe to get just a bit wild. And the locals have always liked to have fun, too, and in the Big Apple the possibilities are endless. But what exactly is "fun"? The dictionary says "what provides amusement or enjoyment," and in distinguishing it from words like "game" and "play," it says that fun "implies laughter or gaiety, but may imply merely a lack of serious or ulterior purpose." Okay, I'll go along with that, though I may stretch the definition just a bit.

I asked several of my friends what they do, or what they have done in the past, to have fun. One said that he didn't have fun anymore, though he has never struck me as glum. And the others said:

+ Cook a dinner for friends you've invited over.

+ Hiking.

+ A good book.

+ A congenial bar with a good piano player.

✦ A good dinner out.

✦ A club with loud music and dancing.

No, not a single orgy; sorry to disappoint. My friends don't go for orgies, or if they do, they won't admit to it. There are wild things to do in New York, and I'll get to them later. I see fun in New York as either Gentle Fun, Hot Fun, or Weird Fun. Let's start with gentle.

Gentle Fun

One of my friends mentioned a good dinner out. Quiet fun, but fun nevertheless, and very New York. New Yorkers like to dine out and have the choice of cheap, moderate, or very expensive and exclusive restaurants, and every ethnic variety conceivable. Over the years Bob and I patronized Italian, French, Spanish, German, Irish, Chinese, and Thai restaurants, with special emphasis on Italian and Chinese.

For a really good meal Bob and I used to go to Gargiulo's, an old family-run Italian restaurant on West 15th Street in Coney Island, but a few blocks from the boardwalk. We went by subway, an hour's ride mostly aboveground, with views of the rooftops of Brooklyn. Gargiulo's is famous for classic Neapolitan fare, but to sample it you have to observe their dress code: no shorts, and God knows, no bare feet. This may be Coney Island, but it's a very special Coney Island, catering to middle-class families of taste. My preferred dishes: for an appetizer, mozzarella in carrozza (mozzarella cheese on toast); for the main dish, fettuccine Alfredo; and for dessert, cannoli: fingerlike shells of fried pastry dough with a sweet, creamy filling.

Going often, we had our favorite waiter, Giancarlo, and got to know the management. With their approval I even invaded the kitchen to say hello to Lula, a longtime employee with the warmest smile, and thank her and everyone for the dinner. For us as veteran New Yorkers, such a meal was the evening's entertainment. There was no thought of doing anything else, except the long subway ride home at night, looking at the lights of Brooklyn, and savoring in memory the dishes we had just enjoyed. When we saw other diners—a few—rush through their meal and dash off to some other engagement, we were amazed. What could possibly top a dinner at Gargiulo's?

One summer evening, returning from an alumni gathering in the West Village near my building, I walked along West Fourth and heard, in the restaurants and cafés along the way, the gentle murmur of conversation. This, I thought, is New York at its best: people dining quietly and talking softly with friends. No hint here of the frenzied pace of the city, the blaring horns, screaming ambulances, and screeching jackhammers. Doers though they are, New Yorkers know how to relax and be civilized. And as I reached the corner of West 4th and West 11th Streets (yes, they do intersect—that's the Village for you), I found a cellist on the corner, sitting quietly and playing his cello, eyes shut, a blissful look on his face. The cello case was on the sidewalk in front of him, open and inviting donations. But whether you gave or not, or stopped to listen or walked on, was of little importance to him. He was totally into the moment, doing what he loved best.

What else do New Yorkers (as opposed to tourists) do for gentle fun? Many of us go to the Union Square greenmarket, the granddaddy of all greenmarkets, to buy such specialties as ostrich eggs, bison meat, sprigs of lavender, organic garlic, or a tangy herb-flavored goat cheese from an upstate goat farm. There is also wine from vineyards in the Finger Lakes, bringing which requires a five-hour trip to New York, as well as locally made beer and liquor ("drink local"), and honey harvested from rooftop gardens in the city.

Sometimes we stay in and cook. Every so often I have done a thick black bean soup, enough for at least four servings. I put garlic, carrots, celery, onions, scallions, parsley, and cabbage into it. To season it I use cumin, coriander, and black pepper, and for a final and absolutely essential touch, the juice of four limes. And a young man of my acquaintance, a millennial, makes white chocolate candy with homemade champagne jam and sends me pictures of it by e-mail. (Hopefully I'll someday get to taste it.)

Here are some other things New Yorkers do in their spare time:

✦   Feed raccoons at night in Central Park.

✦   Join the Greenwich Village Society for Historical Preservation (GVSHP) and help save old buildings from the wrecking ball.

✦   Look for rare editions in the few bookstores that remain.

✦   In season, harvest wild raspberries in Pelham Bay Park (but don't let the park police catch you).

✦   Write letters, sign petitions, join demonstrations, and otherwise protest the antics of the president (any president).

✦   Scavenge discarded furniture put out for collection.

✦   Watch penguins being fed at the Aquarium, or dolphins romp in a tank.

✦   Take a "Scoundrels of Wall Street" tour; you'll learn a lot.

✦   Go foraging with Wildman Steve Brill, who was once arrested for eating a dandelion in Central Park (the case was laughed out of court), and with his guidance gather wild mushrooms, burdock, garlic mustard, mugwort, poor man's pepper, and other edibles in the city's parks.

✦ Relax in an old cemetery and see the graves of Boss Tweed and Leonard Bernstein in Green-Wood, or Miles Davis and the notorious Lola Montez at Woodlawn.

And now for something wilder.

Hot Fun

One friend of mine mentioned The Monster, a gay bar in the West Village on Grove Street at Sheridan Square with a bar/piano lounge at ground level. He described it as having three personalities. The pianist often plays show tunes from the storied past, to the delight of the older gays present, which is personality no. 1. But he also plays tunes from recent shows, to the delight of the younger gay set—personality no. 2. And no. 3? For that you go downstairs to the dance floor, where Hispanic males dance up a storm. The bar has been going since 1970 and is definitely a hot fun scene. One of the online reviews by a young man from Brooklyn tells how his girlfriend wanted to take him out to a fun gay bar for his birthday and chose The Monster on a Sunday night. "We happened to be thrown into a sea of fun bartenders and staff that were hosting an underwear party that night. What a blast we had." And if his girlfriend was one of only three women there, everyone seemed to love her. His conclusion: "Will definitely be back!" Which sounds like a real New York scene.

Though it's in my neck of the woods, I've never been to The Monster, so I'll mention instead the Goldbug, a gay disco that Bob and I went to in the late 1960s and 1970s, when discos were all the rage. It was a Mafia-run joint in the West Village, with the inevitable thug at the door to keep the non-gay element out. Inside you were obliged to have a drink first at the bar, before proceeding to the dance floor in back. And what a dance floor it was! Male and female couples (rarely mixed) bouncing and jiggling to ear-splitting piped-in music, while strobe lights flashed splashes of color that made you think you were high on LSD. And as if that weren't enough, a male go-go dancer in a bikini exposing his pulsating charms. It was wild, it was crazy, it was fun.

Hot too, in the sense of strenuous, is hiking the Palisades, those towering gray rocks across the Hudson in New Jersey. I used to do it on the Shore Path, scrambling over the Giant Stairs, a jumble of fallen boulders with hidden dark caverns and crevices where copperheads lurk (hearing your footsteps, they'll get out of the way).

Or you can attend auctions at Sotheby's and Christie's, those two veteran auction houses where the bidding can get frenzied. But a friend of mine has attended them for years and assures me that, if you know what you're doing, you can pick up fine furniture at bargain prices. Fun for a savvy New Yorker.

More hot fun: cycling in the parks, or riding in Central Park or Van Cortlandt. And for really hot fun, bingo in a Brooklyn bingo parlor, where the frustrated players yell at the game host, "Shake up your balls!" (No, not *that* kind of balls; they're referring to the bowl where he dips his hand to pull out the numbers.)

That stuff is wild, but I wouldn't call it weird. So here we go with weird.

Weird Fun

This isn't my kind of fun, but it's what my friend Ann, a nurse, indulges in, when not looking after others. It's crazy stuff that I didn't know existed, all of it right here in this city. Aside from attending a no-pants party with her boyfriend, Ann has done the following:

✦ GORUCK drills, marches, and water push-ups in the harbor off Brooklyn.

✦ A Color Mob 5k race where she ended up splotched with many colors and looking like a piece of abstract art.

✦ The Walking Dead Escape, an obstacle course where survivors who run the course without being touched by zombies can then become zombies and try to contaminate others.

This is all about keeping fit. GORUCK is an organization that stages challenging military-style programs for civilians staffed by Special Operations combat veterans. Civilians who volunteer for the program can select one of several options that vary in length of time and distance. They join a team, carry heavy rucksacks, do military drills, and learn survival skills. Ann chose GORUCK Light, which involves a mere four to five hours and seven to ten miles. (GORUCK Selection, the most challenging option, involves 48+ hours and 80+ miles!) She did physical drills that included carrying heavy packs and the American flag through the streets, then crossing the Brooklyn Bridge to do push-ups in the harbor. This is fun? Maybe not for you or me, but for Ann, yes, though she also calls the experience awesome. She's a real fitness freak, and adventurous to boot.

Color Mob 5k stages five-kilometer races where runners of all ages get splattered with wild colors as they run, then party at the finish line with music and beer. You are advised to wear clothes you want to have colored permanently, since some of the colors will never wash out. The runners aren't timed; everyone is a winner. Coming back on the subway, their clothes all splotched with colors, Ann and her friends were quite a spectacle. When a woman asked if she could photograph them, they said yes; she then sent them a copy of the photo. This, at least, sounds like fun—honest, wild, weird, and crazy fun.

Walking Dead Escape was staged one October evening at the Intrepid Sea, Air & Space Museum at Pier 86, West 46th Street and 12th Avenue, Manhattan. The museum features the aircraft carrier *Intrepid,* a veteran of World War II and Vietnam that is now a National Historic Monument. Walking Dead Escape participants were invited to climb, crawl, and slide through an obstacle course on the *Intrepid* that included overturned buses, while trying to avoid being touched and contaminated by zombies. Or you can choose to be a Walker (zombie), or just watch as a spectator. When Ann and her friends finished the course, they became zombies and then were professionally made up, their faces smeared to look like zombies, following which they spent several hours trying to touch and contaminate others. At the end, the contaminated zombies were taken into quarantine and subjected to a fake execution, since there is no cure for the zombie virus. Again, pretty strenuous fun, but fun nonetheless. For Ann and her friends, at least. I'm not sure I'd care to dodge overturned buses or be smeared to look like a zombie. Maybe I'd settle for a good dinner at Gargiulo's, or a good book while sitting snug and warm inside on a cold, rainy night.

Chapter 11

Booze

N ew Yorkers haVe aLWaYs had a love affair with liquor.

Not that this makes them any different from the rest of the nation. Consider, for instance, all the names Americans have given to the stuff: booze, the ardent, the stimulating, juice, giggle juice, tangle-legs, firewater, hooch, diddle, tiger's milk, rotgut, coffin varnish, crazy water, and the oil of joy. And there are plenty more.

And the terms we have used for the adjective "drunk": drenched, pickled, plastered, soused, snookered, crocked, squiffy, oiled, lubricated, loaded, primed, sloshed, stinko, blotto, flushed, cockeyed, and (a good nautical phrase) three sheets to the wind. And again, that's just a beginning. To which I'll add a friend of mine's charming way of indicating a lush: "a bit too fond of the grape."

There were always saloons in the city, but they weren't called that at first. A "saloon" in the mid-nineteenth century was a large public room or hall. Thus the ladies' saloon on a steamboat was for respectable ladies and their male escorts. It was a refuge from noise and intemperance, and very, very dry. So what were the terms for what we today call a saloon? Grog shop, groggery, pothouse, gin mill, gin shop, dram shop, rum shop. But whatever it was called, it did a good business. Back in those days, on every corner in the slums was a liquor grocery. Inside a typical one you could find piles of cabbage, potatoes, beans, and chestnuts; boxes containing anthracite, charcoal, nails, and plug tobacco; upright casks of lamp oil, molasses, rum, whisky, or brandy; and here and there on the floor, a butter cask or a meal bin. At one end of the room there was usually a plank stretched across some barrels, and on it some species of grog doled out at three cents a glass. Also, in one corner there might be another short counter with three-cent pies kept smoking hot, where patrons could get coffee also at three cents a cup, and for a penny, a hatful of cigars. Offering all that a tenement household might need, these places were well patronized by the locals, both men and women, and their mix of products show how drinking and grocery shopping and socializing were all jumbled together in a rich and complex tangle. Not fertile grounds for prohibitionists, one might think.

But prohibitionists there were. Not in Babylon on the Hudson, as some ministers were wont to call the Empire City, but in upstate rural counties and elsewhere. In 1851 the Maine legislature passed what would become known as the Maine Law, prohibiting the sale of alcoholic beverages except for medicinal and industrial purposes. Many states followed suit, and seemingly for good reason, since alcoholism was rampant. When two American males met, their greetings were often followed by, "Let's liquor." Mindful of this, many a patriarch enjoined his son departing for college, "Beware the flowing bowl!" Which was about as effective, I suspect, as similar admonishments today.

So would prohibition come to that den of inebriation, New York? Yes indeed, or so it seemed, for if the city was notoriously "wet," the upstate rural counties were adamantly "dry." In 1854 the legislature passed an Act for the Prevention of Pauperism, Crime, and Intemperance whereby, as of the following July 4 (a date the city hailed with whiskey- and rum-soaked revels), liquor would be banned throughout the state and public drunkenness forbidden. The law was vetoed by the governor, but his successor was a "dry," and in 1855 the law was passed again by the legislature.

Prohibition in booze-ridden Gotham? Was it conceivable? The city was now full of newly arrived immigrants who were just as opposed to the law as many citizens. At the thought of prohibition the Irish in their grog shops, downing tumblers of cheap whiskey, muttered dark oaths. At the mere hint of it the Germans in their beer gardens, clinking steins, scowled under frothy noses, while behind the elegant façades of certain brownstones genteel mutterings accompanied the imbibing of delicate wines. All eyes turned to the city's newly elected mayor, Fernando Wood. Himself once the proprietor of a groggery, "Fernandy" was a known "wet" who over the years had frequented the city's finest barrooms, his elegant form reflected in the huge gilt mirrors backing counters adorned with nippled Venuses. So what was he to do?

Tall and dapper, Mayor Wood was as slick a customer as had ever ruled the city (if anyone *could* rule it). Having consulted legal experts, he announced that he would of course enforce the law, however needless and impolitic, while giving full attention to exceptions, technicalities, and the rights of citizens, violating which, officers would be held to strict account.

The city understood the mayor only too well, and its tippling did not notably decrease. Luckily, within a year the law was voided in the courts, and Gotham's Sabbath quiet continued to be tainted by the din of unlicensed grog shops, and drunks staggering out on the street.

So ended the city's first brush with legislated temperance. But the campaign for prohibition had only begun, aided and abetted—indeed, championed and promoted—by a host of female reformers determined to see the matter through. The movement was sidelined by the Civil War, but afterward it regained strength, especially following the founding of the Women's Christian Temperance Union (WCTU) in 1873. Successes followed. In 1881 Kansas became the first state to outlaw alcohol in its constitution. Later in the century Carrie Nation achieved notoriety in other states by entering saloons to smash liquor bottles by the dozen with a fiercely wielded hatchet. Described as sporting the biceps of a stevedore, the face of a prison warden, and the persistence of a toothache, Carrie was a formidable activist, but hardly typical of the crusading women, who preferred hymns, prayers, and arguments to hatchets. But they were dedicated to the cause for good reason, having often suffered humiliation and abuse from a drunkard father, brother, spouse, or son.

Prominent among the drys were Methodists, Baptists, Quakers, and other Protestant groups, as opposed to Roman Catholics, Episcopalians, and German Lutherans. Not that everyone involved was motivated by lofty ideals: tea merchants and soda manufacturers sided with the drys in hopes of increased sales following a ban on alcoholic drinks. The conflict between rural upstate citizens and downstate urban residents in New York State was replicated throughout the country. Rural populations viewed cities as rum-soaked, crime-ridden, and corrupt, while city dwellers decried their rural cousins as spoilsports, puritans, and hicks. And when the WCTU expanded its campaign to include women's suffrage, the leading group focused solely on Prohibition became the male-dominated Anti-Saloon League, founded in 1893 in Ohio but soon active throughout the nation and especially influential in the South and the rural North.

Though beset at times by local prohibitionists, New York City remained passionately and determinedly wet. Female reformers were especially resented by working-class males, who saw the reformers' activities as an assault on a whole way of life centered in what was now called the saloon. The saloon was their refuge and social center, a place to get momentarily free from family obligations, a place to down a few with their pals after work, before trudging homeward with diminished funds to face the scolding tongues of their wives. ("Women," went a saying, "you can't live with 'em and you can't live without 'em.") And in Tammany-dominated New York the saloon was also the political base of the proprietor, often an alderman, who dispensed liquor and salty eats freely toward election time and so corralled the necessary votes for his own or his cronies' reelection. All this, the wets lamented, was threatened by these misguided and depraved reformers, well-scrubbed preachers and goody-goodies who had no understanding of the city's raw needs. To put it bluntly:

meddling females + preachers + hicks = Prohibition

On the other hand,

no Prohibition = freedom = sanity = bliss

And there is little doubt that the reformers had their sights on New York City. Out-of-town ministers had long visited it on whirlwind tours to see firsthand its sins, so they could go home to shock and titillate their congregations with descriptions of this sink of depravity. It was Babylon on the Hudson, Sodom and Gomorrah, Satan's Seat. So Prohibition was deemed especially appropriate for Gotham, where it was most needed; there it would breed virtue and sobriety.

By January 1919 enough states had ratified the Eighteenth Amendment to make nationwide prohibition a certainty, and on January 16, 1920—a day that for New Yorkers would live in infamy—the ban went into effect. Police smashed confiscated barrels of wine and beer, smashed them, and dumped their contents into gutters or the harbor, while stunned Gothamites watched in horror and dismay. Huge vats of alcohol were discovered in outlying areas, and the Coast Guard began intercepting liquor-laden boats bringing thirsty Americans the hooch they longed for.

The lower classes were at once deprived, but their betters had already stockpiled vast quantities of their preferred labels. Significantly, President Woodrow Wilson had promptly moved his personal supply to his Washington residence when his term of office ended, while immediately after inauguration Warren G. Harding, his successor, moved his own stash into the White House. Harding got the stuff more or less legally, through an acquaintance who had a permit allowing him to obtain it for medical purposes.

Such maneuvers were fine for the moneyed elite, but New York City had an answer of its own: the speakeasy. Within a year or two there were between 20,000 and 100,000 in the city, and all of them thriving, since to tell New Yorkers they can't do something at once kindles in them a passionate desire to do it. At first the speakeasies operated clandestinely and required patrons, viewed suspiciously through a peephole, to give a password to enter. But soon enough there was little need for pretense, since the police were amply rewarded for looking the other way.

The speakeasies ranged from the lowest dives offering cheap rotgut of dubious provenance, to well-appointed establishments catering to the wealthy and elite. And if the now-banished saloons had enjoyed a strictly male clientele, these new nightspots went defiantly coed. Patrons included Charleston-dancing flappers and their callow escorts, cavorting businessmen from Cleveland or Pittsburgh and their intrepid spouses, assorted judges and aldermen, visiting dignitaries, silent film stars, and from 1926 on, the mayor.

And where did all this liquor come from? Some was home-made, with all the perils that entailed: foul-tasting brews, explosions, aftereffects ranging from atrocious hangovers to departures for the beyond. But much of the booze came from elsewhere. In a fit of neighborliness the distilleries of Canada labored diligently to supply the needs of a deprived population to the south. And visible off the Rockaways was Rum Row, a fleet of ships at permanent anchor just outside the three-mile limit, where U.S. jurisdiction ended: floating warehouses for smugglers who, dodging the Coast Guard under cover of darkness, brought the precious stuff to land in speedboats.

The queen of speakeasies was Texas Guinan, who quipped her way through multiple arrests, always surviving a raid to open another nightspot that brought patrons flocking to receive her signature greeting, "Hiya, suckers!" But if her series of clubs were the most popular, there were plenty of others in all the boroughs. The most celebrated and frequented were clustered in midtown Manhattan, with thirty-eight on 52nd Street alone. Prominent among them was the 21 Club, whose final address was 21 West 52nd Street, made famous by its ingenious engineering: in the event of a raid, a system of levers tipped the shelves of the bar, sending liquor bottles through a chute into the city's sewers. There was also a secret wine cellar accessed through a hidden door in a brick wall, opening into the basement of the building next door. In the 1950s workers expanding the 53rd Street branch of the New York Public Library are said to have encountered the soil there still reeking of alcohol.

Other joints of the day included the Hi Hat, the Kit-Kat, and the Ha-Ha Club. Noel Coward liked the elegant Marlborough House at 16 East 61st Street, where black-jacketed waiters served partying socialites. Fred and Adele Astaire danced at the Trocadero at 35 East 53rd Street, while pilots flocked to the Wing Club at 8 West 52nd Street, and artists to the Artists and Writers Club at 213 West 40th Street. The Central Park Casino, in the park near the 72nd Street entrance, was the favorite hangout

of fun-loving Mayor Jimmy Walker, who spent more time there
than at City Hall.

But New Yorkers had other ways as well of coping with
Prohibition. Nathan Musher's Menorah Wine Company imported
750,000 gallons of fortified Malaga wine that, certified as kosher,
he sold to "rabbis" with sacramental wine permits, some of
whom sported such names as Houlihan and Maguire. In a more
sinister mode, Meyer Lansky's car and truck rental business in a
garage underneath the Williamsburg Bridge became a warehouse
for stolen goods and rented out vehicles to bootleggers. Lansky
went on to become a major gangland figure, associating with
such stellar operators as Bugsy Siegel and Lucky Luciano. As a
Jewish gangster, he figures in my eyes as a supreme example of
successful assimilation.

As time passed, enthusiasm for Prohibition waned. Far from
reducing crime, as had been hoped, it promoted it by creating
a bootlegging industry dominated by warring gangs. Far from
eliminating alcoholic consumption, it made it fashionable and
prompted the fair sex to join their thirsty males in imbibing.
Flouting the law was "in," it was fun. Nor was Prohibition an
inducement to better health, since drinking bad booze from a
bottle with a counterfeit label could on occasion be lethal.

The coup de grâce for Prohibition came in October 1930,
just two weeks before congressional midterm elections, when
the bootlegger George Cassiday contributed five articles to the
Washington Post telling how for the last ten years he had supplied booze to the honorable members of Congress, of whom he
estimated that 80 percent drank. As a result, in the following
election Congress shifted from a dry Republican majority to a
wet Democratic majority eager for the Eighteenth Amendment's
repeal. To bring that about, states began ratifying the Twenty-
first Amendment. In New York City anticipation mounted, and
bystanders were astonished or amused to see phalanxes of sturdy

matrons, who now had the vote, marching together under bold-lettered signs: WE WANT BEER! Yes, the times had changed. On December 5, 1933, the Twenty-first Amendment was ratified, repealing the now despised Eighteenth; New Yorkers cheered ... and drank.

There are many morals to this story, chief among them the folly of imposing morality from above by law, when vast numbers of those below have only scorn for the law enacted. For better and for worse, New Yorkers have always guzzled and surely always will. Prohibition in the Big Apple? Fuhgedaboudit! And so ... Cheers! Salute! Prosit! A la tienne! Salud!

Chapter 12
Smells

I F YoU ask neW Yorkers what their city smells like, their immediate and vigorous answer will include such items as these:

+ Garbage.

+ Dog poop.

+ Urine.

+ Sweat (from other people, as in the subway).

+ Chemical vapors.

+ Gas.

+ Mold.

+ Grilled meat from block parties.

+ Diesel fumes.

+ Smells from halal and hot dog vendors.

Summer, of course, is the worst season for unpleasant smells, since the heat "cooks" the garbage and other undesirable deposits.

To these I'll add another provided by a friend who lived for many years in Brooklyn. He described the sickly sweet smell of mice dying in the walls after the landlord has spread poison, a smell that lasts from ten days to two weeks until their little bodies desiccate. For my friend this is quintessential olfactory New York.

And if you press New Yorkers for some positive olfactory experiences, they'll think a minute and perhaps come up with these:

+ Toasted bagels, a true New York experience.

+ Fruit tree blossoms in spring.

+ The aroma from a pizzeria, with hints of yeasty bread, cheese, and sausage.

+ In Brooklyn, the aroma of freshly roasted coffee emanating from several little wholesale coffee companies hidden in brick buildings.

+ Italian sausage cooking at stands at the annual Feast of San Gennaro in Little Italy, Manhattan.

Obviously, the negative experiences outweigh the positive ones. And New Yorkers complain: 13,054 odor complaints to 311 (the city's complaint and information number) over four years, or about eight gripes per thousand residents. And to judge by the number of complaints, Manhattan is the smelliest borough by far. Unless, of course, it simply has the most residents willing to lodge a complaint, which may well be the case.

(A personal note: What could be more New York than a bagel? Coming from the Midwest via Europe, I had never heard of them when I arrived here, but I was soon initiated. When introduced by Jewish friends to lochs and bagels, I disliked lochs but fell in love with bagels. When I was invited by a friend, a former New Yorker, to visit him in Massachusetts, and I asked him what I could bring him from New York, he answered without hesitation: bagels. So I brought him a bunch.)

To the smells already mentioned, I'll provide a few more, both pleasant and unpleasant, from my own experience.

✦ The aroma of fresh-baked bread emanating from some hidden bakery nearby, especially delicious on a cold winter night.

✦ On the street, the acrid smell of fresh asphalt when a pothole has just been filled.

✦ Roasted chestnuts from sidewalk stands in the fall.

✦ Hot air from dry cleaners, sometimes with a chemical edge to it that is surely toxic.

✦ A smell of rubble, plaster, and splintered wood heaped in dumpsters outside residences or shops undergoing renovation. Their interiors, when glimpsed from the sidewalk, look totally gutted and devastated.

✦ Exhaust fumes from buses as they pull away from the curb.

✦ In parks, the cloyingly sweet summer fragrance of Canada thistle and milkweed flowers, the soothing scent of a wild mint and, in the fall, a rich cidery tang from rotting apples scattered on the ground under apple trees.

✦ When pavement is being replaced, a smell of wet cement.

Yet many smells escape me, for my sniffer isn't the most sensitive. So let's consult an expert. A neuroscientist, in town one spring to register the smells of a New York morning, stood outside Grand Central Station during the morning rush hour and reported a toasted onion bagel, the briny smell of the East River, and a moist, sweet smell from steam rising from underground. And inside the terminal, where shops abound, he detected after-shave, toothpaste, disinfectant from trains, and brown-black shoe polish. There spoke a scientist of smell, and these are only a few of the aromas he experienced.

Every so often an unusual smell, unusual for the city, arrives to spice up our urban living. In April 2014 New Yorkers awoke to a heady smell of windborne smoke whose source was easily located: a brushfire in New Jersey a good hundred miles away. And periodically, from 2005 to 2009, a mysterious maple-syrup-like aroma visited our nostrils, its source an enigma. Finally, in 2009, Mayor Bloomberg announced triumphantly that the probable source had been detected: fragrance-processing plants in New Jersey making use of fenugreek seed, a spice employed in this country more for industrial than culinary purposes. Not an unpleasant odor, but many New Yorkers were of the opinion that New Jersey should keep its smells to itself. (I shan't chronicle the smells of northeastern New Jersey, which I have also experienced in quick succession: a soggy stink of marshland, a pig farm, and an oil refinery.)

Now I'll mention two less-than-enticing aromas imposed on us by those longtime friends of mine, the trees. An import from China, the gingko *(gingko biloba)* is a common shade tree here with distinctive fan-shaped leaves that turn yellow in the fall. At the same time it bears its fruit, tawny or yellowish little balls that litter the ground, the smell of whose fleshy pulp has been likened to dog poop, an odiferous cheese, rancid butter, or vomit.

If, wearing disposable gloves to prevent irritation to the hands, one endures the smell and removes the pulp, one finds a greenish nut that some consider tasty. Having endured the stink, cracked the shell, and fought through to the nut, I once tried it but found it uninteresting, not worth the ordeal of harvesting it. Furthermore, if consumed in quantity, it can be toxic. In the city the fallen nuts get crushed by pedestrians on the sidewalk, and people wonder where that stink comes from. Yet up in the North End of Central Park I have seen older Chinese women gathering the fruit on the ground, whether for culinary or medicinal purposes, I do not know, since Chinese tradition sanctions both. My conclusion: Leave the gingko fruit to the Chinese, who probably know what to do with it.

And if, strolling the city's streets in spring, you should detect an odor that some have described as a mix of semen and rotting fish, though others just say semen, don't assume some oversexed teenager has been active in the vicinity. Instead, look around and see if you don't find one or several trees bearing quantities of little five-petaled white flowers that, if sniffed, prove to be the source of this odor. Such is the callery pear (*Pyrus calleryana*), another import from Asia and the second commonest shade tree in the city, which puzzled me for years until I finally consulted the city and they identified it. I knew it only as a mystery tree with white flowers in the spring; I had never stuck my schnozzola into its blossoms to discover this surprising—and for some, offensive—odor.

New Yorkers do try to create more pleasant olfactory experiences. At 399 Bleecker Street, right next to the Magnolia Bakery, is Bond No. 9. One Sunday afternoon, having passed it many times without really noticing it, I stopped and saw, in the front window, an array of small bottles, all identical in shape, tapering to a waist and flaring again, each one with a distinctive color: orange, gold, blue, lavender, black, and one with a bright patchwork of different colors. "Making scents of New York" proclaimed the logo, so I concluded that these were perfumes. Perfumes are for me *terra incognita,* a vast hinterland of knowledge that I have never ventured to explore. Why, then, did I go in, knowing full well that I had no intention of buying? Probably some obscure intimation that this might be the beginning of an article on New York shops, and the fact that the shop—so unlike the crowded bakery next door—was for the moment devoid of customers. Also, an awareness that the bottles conveyed unmistakably an impression of New York chic.

I at once identified myself as an upstairs neighbor and was greeted cordially by two young people, sleek and chic: a young man with a scarf around his neck, and a young woman whose dash of bold red lipstick suggested the slash of a stiletto. A short conversation followed, and they gave me a small circular tag proclaiming the name of the store and its motto ("Making scents of New York"), with the address of a series of stores on the back.

Of course I checked out their website, which explained that their perfume collection has been launched as an homage to the city of New York, and that many of their scents convey a particular neighborhood: New York Sandalwood, New York Patchouli, Riverside Drive, West Side, Manhattan, and so on. I decided to investigate So New York, a phrase I often use ("That is *so* New York!"), and of course Bleecker Street, which their staff told me was their most popular scent, Here's how these two perfumes are described:

So New York
A whiff of New York's consuming passion above-
all-else for chocolate desserts and frothy lattes. For
sensualists of sweets, a grown-up perfume liqueur
doused with bittersweet espresso and warm-milk
accords, plus a hint of spice.

Bleecker Street
Art, fashion, seduction, and dessert in liquid form.
A warm and sensual aphrodisiac that glides from
day into evening.

Enticing as the perfume is, this resident of Bleecker Street isn't sure that the street itself is sensual and glides from day into evening. When I offered a sample of the perfume to Bob, who knows perfumes, he found it lacking in distinction. And come to think of it, a really fine perfume must take time and effort and maybe genius to create. How could one outfit produce such a scent for dozens of New York neighborhoods? Buyer, beware. Nor are these scents for everyone's budget. A 100 ml flask of Bleecker Street goes for $280.00, and a mere 50 ml flask for $205.00. But Bob assured me that such prices are not out of line for a really fine product. So take your pick, denizens of Brooklyn, Manhattan, or wherever; Bond No. 9 has a scent for you. And for those who don't live in or near New York, their collection is also available in Vancouver, Montreal, Dubai, and elsewhere abroad.

Finally, I'll end with a new smell that, some say, will soon flood our streets. "A mostly skunky smell with notes of fruit and jet fuel"—that's how Wonder Woman is described. But what is Wonder Woman? A hot new strain of *Cannabis sativa*, aka marijuana, pot, weed, and what have you. Yes, with a growing movement to decriminalize marijuana, the smell of it is becoming ever more pervasive in the city, including Wonder Woman, a strain produced by combining two female plants, one of which has been manipulated to produce male flowers. (If readers are confused by this, so am I, all the more so since I have never indulged in any form of the stuff.) So potent is Wonder Woman, that consumers are warned to anticipate two and a half hours of hand-to-hand combat with reality, their stress banished into the stratosphere and their body limp. So the skunk-like smell of pot is now invading even the thick walls of brownstones, to the point that one mother reported that her teenage daughter was afraid of getting high while doing her homework. So one more smell is added to the roster of the city's smells, with "stench nuisance" fast becoming a problem as more and more New Yorkers struggle to achieve serenity.

Chapter 13
Graffiti

Y oU see them eVerYWhere—on sidewalks, on fences, on mailboxes, wherever there is space and a chance to be seen by passersby. On the pavement of the Union Square greenmarket on March 23, 2016, in the wake of the terrorist attacks in Brussels:

Pray
4
Brussels

We gon
be alright

On the Horatio Street sidewalk near an entrance to Jackson Square Park, just south of West 14th Street:

I was caged
but I fought back

In white chalk, so I thought, but it must have been white paint, since it subsequently survived many days of rain. Under the words were two crudely drawn chickens, or maybe two squawking ducks; the artist's skills were limited.

On a mail storage box on West 13th Street, squeezed in with a host of scribblings and crazy art:

> FAME
> KILLS

Some are problematic, as for instance, on the sidewalk at an intersection:

> TAKE CARE

Good advice, but for whom? Similarly, on East Fourth Street:

> PAY YOUR
> DEBTS

And on Eighth Avenue near Jane Street:

> PROTECT
> YO
> HEART
> PYH

And on the scaffolding masking renovation of a building on West Fourth Street:

> TAKE ME TO THE ALLEY

But there was no alley in sight. Just as enigmatic, also on West Fourth Street:

I DON'T WANT
TO DIE
MOTHERCOW

You rarely know who the graffiti artists are, but in some cases I assume young teenage males, known for their blatant candor, as in these two instances, seen by me long ago, though I don't remember where:

If Satan gets my balls we'll play tennis

farts are healthy

And in the Union Square greenmarket, scrawled on the pavement in fading chalk trampled by busy New Yorkers who pay no heed:

NEW YORK
R U
HUNG?

Some show signs of sophistication, as for instance this one, scrawled on the wall of a men's room on the Columbia University campus eons ago, which was much quoted and became legendary:

God = mc2

For the knowing few, of course, this was a take-off of Einstein's renowned physics equation, E = mc2, meaning that energy equals mass multiplied by the speed of light, squared.

But my favorite graffito (yes, that's the singular) was one I glimpsed, I don't know where, back in the rebellious 1960s:

Jesus saves
but Moses invests

Modern graffiti originated in Philadelphia but soon spread to New York. Here they evolved from crude sidewalk scribbles to the exuberant multicolored art of minority youth spray-painting the sides of the city's subway cars in the 1970s. Graffiti were associated in the public mind with gangs and rap, and in the 1980s the authorities with great effort eliminated the art—and art it was, in my opinion, however misplaced. Guard dogs and razor wire denied access to the subway yards, and workers scrubbed the cars relentlessly clean. For some, the graffiti-ridden cars symbolized the city's moral and physical decline, which goes to show that one man's art is another's vandalism.

But that was just the beginning of the fight. Denied access to the subways, artists invaded the streets. The debate continued, with a resurgence of graffiti art prompting the *New York Post* to declare that the city must beat the "cancer of graffiti." In 1995 Mayor Rudolph Giuliani set up the Anti-Graffiti Task Force as part of his crackdown on "quality-of-life crimes," and the sale of aerosol spray-paint cans to children under eighteen was banned.

But the cancer persisted, showing such originality and flare that gallery and building owners began commissioning street artists to adorn their storefront gates and walls. Artists with names like Taki 183, Blade, Cope 2, Juice 177, and Zephyr emerged, adding fantastic scenery and cartoon characters, and acquiring a special kind of fame. Today street art is an accepted part of youth culture, celebrated in museums and galleries and in graffiti websites on the Internet. There are even walking tours to view "vivid tags, ornate murals, & intricate posters," and lessons to teach the techniques and tools used by local artists. And in February 2018 a federal judge awarded $6.7 million in damages to twenty-one graffiti artists whose works had been destroyed by a real estate developer in Brooklyn. In 2013 the developer had whitewashed away their swirling murals on the walls of his warehouse, obliterating what the artists' lawyer described as the world's largest open-air aerosol museum. The judge had decided that forty-five of the lost murals had enough artistic value to merit protection.

Street art has now so evolved that it appears in living rooms, especially that of Lee Quiñones. As a teenager in the 1970s, he snuck into train yards at night to scrawl his graffiti on subway cars. But today his art, often introspective and ethereal, appears not only in his home in Bedford-Stuyvesant, Brooklyn, but also in museums like New York's Whitney and Berlin's Staatliche. His work lies somewhere between graffiti and contemporary art, and museums definitely want it—another example of the irrepressible creativity of the city of New York.

One graffiti artist who announces himself is Hans ("Ace") Honschar, a man in his forties, dark-haired with a black mustache, whose colored chalk snippets appear all over the Upper West Side. In 2016 he briefly invaded the West Village—my turf—and left messages on the sidewalk outside the D'Agostino supermarket. His messages—at least, the ones that I have seen—are relentlessly upbeat:

the two most
joyous times
of the year
are Christmas
morning and

the end of
School

find ur talent
& fulfill your
purpose
for you are
the embodiment
of infinite
possibilities

I saw that
my life was
a vast, glowing
empty page
and I could do
anything

In producing these multicolored bits of wisdom he even makes a buck or two, for shop owners pay him to leave an inscription in front of their shop, and passersby pay him to take their picture for five dollars or, for double that, to have their picture taken with him.

Fulfilling his destiny, alas, has led to a tangle or two with the police, since graffiti are technically forbidden, but like a good New Yorker he persists. Born in Halifax, Nova Scotia, to a strict religious family that attended a Pentecostal church, he grew up in Florida and migrated all over Canada before landing in New York. There, like so many, he knew he had to stay, with a special fondness for the Upper West Side.

I wake up
every morning

and I say
to myself
'Well, I'm still
in New York,
thank you God'

No matter what the outcome of his skirmishes with the police, he continues to fulfill his chalky, polychrome destiny.

Graffiti have always been with us and always will be. They have been found in the ruins of ancient Egypt and Pompeii and surely go back eons, probably to the dawn of writing. I can well imagine some enterprising young caveman sneaking a few raw squiggles onto the walls of a cave otherwise adorned with marvelous drawings of the animals hunted by our ancestors in prehistoric times. Graffiti are usually anonymous, often irreverent, often bawdy, but sometimes uplifting and inspiring. And by their very nature subversive. No city has contributed more to their fame and notoriety than New York.

Chapter 14
Construction and Destruction

New York has always been a tear-down, build-up city: tear down the old, put up something new on the site. In the nineteenth century there was a constant rattle and screech and grind and thud as workmen hammered and sawed and bolted materials into place, or hauled them in wagons, or hoisted them by means of a horse-powered windlass or derrick. Such operations raised up clouds of dust and plaster, and sent avalanches of brickbats and splintered wood and slate down upon the heads of luckless pedestrians. And on one occasion, when construction involved blasting, a boulder crashed through the roof and three floors of a mansion to lodge between two ceiling beams in a gentleman's parlor; the contractor apologized.

If such an intrusion violated that revered sanctum, that shrine of Victorian gentility, what can one say of the cemeteries, those sanctuaries of the dear departed, when development decreed their closing? Only too often workmen excavating the site shoveled out onto the pavement shreds of grave clothes, bones, and bits of skull with tufts of hair. The kin of those buried there had been notified of the cemetery's closing and been given time to remove the loved ones, but sometimes no kin could be located, with desecration the result.

What was the city up to? It was called Go Ahead: the passionate belief then gripping the nation that More + Bigger + Faster = Better. Go Ahead proclaimed that the city and the nation were vehicles of Progress, that old fogyism and reverence for the past must yield to Young America and its fervent embrace of the New. And who could doubt the cult of Progress, since in a single lifetime citizens could witness the coming of gaslight, replacing candles and whale-oil lamps, and then the electric light. In their lifetime they welcomed steamboats and railroads and the telegraph, making travel and communication easier. Not to mention that wondrous amenity, the flush toilet, right inside one's home, replacing wells and cisterns and the indignity of the chamber pot.

Americans were gaga over material progress, and for New Yorkers this meant tearing down old buildings to replace them with new and better ones, while pushing the city's limits farther and farther north on the narrow island of Manhattan. The Commissioners' Plan of 1811 imposed on the city's expansion, "for beauty, order, and convenience," a grid plan of rectangular blocks that would discipline the city's growth for the full length of Manhattan and on into the Bronx, all the way to the border with Yonkers. From then on, as the city expanded northward, hills were leveled, valleys filled in, and marshes drained. Browsing goats, squatters' shanties with gardens, skulking woodcock, and rutted country roads gave way to paved streets, hammerings and sawings and poundings, and the rising walls of stores and tenements. A few preexisting neighborhoods like Greenwich Village, with its crazy pattern of streets, were spared, but otherwise the grid pushed relentlessly northward. And in the later nineteenth century, with the coming of better construction materials and the elevator, the city could be pushed up as well—up to eight-, ten-, and 12-story buildings. And who knew how much farther they could jab into the blue vault of heaven? With the twentieth century the answer came in the form of soaring Art Deco masterpieces like the Chrysler Building and the Empire State Building, skyscrapers emblematic of a city and nation eager to cast off Old World vestiges and lurch boldly into the intoxicating realm of the New. (The great influence in this development, ironically, was the avant-garde of European architects, who likewise were plunging headlong into the New.) Hence the construction of the Twin Towers, for which there was no pressing need, and after their destruction, the Freedom Tower. Yes, in New York today Go Ahead is exuberantly, even savagely alive, devising strange low-level monstrosities and thrusting glass-pinnacled high-rises far into the sky.

This fever affects even my neighborhood, the West Village, landmarked though it is. When I go out on errands, I am constantly forced into detours because of construction. I pass graffiti-adorned scaffoldings masking construction or renovation within, and see trucks coming and going with lettering on their flanks announcing

PLUMBING HEATING ELECTRICAL
LUMBER
INSTALLATIONS
DEMOLITION & CARTING
INTERIOR DEMOLITION

When I get a glimpse of an excavation site, I see a deep pit with rubble and debris. At the curb outside any building undergoing renovation there is a big dumpster overloaded with bricks, bits of wood and plaster, twisted steel, bits of pipe, and heaps of bent nails and rubble. Often I get a peek through the open doorway of an old brownstone, its façade intact, its interior gutted and strewn with debris. That glance often goes the whole length of the interior to a gaping window frame in the rear wall that affords a glimpse of the back garden, or what remains of it. Yes, the West Village is a historical district, but interiors can be revamped inordinately, as long as the exterior is preserved.

And the cranes—those towering devices whose installation may cause the closing of a whole block to traffic. Their soaring spikes reach up high to remove debris from the topmost floors of a building, or to hoist materials onto the structure, or to do whatever is necessary at those dizzying heights. Like many passersby, I often pause a few minutes to watch them in operation, staring in disbelief at the compact powerhouse at street level, amazed that this little structure can command the metal giraffe neck of a monster reaching high into the sky.

Do these towering monsters ever collapse? Yes, alas. At 8:00 a.m. on the morning of February 5, 2016, when falling snow was accompanied by wind gusts, the crew of a crane rising 565 feet into the air in TriBeCa in Lower Manhattan decided to lower the crane to a more secure level. But as the crane descended, it suddenly toppled over and came crashing down on Worth Street, killing a pedestrian, injuring three others, shaking nearby buildings, and littering the surrounding blocks with debris. Thinking a bomb had exploded, people going to work panicked and fled from the scene. Firefighters, policemen, and utility workers rushed to repair the damage to a water main and a number of gas lines. Gas was shut off in the immediate area, streets were closed, and subway lines skipped nearby stops—all this during the morning rush hour. Photographs show the toppled crane stretching the length of a city block.

The sole fatality of this incident was a Czech-born immigrant of thirty-eight who had a mathematics degree from Harvard. To die in a crane collapse strikes me as one of the weirdest possible deaths in this city, topped only, perhaps, by being killed by a falling branch while crossing Central Park on a windy day. And what was the crane doing there? Installing generators and air-conditioning units atop the building at 60 Hudson Street. As a precaution, after the collapse city officials ordered 419 other cranes then operating in the city to be secured, and the mayor promised that inspectors would be tough on the companies responsible for construction site accidents.

Will cranes continue to be a feature of life in the city? Of course. In 2016 Rockefeller University on the Upper East Side began moving horizontally instead of vertically, this being the only way it could expand. It built over (yes, *over*) the FDR Drive, and a huge crane soon hoisted a prefabricated 800,000-pound metal structure from a barge in the East River and lowered it into place over the Drive. This was the first of nineteen such structures, and the crane was the largest marine crane on the East Coast, able to reach as high as a 21-story building and carry up to two million pounds. The hoisting was to be done at night, with the Drive closed for the operation. Even so, good luck, East Side motorists! Heavy heavy hangs over thy head.

If dying in a crane collapse is weird, how about being buried alive? On April 6, 2015, a fourteen-foot trench at a construction site on Ninth Avenue collapsed, crushing an Ecuadorean immigrant worker under thousands of pounds of dirt. The machinery of justice grinds slowly, but on June 10, 2016, the contracting company was convicted of second-degree manslaughter and criminally negligent homicide, both felonies, and of reckless endangerment, a misdemeanor. When the jury verdict was announced, relatives of the victim, including his mother who had come all the way from Ecuador, broke down in tears and were hugged by the prosecutor. The verdict was significant, since criminal liability in such cases is hard to prove. Two construction managers were also indicted on homicide charges, and the company itself faced possible fines of up to $35,000.

Crane collapses, alas, have become a common feature of life in New York City. At 10:00 a.m. on September 11, 2018, a crane on a construction site on 12th Avenue near West 34th Street was hoisting a steel beam, when the load knocked over a second beam, and both beams crashed to the ground. A double whammy, closing traffic on the West Side Highway near the Jacob Javits Convention Center, though no fatalities or injuries resulted. More such accidents must be anticipated.

The constant destruction of old buildings and neighborhoods, often to make room for luxury apartment buildings with astronomical rents, has provoked a countermovement for preservation. Old buildings and even whole neighborhoods are landmarked, preventing drastic changes to their exteriors. Outside of landmarked districts, fierce battles pit the New York Real Estate Board (NYREB) and developers against preservationists and local residents. In Greenwich Village, as in SOHO (south of Houston Street) and NOHO (north of Houston), the Greenwich Village Society for Historic Preservation fights for the preservation of old buildings with aesthetic and historical significance. Some battles it wins, and some it loses, depending on the decisions of city authorities. It's a war that never ends.

The West Village is an old neighborhood full of Greek Revival and brownstone houses, and even a few Federal-style houses, so I support GVSHP and its allies. An example of what can happen outside the limits of the Greenwich Village Historical District is the Palazzo Chupi on West 11th Street between Washington and West Streets. Originally the site was occupied by a plain-fronted three-story brick building that served in turn as a stable, a garage, an office building, and an artist's studio. Then, in 1997, it was bought by artist and filmmaker Julian Schnabel, a Renaissance man of many talents with big dreams and plans to build big as well. He moved his family in and then, in 2005, began construction of a superstructure of additional floors on top of the existing building.

The result was an 11-story addition, a soaring stucco monster of a palace with loggias and balconies and terraces and round-arched windows, its façade receding in stages toward the top. The whole shebang was vaguely and brazenly Italianate, saying which I mean no insult to Italy and its architects, who are in no way responsible for this outlandish palazzo, the creation of an ambitious American developer who had no regard for the West Village setting it so violates.

The original three stories now serve as Mr. Schnabel's studio, a grandiose space for grandiose visions, with a grandiose swimming pool in the basement. On the upper floors, whose trendy Italianate superstructure overtops every other building in the area, are five lavish units. One was for his family (a second wife and twin teenage sons) with bold black-and-white tile floors and super modern furnishings with vibrant colors; the four other units he meant to rent out. He bought the building, he says, first, because he wanted more space, hoping to rent out two or three apartments to pay for that space, and second, because he could. Photographs show a dark-haired man in his sixties with a thick mustache curled over his upper lip, and a dark beard tinged with gray. He looks earnest, resolute.

Far above the street one now sees, in bold letters, **PALAZZO CHUPI.** The moment it appeared, speculation raged as to what it meant. The first word was clear enough, but "Chupi"? It means "kisses" in Italian, and "underpants" in Swahili, investigators discovered, but this and other interpretations were irrelevant. "Chupi" is a pet name for Mr. Schnabel's wife.

Okay, but how could he get away with this oddity in the Greenwich Village Historic District? Because he could. The historic district stops at Washington Street, just short of the palazzo's site. GVSHP had worked hard to get the historic district extended all the way to West Street and the river, but was not successful. The city agreed to downzone much of the Far West Village in 2005, limiting the height of all new construction. Schnabel's neighbors protested his plans the moment they learned of them, but he evidently had his workers doing construction after-hours and on weekends, so as to get the project approved before the new rules went into effect. He gambled and won, for the city allowed him to build under the old, looser zoning rules, rather than the new rules just enacted.

When the black construction netting was removed in June 2007, the newly renovated building was revealed as being, of all colors, *pink.* I don't mean soft feminine pink; I mean bright, vibrant, garish, bubblegum pink. Or "hot pink," as some detractors labeled it, or "neon pink," or "Pepto Bismol pink." "Pompeii red," insisted Schnabel. But for me, it was a pink more garish than I knew pink could be. Only with time—about four years of it—did the palazzo's weathered features fade slightly to a more acceptable "dusty Venetian rose." For this at least, we should be grateful. Or as one commentator put it, "Paler pinks make better neighbors."

Not that the preservationists and their allies have given up. Never has a development been subject to more tweets and twitters. For if Schnabel managed to wiggle past the rules, his ensuing travails have been chronicled on the real-estate blog "Curbed" with vast irreverence and unbounded glee.

And travails there have been. Schnabel's main problem was simply bad timing. He bought the building and "chupified" it at the peak of the real estate boom, and then the bubble burst, convulsing not just the real estate market but the whole financial community and the economy as well. Two of the four units sold fairly quickly. Later a third one, a penthouse triplex

with eighteen-foot ceilings and baronial bathrooms, sold for
$10.5 million, a bit of a comedown from the original asking price
of $32 million. Finally the duplex below it went for $12 million, down from $27 million. Was the pink palazzo becoming a
white elephant? In 2009 Schnabel had to pluck his late Picasso,
Femme au Chapeau, off his bedroom wall and sell it at Christie's
for $7.7 million, so as to pay down some of the debts created by
the construction of his palazzo.

"An unholy shrine to Schnabel's ego," one commentator
grants, but better, he insists, than the glass boxes sprouting up
all over the city like a bad virus. Certainly it is the big dream of
a big man, no pale imitation of someone else's fantasy. Maybe
Schnabel really is a Renaissance man of our own age, bigger
than life, whom we'll all come in time to appreciate. Maybe he
would endorse the words now posted on the front window of
one of the designer clothing stores just down Bleecker Street
from my building: "*Les folies sont les seules choses qu'on ne regrette
jamais*" (Follies are the only things one never regrets—Oscar
Wilde). But from the corner of Bleecker and West 11th, just
across from my building, I can see his pink tower high above
the other rooftops, and it pains my psyche. For me, his pink
palazzo was at first a horror. Now, with its "hot pink" cooling,
I am beginning to accept it for its originality. But it belongs
somewhere else, maybe Vegas.

Mr. Schnabel didn't tear down; he built. But many buildings
are indeed torn down, and when that happens, what becomes of
the debris? It is carted off, one assumes. But what of the ornamental fixtures and furnishings that once adorned them—the
ornate fireplaces, carved oak paneling, stained glass, vintage
plumbing, terra-cotta curlicues, and antique lighting fixtures?
They are rescued by a special breed of scavengers who, by prior
arrangement with the demolisher, rush in to collect architectural
artifacts and either preserve them or offer them for sale.

And where do they end up? One huge trove is in a sprawling complex of buildings on Main Street in the sleepy little town of Ivoryton, Connecticut, a two-hour drive northeast of New York. Inside the buildings is a vast array of scavenged artifacts:

+ carved oak transoms from the first Helen Hayes Theater on West 46th Street in Manhattan.

+ seven phone booths covered with band stickers and graffiti from the famous Roseland Ballroom, which closed in 2014.

+ antique carved oak paneling from art patron Gertrude Vanderbilt Whitney's Fifth Avenue mansion.

+ marble fireplaces from the elegant Plaza Hotel.

+ Tudor-style stained glass from a penthouse on 57th Street where actor Errol Flynn once lived.

+ bars from Gino's restaurant on Lexington Avenue, which closed in 2010.

+ the reception counter and display cases from Manhattan's prestigious 21 Club.

+ the terra-cotta façade of the Savoy Theater on Bedford Avenue in Brooklyn.

And this is only a fraction of the trove.

So what is all this stuff doing in Connecticut? It is the collection, assembled over many years, of Evan Blum, who calls it the "Sixth Borough" and offers the items for sale at prices you might not want to pay. And how does he get the stuff? By making an agreement, often for a fee, with the company doing the demolition. Some preservationists criticize him for selling the artifacts, arguing that this creates a market for items that should be placed in museums. But he insists that he hates to see old buildings demolished, and that he is rescuing the stuff from a trip to the landfill. The Connecticut trove isn't open to the public, but a sampling of his collection can be seen at Demolition Depot & Irreplaceable Artifacts, his showroom on East 125th Street in Harlem, well known to collectors and designers. But demolition keeps Mr. Blum busy. In 2016 he told a *Times* reporter that they're taking down and gutting buildings faster than he can keep up. "I have twenty-five churches to do before the end of the year."

Chapter 15
Fires and Firemen

n this City i have been through 2½ fires.

Fire No. 1

My partner Bob and I heard a commotion downstairs, poked our noses out the apartment door, saw a haze of smoke coming up the staircase, and a fireman knocking on doors one flight down.

"Do you want us out of the building?" I yelled.

"Yes," came the fireman's answer. "And fast!"

That said, he darted down the stairs into the hazy smoke. So Bob and I tossed on our light jackets and followed him down the stairs into the smoke. Ahead of us we saw the landlady, who was housebound with arthritis, being carried down the last flight of stairs. Only when we were safe outside, joining the crowd watching the firemen at work, did we realize that we had done exactly what you're told not to do in a fire: to go in the direction of the smoke.

The fire was in the basement. Later we learned that the landlady had once had a perfume business and stored some chemicals there. Another no-no: don't store inflammables in the basement, and above all, don't leave them there, forgotten, for years. The chemicals had been a fire just waiting to happen. The fire was quickly put out, and after the firemen had aired the building to get rid of the smoke, we were allowed back in. No damage except in the basement, so it ended well. Being a bit shook up, Bob and I and our downstairs neighbor Hans joined another neighbor in her room for an after-crisis drink. A real Village scene, we thought: four survivors tippling together in a tastefully shabby apartment

"Like in *La Bohème*," said Hans, a great opera buff.

"Or *Götterdämmerung*," I quipped, mindful of Wagner's fiery finale.

So ended my first fire in the city. No word of it in the newspapers, since such non-events occur all the time, too numerous and routine to merit a mention in the newspaper of record. But I had learned to be leery of accumulating inflammables. Once, when our trash area was piled high for days with boxes and newspapers that the super hadn't put out for collection, I informed the Fire Department, and they were on the spot inspecting the place within twenty-four hours. And every time I walk past the Magnolia Bakery, our celebrated ground-floor neighbor, and the Bleecker Street entrance to our basement is open, I peer down the steep stairs, wondering if that shadowy underworld is piled high with the bakery's empty cartons, as it once was, when I went down to have access to our circuit breaker.

Fire No. 2

One summer many years later there came a sudden knock on the door. Bob was away, so I was in the apartment alone. At the door was our young next-door neighbor, and behind her, once again, smoke pouring up the staircase, this time much thicker and more threatening.

"Get out of the building!" I said, before she could say a word. "Don't go down the stairs. Use the fire escape. I'll see you down on the street."

So she went down the front fire escape to West 11th Street, and after phoning Hans to alert him, I went down the other fire escape to Bleecker Street. It was a mild summer afternoon, so all the tenants joined the inevitable throng watching the fire from the street. Hans told me that another of our neighbors, who was watching the scene with visible anguish, had apologized to him: The fire had started in his kitchen. Long out of work, he watched television day and night and had probably been watching it when he had something on the stove. A quiet, harmless guy, but sad. Another neighbor had told us once of helping him get an ambulance on Christmas Eve. "I'm the loneliest man in the city," he had confessed, before being whisked off in the ambulance to an emergency room—not a cheerful prospect on Christmas Eve. And now, a fire in his apartment, and all of us routed out to the street.

Again, the firemen had come quickly and soon the fire was out, with damage only to our neighbor's kitchen. Hans had three cats, but they had taken refuge under the furniture and emerged unharmed. For several days afterward, going up or down the stairs, through an open door I could see workmen in the fire-damaged kitchen, and our neighbor, seemingly oblivious of them, watching television. In time he moved out; I have no idea what became of him. And that is the story of my second fire in the city.

As fires go, not much, you might say. No roaring infernos, no charred bodies, no tangled, blackened wreckage. Agreed. But I have one more fire to offer

Fire No. 2½

Why 2½? Because this fire wasn't in my building, so I wasn't routed out to the street. One summer night, long past midnight, I heard a commotion on the roof next to mine. Going to a window, I looked out and saw firemen on the roof next door, training hoses on a fire on the next roof over, where the residents had partied quietly the night before. The flames were leaping skyward: a real conflagration devouring everything in its path. I hadn't even heard the sirens, but there were the firemen, dousing the fire with torrents of water until the flames shrank down, flickered, and went out. It was all over in a matter of minutes, but I'll never forget the sight of those flames leaping high. The excitement over, I went back to bed.

The next morning I looked out and saw two of the residents poking about in the charred ruins of what had once been a charming roof garden. Among the wreckage were glasses from the partying of the night before. They saw me, gestured, shrugged. I shrugged too and told them of the spectacle I had witnessed well past midnight. And that was the end of the rooftop partying. One cigarette, not quite out, had probably been left behind, when the revelers quit the roof and went downstairs; that's all it took to kindle a blaze.

New Yorkers tend to shrug off fires. Not in their own building, of course, or in a building nearby, but otherwise they don't pay much attention. Fire engines race down the streets every day, their sirens wailing, and they're just a part of the usual hullabaloo, along with police and ambulance sirens, rumbling trucks with screeching brakes, horn blasts of irate drivers, and altercations—often shrill—of motorists. But New Yorkers don't resent those ambulance and fire engine sirens, annoying as they can be, since they are rushing aid to residents who need it. Here the city's congestion is advantageous, since firemen, once an alarm is sounded, can be at the scene of the fire within minutes. Congested cities don't harbor the worst risk of fires. It's those handsome residences out in the country, in idyllic settings, that risk burning to the ground before fire engines from some distant location can arrive. There are fires in the city, but they tend to be put out fast.

An exception to my statement that New Yorkers shrug off sirens: my partner Bob. Once, when he was fourteen, he and his family were routed out of their apartment in a three-story tenement in Jersey City, when in the wee hours of the morning, a fire raged next door. They were soon allowed back in, with no damage to their building, but the experience marked him for life. Whenever he heard a fire engine's siren in the street below our West Village apartment, he would listen intently, nervously, until the engine raced on past our building. And if the siren stopped near us, he would peer out the window to see if our building was involved. It never was, and he always breathed a sigh of relief. Needlessly fearful? Maybe. But he was the best fire detector our apartment could have had.

New York City firemen have a long and colorful history. Back in colonial times all able-bodied men were expected to fight fires. By the nineteenth century there were many wooden buildings in the city, and many fires. The city was spared a citywide conflagration like those that leveled Chicago in 1871 and San Francisco in 1906, but there were fires that raged and terrified.

On the night of December 16, 1835, fire broke out in a store on Merchant Street and immediately spread in all directions. Fire companies raced to the scene, but the men were exhausted from the previous night's work, and the intense cold froze the water in the hydrants. First, the dry-goods stores on Pearl Street were engulfed. Then the flames reached the Merchants' Exchange on Wall Street, a handsome building fronted with

marble columns and topped by a dome—the very symbol of the
city's prosperity—and it came crashing down, all of it but the
façade and its columns reduced to rubble. One citizen crossed
the ice-filled East River to the Navy Yard, loaded a brig with
kegs of gunpowder, and with the help of sailors and firemen
returned to Manhattan to blow up several large buildings and
create a firebreak that stopped the flames from spreading. But
a vast stretch of downtown New York around Wall, Broad,
and South Streets had been leveled, with the loss of 674 buildings. Looters soon began prowling the ruins, getting drunk
on champagne and other liquors littering the streets, while
exclaiming, "They'll make no more five percent dividends,"
and "This will make the aristocracy haul in their horns." But
the city's merchants were soon clearing the smoking rubble,
and with the ground still hot, began rebuilding.

Ten years later, early in the morning of July 19, 1845, fire
broke out in a factory on New Street and spread to a warehouse
filled with saltpeter. The warehouse then exploded with such
force that windows within a mile's radius were shattered, and the
fire spread, unchecked, to the whole area, much of it ravaged by
the fire of 1835. Buildings seemed to wither away in the flames
and melt down in white heat. When daylight came, the fire was
still raging. Even on streets far removed from the conflagration,
terrified storekeepers began tumbling boxes and barrels into
the street in hopes of saving their stores, and clerks poured
out of offices carrying loads of account books and papers. By
late morning the fire had been checked, but only when a thun-
dershower cooled the city on the night of July 21 were the last
embers extinguished. A large area around Broad and William
Streets and Exchange Place had been destroyed, including some
300 buildings.

A fire of a different kind engulfed Barnum's Museum on
Broadway on July 13, 1865. Firemen opened the museum's cages

to free the birds, which then flew about the city to the amazement and wonder of the populace. A huge Bengal tiger broke loose from its cage and leaped from a second-story window to the street. Onlookers froze in their tracks or stampeded in terror, while several policemen banged away ineffectively with their pistols. Then a fireman felled the tiger with a mighty blow of his ax. Even as spectators cheered, the fireman ran into the blazing building and carried out a fat lady weighing 400 pounds, returned to fetch out two children, and on a third trip rescued a woolly-headed albino woman. Inside the building two whales were boiled alive in their tanks. Seeing a caged thirty-foot python writhing in pain as it began to burn, another fireman broke open the cage and ended the creature's misery with two swift strokes of his ax. Many animals died in the fire, though some escaped to the street and were never seen again. Amazingly, no human lives were lost, but the fire, much smaller than those of 1835 and 1845, was long remembered.

And who were the firemen who so heroically battled these blazes? From the 1830s on, many young men of the working class joined volunteer fire companies that hauled their engines to the scene of a fire. Rivalry among the companies was fierce, and all too often one company would tangle with another for the use of a hydrant, even to the point of beating one another's skulls with pipes or the blunt ends of axes, while a fire roared merrily on. But joining Old Turk or Red Rover or the Honey Bee gave a young man more than a chance for a ruckus; it gave him status, and often paved the way to a career in politics. Mayors got started in this fashion, and Big Bill Tweed, the future Boss, formed the Americus Engine Company No. 6 and ran with it through the streets to a fire, shouting to his men through a silver trumpet, "Jump her, boys! Jump her!" In later years he would look back to that time as maybe the happiest in his life, and give a handout to any former member who came to him in need.

More glory came to the volunteer firemen on February 15, 1848, when a mediocre sketch of city life at Mitchell's Olympic Theatre was suddenly transformed by the appearance of a new character, Mose the Fireboy, played by Frank Chanfrau. Mose was courageous, outspoken, and blunt, a perfect portrayal of the Bowery Boy of the day, the "Bhoy dat ran wid der mersheen." Recognizing the character at once, the working-class audience erupted in applause. Chanfrau made his name doing Mose, flaunting the Bowery Boy's black plug hat and red shirt, and the hair on his temples greased and combed forward in soap-locks. Mose's black trousers were tucked into high-heeled boots, and the cigar clamped between his teeth was cocked upward in a feisty tilt. Most typical of all, his speech inflicted mayhem on the English language, and for that alone the audiences loved him.

But these were the days of Tammany, the Democratic organization that ran the city, and lots of money appropriated for fire equipment ended up in some politician's pocket. Finally, in 1865, the Republican-dominated state legislature replaced the volunteer companies with the Metropolitan Fire Department, a paid professional force governed by a Republican-dominated board of commissioners. Steam engines, horses, and the telegraph soon modernized the force, and from then on, firemen were more likely to fight fires than each other.

Today, New York City firemen are generally admired. Yes, their union long resisted admitting minority applicants and had to be coerced by the courts. And yes, occasionally a few of them get into off-duty brawls and scrapes. But the city's firemen emerged as the heroes of 9/11, when many of them were isolated in the flaming North Tower, unaware of the South Tower's collapse, and unaware as well of warnings from their commanders on the ground, and from police helicopters in the sky above, that the North Tower too was on the verge of collapse. Of the 343 firemen who died that day, an estimated 200 or so were lost inside or at the base of the North Tower.

We need the police too, but they have been tainted by corruption in the past. Stop-and-frisk practices have offended minority youths who were arbitrarily harassed, and have alienated the general public as well. The firemen have escaped such controversy. When my friend Barbara visited from Maine, she watched in admiration and awe as firemen packed up their gear and departed, having seen to some problem other than a fire on West 14th Street. Another woman, a passerby who was a total stranger, joined her, professing the same admiration of these burly stalwarts going about their business, totally unaware of two admiring females watching discreetly from a distance.

Chapter 16
Are New Yorkers Rude?

"With aLL the opULenCe and splendor of this city, there is very little good breeding to be found…. They talk very loud, very fast and altogether. If they ask you a question, before you can utter three words of your answer they will break in upon you again and talk away." So wrote John Adams, a Massachusetts man, in his diary for August 23, 1774, on the eve of the Revolution. He was writing about New York and New Yorkers.

And Thomas Jefferson, a Virginia gentleman suspicious of big cities and of New York in particular, called the city "the cloacina [cesspool] of all the depravities of human nature."

The Founding Fathers got to know the city well, since it served as the first national capital from 1785 until 1790, at which time the capital was moved temporarily to Philadelphia, pending the construction of a new capital on the banks of the Potomac. But the Founders don't seem to have loved New York or New Yorkers, which shows that the city and its residents had an image problem right from the start.

And today? One would like to think that New Yorkers are a courteous and welcoming lot, since over 60 million people visit the city annually, adding billions of dollars to the economy. But New Yorkers are often said to be arrogant, brusque, and rude. This I can understand, remembering my own first experience of the city and seeing hordes of people pacing briskly on the sidewalks and jamming into the subway system, with its confusing maze of corridors and stairs and platforms, and the constant comings and goings of crowded, screeching trains. And it didn't enhance the city's image when I took a taxi to the docks, and on arriving at my destination, heard the cabbie exclaim, with a slick look on his face, "Oh, I forgot to turn on my meter! Well, let's say five dollars." Young and green as I was, I knew I was being taken, so I gave him the five minus a tip.

If one looks online at posts on the subject of New Yorkers and their perceived rudeness today, what does one find? Here are some answers to the question, "Why are New Yorkers stereotyped as rude or mean?"

1. A fourth-generation New Yorker who knows all the boroughs finds most New Yorkers to be polite, helpful, and respectful. Where does this dumb stereotype about New Yorkers being rude and mean come from? Elsewhere in the country it would be hard to find first responders like the writer's father, who still has health problems from 9/11, risking their lives on 9/11 and after Hurricane Sandy.

2. New Yorkers tend to be direct and to the point, which is perceived as rudeness in some parts of the country. But the city also attracts ruthlessly ambitious people who can indeed be rude and mean.

3. Most New Yorkers are nice and often surprisingly generous. In the writer's hometown you can't get anyone to do anything for you unless you pay them first.

4. New Yorkers can be rude. When the writer gets coffee, people shout out, "Small coffee, three sugars!" and they don't say "please." This seeming rudeness occurs because there's a long line to get coffee and people are in a hurry. New Yorkers are rude, but it comes with the territory.

5. When we New Yorkers order a sandwich at a deli, the polite thing is to order it fast and not make other people wait; no time for "May I please..." But we do say "thank you," because that doesn't make anyone wait. We're not savages.

These are the voices of New Yorkers, whether born here or not, and maybe self-interested. But the points they make are valid. What's rude in other places isn't necessarily rude in New York, where getting to the point quickly often shows consideration for others.

There are interesting comments online about New Yorkers' directness vs. Southern or Midwestern politeness. For instance (I'll paraphrase):

✦ I just moved from New York to Minnesota. Minnesota residents have a reputation for being nice without being friendly, cheerful but bland, passive aggressive, and often not saying what they mean. It's weird.

✦ I grew up in the South and have never lived in New York, but I've never thought New Yorkers rude. I appreciate straight-talking New Yorkers more than the beat-around-the-bush niceties that you find in the South, where "hello" often means "fuck you."

✦ I've been living in Texas for ten years and I know, I know, I know that when my partner's mom acts real sweet and friendly to your face and then complains about you behind your back, it's because that's what's taught as politeness down here. You aren't ever supposed to forgo the "Southern hospitality" thing, especially if you're a woman, so all the value is placed upon "making nice" in public. But I was raised in a different culture where being blunt and to-the-point is valued.

Another blogger asks visitors not to make fun of "our 'New Yawka'" accent, and cites as an example "Ahright yous guys, let's get outa hea'." Yes, there is a New York accent. I remember years ago the amusement of my suburban Midwestern neighbors at a visiting New Yorker's saying "commoicial." But my Manhattan friends are all middle-class professionals or artists from elsewhere and don't have a trace of that accent. As for "Fuhgeddaboudit!"—a legendary saying attributed to natives of Brooklyn—I've never actually heard it, but it does sum up the New York attitude perfectly in conveying "no way" or "impossible": "The Democratic convention in Brooklyn? Fuhgeddaboudit!"

How about the views of out-of-towners? A poll conducted by Business Insider, a business news website based in New York City, interviewed 1,600 Americans and discovered these interesting opinions:

✦ Americans do indeed think New Yorkers are rude and arrogant, but also think New Yorkers serve the best food.

✦ The residents of Georgia and Minnesota are deemed the nicest.

✦ Alaska has the worst food.

✦ Colorado has the most beautiful scenery.

✦ Texas should be kicked out of the United States.

New Yorkers can be too critical of themselves. Here are some items from a 2012 blog, apparently by a resident New Yorker, listing fifty-five of the rudest things New Yorkers do:

1. Claim that you are poor when you make $700,000 a year.

2. Drink the milk directly out of the container.

3. Act like elderly people don't have a right to exist in this city.

4. Cheat.

5. Cut the wallet out of drunk people's pockets when they pass out while riding the subway.

6. Chuckle, even audibly, when the subway door slams in the face of that loser.

7. Think that you are better than other people because you are a New Yorker.

8. Claim that New Yorkers are rude.

What world is this blogger living in? I either haven't observed any of these behaviors (#1, 3, 5, 6), or consider them too universal to blame on New Yorkers (#2, 4). And as regards #3, I can testify that, having attained the status of white-haired codger still traveling by subway, I am often offered a seat by a seated fellow passenger. I might agree with #7, but suggest that residents of many cities, big and small, are inclined to do the same. As for #8, some of us do, rightly or wrongly, claim this, but isn't that more honest than rude?

Here, for the sake of visitors to the city, are three things that New Yorkers feel they have an inalienable right to do:

1. Boast. (About New York, of course.)
2. Complain. (About New York, of course.)
3. Jaywalk. (Which is why they get fined when visiting other communities with laws against it.)

When you visit another community, you are a guest there and need to learn the unwritten rules of conduct, if you wish to be accepted. In New York, too, visitors should be aware of this, so as to avoid unpleasant experiences. This is a crowded city where people hurry because they value their time. It is also a city—especially Manhattan, the most visited borough—where many people don't have cars and get about by walking and using public transportation. So here are some tips for visitors:

1. Don't walk three or four abreast on the sidewalk; you obstruct pedestrian traffic.

2. For the same reason, don't pause at the top of a stairway as you exit the subway system. If you need to get your bearings, move out of the way before stopping.

3. Don't hold subway train doors open or try to force them open. Let the frenzied natives commit this folly; there'll soon be another train.

4. Don't enter a subway train before all the exiting passengers have left.

5. When you ask a question, don't beat around the bush. If you get right to the point, most New Yorkers will be glad to help you, as I myself have often done.

6. Don't go to Times Square on New Year's Eve, unless you enjoy claustrophobia. You'll be packed in for hours with thousands of other celebrants.

7. And if you value your life, during rush hour don't ever,
   ever get between a hurrying New Yorker and his bus or
   train.

Here now is the report of a cousin from Kokomo, Indiana,
who visited New York with her twenty-year-old son. Wanting to
have a view of the Statue of Liberty, they got on a subway train but
soon sensed something was wrong. In the car with them were a
foreign family who spoke no English, and a middle-aged woman
who was sound asleep. As my cousin and her son discussed their
predicament, the middle-aged woman woke up and asked if they
were lost. "Absolutely!" my cousin replied, and told her where
they wanted to go. "Well, you're in the Bronx," she said, which
meant that they were going in the opposite direction. Shouting
"Thank you!" they immediately got off the train, took one in
the opposite direction, and finally, after an unintended visit to
Chinatown and with more help from New Yorkers, got to their
destination. At one point other lost souls also asked for help,
and everyone was helping everyone. My cousin's conclusion:
No, New Yorkers aren't rude, they're helpful. And she decided
that a bit of Kokomo courtesy, with a good dose of "please" and
"thank you," would see her through in the future.

So what do I conclude? New Yorkers don't mean to be rude, but
they can seem so when judged by the standards of other communities where life is less pressured and hectic … but also less
exciting. My advice to visitors: By all means come, for New York
is an experience not to be missed. You'll be thrilled, entertained,
and dazzled. But come prepared.

Chapter 17
Scams, Cheats, and Cons

O nCe, Long ago, When m Y brother met me at an airport to give me a lift to the family apartment, he said with a canny look, "Let me tell you about my new scam." His "scam" was simply a plan to redeem hundreds of coupons in newspapers, so as to acquire a lifetime supply of whatever at a reduced price. Being in the newspaper distribution business, he had access to reams of unsold papers and so had a free hand in clipping reams of coupons. There was nothing illegal about this; he was simply taking advantage of his position to buy things cheap. Years later, when I came back to bury him, I found the apartment crammed with his spoils: a lifetime supply of deodorants, ditto of detergent, car repair equipment that only a grease monkey could appreciate, and I don't recall what else. It took me weeks to clear it all out. But what I still remember most vividly, was that look on his face when he announced his so-called scam: canny, shrewd, knowing, worthy of Wily Coyote, the trickster of many Native American legends. It was indeed the look of an operator about to put something over on others—in other words, the look of a con man.

New York, like any big city, is a mecca for con men, cheats, and thieves, and as such reinforces the timeworn image of the wicked big city, full of urban wiles, as opposed to quiet, decent, clean-living small-town and rural America. A stereotype, and as such suspect, but not wholly devoid of truth. Here are some of my experiences.

An African American cruising the streets in a fancy limousine stuffed with clothing once asked with a winning smile if I'd like to buy some clothes. I declined, convinced that they were stolen items. He was surely a thief or a fence.

On another occasion when I found myself at night in midtown, I saw a man trying to sell some paper dolls to some sailors. Aligned side by side, the dolls were dancing on the sidewalk as if by magic. It was an old trick still being played. But the sailors weren't fooled; they were looking for the hidden strings that propelled the dolls. Seeing this, another man standing nearby announced in a resonant voice, "It's showtime!" He repeated his warning a second time, and the vendor of the dolls packed them up and moved on down the street. "I knew there was a hidden string," said one sailor, "and here it is." Looking closely, he had detected the almost invisible string.

Another scam that used to be practiced in the city involved a man entering into conversation with a stranger outside a bank and telling him that banks were frauds, they took your money but wouldn't give it back. He would repeat this assertion so consistently, and so smugly, that the other man would wax indignant and tell him he was crazy. "Go ahead, just try," the first man would dare him, "try to withdraw a sizable sum, and you'll see that I am right." So the dupe would do so, and it was just a matter of time before he and his money were separated.

How could anyone fall for such an obvious scam, you and I and almost everyone would wonder, and the victim, once disabused, would wonder the same. But at the time, he fell for it hook, line, and sinker, and—to mix metaphors—got royally fleeced. Other common New York scams, cheats, and cons that visitors may encounter:

1. Costumed characters in Times Square who invite you to pose with them for a photo and then demand a tip. No tip is required.

2. Someone offers to sell you a ticket for the Staten Island ferry at a bargain price, when the ferry is free.

3. Restaurants in places frequented by tourists that charge for dishes you didn't order, and leave a space for an additional tip, when the mandatory 15 percent tip for parties of eight or more is already included in the bill. (Note: In my experience, most New York restaurants are honest.)

4. Pickpockets in crowded places like subway cars and greenmarkets.

5. People with badges saying "Authorized Ticket Agent" who offer to sell you a fake ticket to visit the Empire State Building, with an added fee to skip the long line at the entrance, or to take a nonexistent "skyride."

6. People who offer to sell you fake tickets for the ferry service to the Statue of Liberty.

7. Someone who bumps into you and claims you broke his glasses, which he shows you, and demands compensation.

These are scams that primarily target unwary tourists visiting the city. But today the cheats take advantage of the Internet to reach everyone in their home. Once, out of nowhere, I got an

e-mail: "Aloha! I'd like to get to know you. From your profile
I think we have lots in common." The sender seemed to be a
pleasant young woman. Surprised and charmed, I was tempted
to respond, but some good spirit deep within me, some demon
of skepticism, held me back, and I quickly realized that this was
probably a scam, tempting you to interact and yield personal
information useful to the scammer. Like all such greetings since,
I deleted it.

On another occasion I got an e-mail purporting to be from
my publisher, saying that on the spur of the moment he had
taken a trip abroad—I think he said to the Philippines—was
in trouble there and needed money. If I could send him several
hundred, he'd repay me as soon as he got back. This smelled
fishy, so I asked for more information. The appeal was repeated
urgently, but it seemed fishier than ever, so I asked how he knew
me, what was the connection? No answer came. I then e-mailed
the publisher and got an immediate reply: An account of his
had been hacked, and this appeal was going out to many of his
authors and acquaintances whose e-mail addresses had been
discovered; he was now closing the account and opening another
with a different password. Beware of sudden e-mail appeals. With
hindsight, I realize that I shouldn't even have answered the first
appeal before contacting him for verification.

I'm not always so canny. I once got an envelope labeled
Social Security & Medicare, personal statement enclosed,
and in bold red ink, **EXPIRATION NOTICE.** At the very thought
of my Social Security and Medicare expiring, I almost panicked
and hurriedly opened the envelope. So what did I discover? It
was an appeal from the National Committee to Preserve Social
Security & Medicare, urging me to renew my membership—in
other words, give them more money. Looking closely at the envelope, I now saw that the words "National Committee to Preserve"
were indeed there, but in small print. They had tricked me into

opening the envelope. But this so annoyed me that I vowed never to give them money again.

Being a bit of a tightwad and suspicious by nature, I've never fallen for a con, but that was not true of one of my friends. Kevin was a natty, sophisticated New Yorker who had helped initiate me, a newcomer to city, into the savvy ways of New York. He introduced me to Jewish jokes and idioms, delivered dicta on how I should dress, and told me of attending a cocktail party of Gypsy Rose Lee's where he met Ethel Merman and Gypsy's sister, June Havoc. And it was thanks to Kevin that, quite on the spur of the moment, I joined him in sipping drinks at the bar of the Latin Quarter, the famous nightclub near Times Square, so we could see Mae West perform with her squad of hulking musclemen.. A veteran New Yorker, then, and not a prime target for a con.

One day Kevin told me he had just met an interesting visitor from South America (I forget which country) named Vergilio and was quite taken with him. The next thing I knew, Kevin had arranged with a friend who was going away on vacation to let Vergilio move into her place temporarily. Kevin's praise of Vergilio grew ever more intense, and finally I met this paragon when Kevin invited me over for cocktails at his apartment on West 13th Street. Vergilio was a good-looking young man of about thirty, no kid, well-groomed and well-mannered, with a soft, pleasing voice and a gracious smile. Good enough, but everything about him, while pleasing, seemed strangely vague. He was right there in the present, but he seemed to have no past and no discoverable future—a mysteriousness that made him just that more interesting to Kevin.

"What is it about this guy that so gets to you?" I asked Kevin later.

Kevin flashed a look of intensity. "I've never known anyone like him. He's fascinating. He has *glamour!*"

Glamour—a word I associate with Hollywood ballyhoo—was something I had never hankered for, but it was clear that it appealed to some need deep in Kevin's psyche. But I was worried. For me, Vergilio, who had appeared out of nowhere, was a smile over a cocktail glass, nothing more.

In the weeks that followed, Kevin began evincing alarm: Vergilio was sick. Then he informed me that Vergilio was going to consult a doctor on the doctor's yacht, which struck me as an odd site for a consultation. Next I got a phone call from Kevin, with anguish in his voice: "Vergilio is dying!" His friend had informed him that he was suffering from a long-term fatal ailment, its exact nature undisclosed, that required treatment in Europe; he would be leaving soon. So Vergilio left; Kevin moped about, waited for news, worried. Postcards came from Paris, Monte Carlo, Nice, with only the briefest message and no news about his treatment.

Three weeks later he was back, well-groomed and urbane as ever, the same soft voice, the same smile over a cocktail glass. He showed Kevin and me a series of photographs from his trip, every one featuring a smiling and handsome Vergilio in a well-appointed residence, his host unidentified: photos of a narcissist. By now even Kevin sensed something amiss, but his need of glamour locked him into the spell.

Vergilio now informed Kevin that he had to return to Europe for an operation that might or might not save his life, probably not. Professing embarrassment, he confessed he needed money for the trip. Why he had to turn to a new friend, and not to old friends and family, went unexplained. Kevin at once gave forth of his own meager savings, then phoned any number of friends, entreating them to loan him what they could. Some did, some didn't. I myself, unable and unwilling to label Vergilio a liar or a fraud without convincing evidence, promised five hundred dollars but then, common sense prevailing, gently but firmly declined. "I don't believe in it," I told Kevin, who replied, "I feel like I've been kicked in the teeth."

Vergilio departed once again for Europe, and I heard no more of him, for Kevin and I were now estranged. Finally I phoned a mutual friend, asking how he was. "He's learning what he has to learn," she said, but refrained from saying more. Months passed; other matters claimed me, but I thought often of Kevin. Finally he phoned and invited me over. He looked worn and wan, but got to it right away: "If I ever see him again, I'll say to him, 'What? You're not dead? But that's why I gave you all that money and sent you back to Europe. Dead—you should be *dead!*'" A hard look came over him that I had never seen before.

To my knowledge, Vergilio never reappeared in New York; if he did, it was at a far remove from Kevin. Kevin never mentioned his name again. Since his finances were habitually precarious, I doubt if he ever repaid any of his friends. But of one thing I am sure: Vergilio was off somewhere, on this continent or another, smiling over a cocktail glass and enlisting the sympathy and generosity of friends. *New* friends; to the old ones he wouldn't dare show his face.

Vergilio was a classic example of the con man, and Kevin a classic example of the dupe. (Note my insisting on "con man" and never "con woman" or "con person"; it seems to be a males-only game.) It has been argued that we humans are born to be conned, that the true con artist makes us feel good about ourselves, makes us think he's giving us just what we deserve. The victim is always swept up in a narrative that at the time seems absolutely compelling.

So it was with Kevin. Though in many ways a canny New Yorker, he had a deep need to experience glamour. Vergilio satisfied that need marvelously, to the point that Kevin ignored all the danger signs that I and others saw clearly. Kevin was no fool, but he fell for the con that a shrewd operator offered him, and his awakening was harsh. Kevin's wound was long in healing, if it ever did heal completely.

Chapter 18
How We Worship

"We have here papists, Mennonites and Lutherans among the Dutch and also many Puritans or Independents and many atheists and various other servants of Baal." So wrote a Dutch citizen of New Amsterdam to officials in Holland in 1655, complaining of the diversity of religious faiths in the colony. He supported Governor Peter Stuyvesant's attempt to impose the Dutch Reformed faith on the colonists, but the population was too diverse both ethnically and religiously to be made to conform. When the British seized the colony in 1664, they in turn tried to impose the Anglican faith, but with the same result: The city could not be made to conform. Right from the start New Amsterdam, and subsequently New York, attracted such a mix of peoples that a policy of mutual tolerance was practiced, with occasional attempts at conformity that never had a ghost of a chance. Many residents were too busy making money to find time for religion, and those who did find time went their separate ways.

And since then? According to the 2010 U.S. census and other sources, the city's congregations range in number from 109 Roman Catholic, 77 Orthodox Jewish, 46 Episcopal, 41 Baptist,

35 Mahayana Buddhist, 32 Assemblies of God, 30 Presbyterian, and 21 Muslim, down to a single Baha'i, Serbian Orthodox, Coptic Orthodox, Ethiopian Orthodox, Hungarian Reformed, Tao, and Shinto. And there were plenty of others in between, such as 14 Mormon, 11 Jehovah's Witnesses, 10 Greek Orthodox, 5 Salvation Army, and 2 Mennonite, and many that I have never heard of, for a total of 865 in all. But religion in New York is in flux, so these figures are now out of date. As for my borough, Manhattan, it has the fewest residents who are committed to a religion.

Precisely because New York has always been a place of many faiths, it became a refuge for the persecuted. New Amsterdam had been founded in 1624 by a group of Huguenot Walloons sponsored by the Dutch West India Company. More Huguenots from the Netherlands and Germany followed, including Peter Minuit, famous for buying the island of Manhattan from the native peoples. By 1650 Huguenots were about a fifth of the settlement's population, and when, in 1685, His Solar Majesty Louis XIV revoked the Edict of Nantes, which guaranteed French Protestants certain protections, many more Huguenots fled the Sun King's radiating splendor to find sanctuary in New York. So welcoming was the city that the Huguenots assimilated readily. By the eighteenth century, Huguenot merchants numbered among the city's leaders, and members of the Huguenot community gradually became affiliated with other denominations, especially the Anglican Church. Such is the price of acceptance: loss of identity.

Peter Stuyvesant may have cast a sour glance at the Huguenots, but they had long preceded him to New Amsterdam. But when, in 1654, a group of twenty-three Sephardic Jews arrived, some of them fleeing the fall of Dutch settlements in Brazil to the Portuguese, he put his gubernatorial foot down. The "deceitful race" were barred from buying land or participating in the citizens' militia, and were invited to depart. But the Jewish leaders knew their rights under the laws of the Dutch

Republic, which guaranteed freedom of religion to all. So they appealed to authorities in Holland, and Stuyvesant's superiors reminded him that "each person shall remain free in his religion." He was further advised that certain influential Jews had invested heavily in the Dutch West India Company, which must have settled the matter. The governor was told to back off. But what really ticked Stuyvesant off was the arrival of English Quakers, likewise fleeing discrimination in their homeland. Their aggressive sermonizing, and when moved by the Holy Spirit, their fits of jiggling or quaking (hence their name), invited his disdain. These oddballs, he decided, were a threat to the peace and stability of the colony, and were probably crazy as well. When they persisted despite his disapproval, he forbade the settlement of Vlissingen (today's Flushing, in Queens) to allow their worship. The townsfolk, who were all English, signed a remonstrance to the governor reminding him that Dutch tolerance extended even to Jews, Turks, and Egyptians, in consequence of which they must respectfully refuse to obey. This Flushing Remonstrance of 1657 is now celebrated as a forerunner of the First Amendment of the Bill of Rights; but Stuyvesant, not being conversant with said Bill, arrested four of the remonstrating townsfolk and clapped two of them in jail for a month. Only the coming of the British in 1664 ended his antics of intolerance.

So much for religious diversity in New Amsterdam; it was there from the start, though not without fitful challenges. Now let's fast-forward to the twenty-first century and a vast metropolis that over the centuries has attracted wave after wave of immigrants. What kind of religions are here today? Many, as we've already seen. Using the terms loosely, I'll divide them into three categories: High Church, Low Church, and No Church, meaning the more formal and traditional, the more informal and upstarty, and the Great Unwashed.

No Church

The people I have socialized and worked with in Manhattan are white middle-class professionals—writers, directors, editors, artists, bank employees, teachers, librarians, chefs, and attorneys—who for the most part fall into the category of No Church, or the Great Unwashed. Some of these No Churchers may never have been touched by religion, but most have fallen away, gently or not so gently, from the faith of their childhood. To really know them, you need to know where they've come from religiously, culturally, and geographically. Being No Churchers, they're the ones who create the impression that New York is a city devoid of religion—a place, in fact, where people go to lose their religion, if they ever had any in the first place.

My friend Ed was raised a traditional Roman Catholic in Denver, where he served as an altar boy, and then attended Marquette, a Jesuit university in Milwaukee. When he first came to New York he was an observant Catholic who attended Mass and dutifully went to confession. But as the years passed, he became less dutiful, began questioning his faith, and finally fell away completely, even to the point of denigrating it with, I'm sure, no small amount of bitterness. If Catholicism left its mark upon him, it was visible, I think, in his courteous, soft-spoken manner, very reserved. He was not one to give himself emotionally, to yield to impulse. Which reminds me of a French friend whom I knew at Lyons when I was studying in France. He had attended a Catholic *collège,* rather than the secular secondary school, the *lycée,* and showed the same well-mannered, soft-spoken reserve. We can leave our childhood faith, but it won't necessarily leave us.

My friend John, who was proud of his Finnish descent, was raised a Laestadian Lutheran in Minneapolis and was taken by his mother to a church where the service was in Finnish, of which he understood barely a word. He describes Laestadianism as a freakish, fundamentalist branch of Lutheranism that flourished in northern Minnesota. Its aversion to sin and worldliness went so far as to consider going to movies a sin, as well as alcohol consumption, dancing, and the wearing of makeup. When he attended the University of Minnesota, where he majored in English and philosophy, he lost his faith, and upon coming to New York he became a full-fledged atheist and remained one till the day he died. Religion for him was simply a distant and unpleasant memory from childhood, something he could do quite easily without. But unlike Ed, he felt no biting resentment.

As for me, as a child in Evanston, a suburb of Chicago, I was exposed to a gentle Methodism, quite liberal, that imposed no catechism or ideology, no ban on movies or dancing, but instead inculcated a few basic concepts of morality, and the need for understanding and compassion. In Sunday School the story of Jesus was retold every Easter by a talk with slides, and every Christmas the church presented a well-attended Nativity pageant, superbly dramatic, in which the whole church participated. Even yours truly was involved, musical illiterate though I was, white-garbed and holding my electric candle high, as the triumphant strains of Handel's Hallelujah Chorus brought the whole attendance to their feet, and the high school and adult choirs marched down the aisles singing lustily, till our resounding hallelujahs climaxed and closed the performance with a whopping big musical bang.

Because the Methodism I had known was gentle, even in my later—and inevitable—lapsed state, where I felt no immediate need of religion, I nursed no resentment, only warm memories of the Methodists I had known, their principles, their warmth, their faith. At times I ask myself if I have ever encountered anyone who impressed me as being truly spiritual, and always I recall my junior-year Sunday School teacher, Dr. Edmund D. Soper, white-haired and spectacled, soft-voiced, a teacher and scholar with a mellow wisdom. What it was about him that was spiritual I cannot define or describe; it was simply an intangible aura that you sensed. My partner Bob says the same of his mother's Lutheran pastor in Jersey City, a truly spiritual man such as one rarely encounters.

Even if I'm not myself a believer, I respect those who are. Whenever I'm in the Union Square subway station—a huge labyrinth of passageways giving access to any number of subway lines—I give a smile and a friendly wave to the women, often black or Latino, who have a table there with literature and invite people to learn what the Bible really says. They look so committed, and so ignored by the hurrying commuters, that I can't resist this gesture, which always provokes a warm smile and a friendly wave back. Maybe someday I'll stop and tell them that I still have the Bible I was given by my mother at age sixteen, a bit decrepit but still usable. (The Bible, not my mother.)

Low Church

So much for the No Churchers. So what about the High and Low Churchers? In supposedly godless New York they're all over the place. In a former vaudeville theater in the Corona neighborhood of Queens, some six hundred worshipers leap to their feet to join a Latino band in song, shaking their tambourines. Then a preacher gives a fiery sermon and speaks in tongues, and parishioners with tear-streaked faces raise their arms heavenward, eyes shut, in collective rapture. Nothing quiet or meditative here. It's noisy, public, and passionate. And it is definitely Low Church.

Such is the Sunday morning service of the Pentecostal megachurch Aliento de Vida (Breath of Life), founded in 2003 by the pastor, Victor Tiburcio, and his wife, immigrants from the Dominican Republic. And who are the worshipers? Immigrants from Ecuador, Argentina, El Salvador, Trinidad, Tobago, and just about any country in Latin America. Some of them are legal and some are not. Ordinary people from the bottom of the social heap who want passion in their services, as well as help in learning English and navigating the complexities, legal and otherwise, of realizing the American dream. So great is the demand for Aliento de Vida's services, simulcasts are offered by the church's own TV network.

But this is nothing, compared to a Pentecostal festival in Central Park on July 11, 2015, featuring Luis Palau, the "Hispanic Billy Graham," one of the world's leading evangelical Christian figures. The event drew 60,000 worshipers—the limit allowed on the Great Lawn—for the largest evangelical Christian gathering in the city since Billy Graham's crusade in Queens in 2005. Of the 1,700 churches participating, 900 were Hispanic, reflecting the surging growth of immigrant-led churches in the boroughs outside Manhattan. Yet participants weren't just Hispanic, but Korean American and African American as well. Mayor de Blasio was present to offer a few welcoming words and get prayed for, and the crowd danced and cheered and leaped and prayed, and listened to white-haired Luis Palau in his shirtsleeves preaching in both English and Spanish, as everyone present expressed the collective joy of being Christian and proud of it. And this in the heart of godless New York! Most definitely and exuberantly Low Church.

And little new religions are appearing, or reappearing, all over the place. Outside a humble storefront church in Crown Heights, Brooklyn, hangs a banner: "Faithists meet here." And who are the Faithists? A small congregation who are reviving a religion founded by a Manhattan dentist named John Ballou Newbrough who, inspired by a vision of an angel who put hands on his shoulders, wrote furiously and in 1882 published the Oahspe Bible. This Bible strikes nonbelievers today as a rich mix of sci-fi and myth, with gods, lords, and angels thrown in. He and his followers founded a community in New Mexico, but he and others died in an influenza epidemic in 1891. Following this, his religion was plagued by disputes and setbacks and faded away, only to be revived decades later in Brooklyn. Now the Faithists' Kosmon Temple offers weekly Sunday services, guided meditations, and testimonials by members. And their website states that "the Kosmon Church welcomes all those seeking the Light and TRUTH of JEHOVAH THE CREATOR. May all who enter grow in Spirit, and find inner peace and an expression of the Divine in Man." A bit vague and New Agey, some might say, but walk-ins are welcome and some of them become converts. One more reminder that religion is alive and well in New York.

High Church

Needless to say, it isn't the Faithists who are sweeping New York, the nation, and much of the Third World as well; it's the Pentecostals. And if they are gathering new converts by the thousands and tens of thousands, who is losing out? That most High Church of all High Churches, Roman Catholicism. Some years ago the Archdiocese of New York, faced with declining attendance, aging priests, and mounting maintenance costs, initiated a broad reorganization that led to the closing of dozens of churches in the metropolitan region. Thus Our Lady Queen of Angels parish in East Harlem closed in 2007, and its church on East 113th Street was boarded up. But a handful of parishioners refused to accept this change, which some denounced as "betrayal" by the Church, and ever since the closing they have met on park benches in East Harlem housing projects to sing hymns and join hands in prayer. Despite raucous sounds of children playing and dogs barking nearby, they do this every Sunday, braving the scorching heat of summer and the icy rigors of winter. Yet the closing of this and other parishes in East Harlem is understandable, since the Puerto Ricans who once filled the pews have left for other parts of the city, replaced by Dominicans and Mexicans who are drawn to the storefront Pentecostal churches that have popped up in the area. A mere two blocks down the street from me in the West Village is St. John's in the Village at 218 West 11th Street, a welcoming Episcopal church that I have passed many a time while doing errands. Though a No Churcher, I have distantly related to this church over the years. Long ago I visited its predecessor, a handsome Greek Revival edifice dating back to 1846, its temple-like front featuring a portico with fluted columns. This gem of West Village architecture burned down in 1971, the fire probably started inadvertently by a homeless man sleeping on the premises. The cost of restoration being prohibitive, the present brick building in modern style replaced it, affording security not possible with the older structure.

Once, passing the church, I was surprised to see a long procession come out of it, with priests and choristers and then a coffin: a full-fledged funeral with all the trimmings. When they turned and came along the sidewalk toward me, all I could do was press back against a parked car to let them pass. Where they were going I couldn't be sure; presumably, to a hearse nearby. Unwittingly, I had witnessed, and almost interfered with, a real High Church event.

Well aware of the local gay population, St. John's did outreach to gay Episcopalians, and in 1969 the rector denounced police brutality evidenced in the Stonewall riots then occurring. But what drew me and my friend John to the church was the home-baked goods offered on a table at the entrance during their periodic fund-raising sales open to the public. Their pastry was always devilishly good.

What finally got me inside the church building was my interest in Gregorian chants, which I had discovered long before on recordings. Learning that an evening service with plainsong was announced, and that plainsong was the same as Gregorian chants, I attended the service, my first church service in years. Yes, I finally heard the chants being sung, and found myself standing and kneeling, and standing and kneeling again, as required by Episcopal tradition, and at some cost to my creaky knees. At the end of the service a black-garbed clerical gentleman from the front row kneeled, crossed himself, and rose, then came down the aisle to the rear to greet worshipers as they were leaving, and invite them to partake of a supper. I declined the invitation, but thanked him for the service and left. The whole experience had immersed me briefly in the High Church tradition, tasteful, restrained, and quite beautiful, but inevitably lacking the gutsy, noisy communion that revs up Low Church worshipers today.

Pagans

In the month of June, strollers in Central Park have occasionally come upon a secluded forest clearing with a makeshift altar in the middle of it. On the altar are a lantern, a chalice, a bowl of water, a jar of salt, a sunflower, and a wand. Sitting cross-legged around the altar are a number of young people, eyes shut, chanting. Then, led by a woman in a billowy white skirt and flipflops, the worshipers—for such they are—join hands and begin singing, and one by one enter a spiral of flowers carefully arranged on the ground. Inside the spiral they dance vigorously and chant. What is going on?

This spot is known to them as the green cathedral, and in it every year the high priestess, a witch, guides her coven through a ritual celebrating the summer solstice. Yes, there are witches in the city—as of 2018, perhaps as many as ten thousand, organized in some eighty covens. They are pagans, and I place them somewhere between Low Church and No Church. Over the past several years there has been a millennial "witch wave," as young people are drawn to occultism. The witch, after all, is an independent woman with power, and as such she appeals to feminists. Wicca, a decentralized modern pagan religion, is attracting more and more young women. But even though there is a Pagan Pride Day and a pagan street fair, many witches, fearing censure from family, friends, and fellow workers, prefer to keep their practice secret.

The Wiccan Family Temple Academy of Pagan Studies, on Lafayette Street in Manhattan, offers an introduction to the modern pagan witchcraft religion known as Wicca, with classes in magic, the Greater and Lesser Sabbats, the history of witchcraft, god and goddess archetypes, Shamanism, divination, talismans and amulets, voodoo, the use of spells, and countless other topics. With proper training, anyone can become a witch. But they don't worship Satan, they simply want to be in tune with nature and its forces.

To do justice to my announced theme of religion in New York, I'd have to do a whole book. I haven't even mentioned St. Patrick's, the looming Fifth Avenue edifice whose slow beginning in the nineteenth century, with walls rising only as finances permitted, signaled the growing influence of Roman Catholicism in what had hitherto been a WASP city. A prime tourist attraction, it has a souvenir stand inside its sacred walls, which shocks me, a WASP who in his European travels absorbed the notion of the sacredness of Catholic churches, where God is literally present, and souvenir stands are not to be found (not inside, that is, for souvenirs are always to be had). A crypt under the main altar harbors the remains of numerous cardinals and other prominent Catholics, including at least one, Francis Spellman, the Cardinal Archbishop of New York, whose presence there has been questioned, in light of his rumored ... shhh! ... homosexuality.

If you google "places of worship in New York," you'll come up with pictures of the Episcopal Cathedral of St. John the Divine on Amsterdam Avenue near Columbia University; the Islamic Cultural Center of New York at Third Avenue and East 96th Street, its domed mosque overtopped by a towering minaret; various synagogues; and with a little more poking about, the famous Abyssinian Baptist Church in Harlem; the Mahayana Buddhist Temple on Canal Street in Chinatown, with an outsized gold statue of a smiling Buddha, his right hand raised in blessing; and the St. Nicholas Russian Orthodox Cathedral on East 97th Street, its multiple cupolas topped by crosses. And these are only the biggies. There are smaller sites as well, each with a story to tell. So New York, which some think of as rabidly secular, worships in a hundred ways.

Dazzled by thoughts of minarets, Buddhas, and cross-topped cupolas, I now ask myself what I would most want to see, if visiting an unfamiliar place of worship. The answer comes immediately: I would most want to see something truly holy, something awe-inspiring, something to take me out of myself, something with a touch—or a punch—of mystery. And this from a No Churcher!

Chapter 19
Finding the Sacred

A s a no ChUrCher, at the end of the last chapter I expressed a yearning for something awe-inspiring, something mysterious, something to take me out of myself. In a secular sense, something sacred. So can a No Churcher find the sacred in New York? I'll try. And I'll go at it in three parts.

The Sacredness of Water

On the radio I once heard an interview with Vandana Shiva, an Indian environmental activist and author who is fighting against the privatization of water in her country. "For us," she said, "water is sacred." The people of India, she pointed out, see the Ganges as their mother. She then described how Coca-Cola had come to a small village in the state of Kerala in southern India and opened a bottling plant there. This might sound like progress and was no doubt presented as such, but the plant consumed all the water in the area, forcing the women to walk miles to obtain water for their households. Outraged by this, one of the older women organized the others and launched a campaign to get rid of the plant. As a result of their efforts the village council refused to renew the plant's license, causing the plant to shut down. "What shall I tell them back in Delhi?" Vandana Shiva asked the leader of the struggle, Delhi being the capital, where the government was making deals with foreign companies like Coca-Cola. The leader replied, "Tell them they drink the blood of my people."

This whole account impressed me greatly, above all Vandana Shiva's emphasis on the sacredness of water. Primal peoples and traditional societies all over the globe share this belief, just as they see the earth as their mother; but we in the developed societies, being obsessed with science, find this notion strange. Water is certainly necessary, precious, essential, but ... sacred? Yet this belief inspired the village women to take on the mighty Coca-Cola Company, and against all odds, defeat it. To view water as sacred may be a tough sell in a city like New York, the victim at times of powerful hurricanes whose flooding inflicts vast damage, but the water we're talking about is fresh water, not salt. We should ponder this notion: *the sacredness of water.* In some mysterious way it reaches to my depths, it resonates.

New York City came into existence because of water, salt and fresh, and could not exist without it. Its large harbor, and its location at the mouth of a navigable river, the Hudson, stretching deep into the interior of the continent, predestined it to flourish as a trading post and port, then as a metropolis, then as a money center, and finally as a cultural hub, too. Where there is commerce, money will accumulate, and where there is money, culture and the arts will follow. But it all began with water, and the city's fate will always be linked to water.

But will that water be clean? We think of it as something to be exploited, and the result has been pollution. After the pollution reached alarming levels, we began to be aware of the problem. The late Pete Seeger was a pioneer in the fight against pollution in the Hudson. Though he was born in the city, he lived most of his life in Beacon, a river town about midway between New York and Albany. In time he became aware of the river's pollution, which was so bad that wooden boats from the Caribbean would sail up the river, so its poisons would kill the worms and other parasites boring into their hulls. Loving the river, Seeger launched a campaign to clean it up.

In the late 1960s Seeger raised money to build the 106-foot river sloop *Clearwater,* modeled on the Hudson River sloops of yore. Its name proclaimed his goal: to clean up the Hudson's dirty water. To get the sloop built, he and his allies had to go all the way to Friendship, Maine, to find a shipyard capable of the task. Launched in 1969, the sloop has plied the Hudson ever since, educating people about the river's pollution and the dangers it imposes; when hiking in the Hudson Valley, I often encountered it. As a result of his and others' efforts, Congress passed the Clean Water Act of 1972.

To pass a law is one thing; to enforce it is another. There was still plenty of pollution in the Hudson, so the *Clearwater* sailed up and down the river, stopping at river towns along the way to tell schoolchildren and adults about pollution, and posting the names of the greatest polluters, with General Electric at the top of the list. For years GE's facilities at Hudson Falls and Fort Edward, about fifty miles north of Albany, had been dumping tons of toxic polychlorinated biphenyls (PCBs) into the river, contaminating the entire river and its fish, as well as humans who drank that water or ate the fish. In 1977, thanks to efforts by the *Clearwater* and others, PCBs were banned in the United States, but much of the Hudson was polluted already. After resisting for years, GE was finally forced to clean up the river, a process it completed in 2014. Critics insist that the cleanup is only partial to date, but the river is certainly cleaner than before.

So even if we today don't think of water as sacred, we at least appreciate its importance and campaign long and hard—inspired by the likes of Pete Seeger—to keep it pure and clean. His motto: "Think globally, act locally." And that is what he did.

The Idea of the Holy

Pete Seeger's songs were often pacifist and contemplative in nature, even spiritual. Was he religious? In the conventional sense, perhaps not. But one can be spiritual without being overtly religious. Consider what he told an interviewer:

> I feel most spiritual when I'm out in the woods. I feel a part of nature.... I used to say I was an atheist. Now, I say, it's all according to your definition of God. According to my definition of God, I'm not an atheist. Because I think God is everything. Whenever I open my eyes I'm looking at God. Whenever I'm listening to something I'm listening to God.

Saying this, he speaks for many Americans today.

Personally I think that anyone who sees a night sky filled with stars, or a sunrise or sunset, will experience some hint of the spiritual, even of the sacred or holy. But in the city one rarely has the full experience of these things. So how can a city resident experience the sacred or holy?

In his book *The Idea of the Holy* (*Das Heilige*, 1917), Rudolf Otto examined the nature of the holy. (Imagine pursuing such a study when World War I was raging all around you.) Otto saw the experience of the holy as involving three things:

+ a feeling of awe, of something weird or uncanny, yet fascinating;

+ a feeling of powerlessness in the face of overwhelming might;

+ an awareness of tremendous energy.

Deep in all of us, Otto insisted, is an irrational yearning, a need of the overabounding and unutterable.

To experience such feelings in a noisy, congested city isn't easy. The Hebrew prophets forsook the settled areas of Palestine and went out into the wilderness to get clean with God and hear his commands, then returned to the cities to preach and proclaim and inveigh. To experience the holy requires silence, and in the city there isn't much of it. Yes, a believer can take refuge in a church or temple or synagogue, but many of us today are not true believers. We need silence, for in silence the spirit speaks. But where can we find that silence? Pete Seeger points the way, for even in the city or near it, we can find places of sanctuary and silence, places where we can be alone and experience something akin to the holy. In my experience I can name five. They won't work for everyone, but they have worked modestly for me.

My Five Secret Spots

Of course they aren't really secret; they are there for all to see. But most people ignore them or pass them quickly by.

Tanner's Spring

Well known to bird watchers and photographers, but to almost no one else, Tanner's Spring is a small pool of water in a wooded area on the west side of Central Park near the park's 81st Street entrance, accessed by either of two short paths of wood chips. One of two natural springs in the park, it is named for Dr. Henry S. Tanner, an advocate of therapeutic fasting, who in the summer of 1880 fasted for forty days and nights, drinking only water from this spring. Since he survived, it was thought that the spring must have magically concentrated nutrients, but this seems doubtful. It is simply a spot where migrating birds often gather to drink and bathe. I have seen warblers and tanagers and sparrows there, but even when there are no birds, it is a quiet spot where you can sit on a stone bench, relax, reflect, and feel a bit of what Pete Seeger felt in the woods: something spiritual, maybe even, in the woods all around you, God. In silence the spirit speaks. And a spring gives forth water, which means it gives forth life. Again, the sacredness of water.

The Wildflower Meadow

Another special spot for me is the Wildflower Meadow at the North End of Central Park, especially in late August, when many of the flowers achieve full growth. We think of wildflowers as dainty little earth-hugging plants flaunting charming bits of color, but here, towering above me, I have seen tall coreopsis and cup plant and green-headed coneflower. These hardy composites rise to nine or ten or twelve or rarely even fifteen feet above the ground, thrusting their light-gobbling, greedy yellow flowers at the sun. They are dazzling, and for us lowly earth-bound mortals, humbling.

Here I always get a hint of what visitors feel upon viewing the giant sequoias of California: awe at the mightiness of nature, its ability to put us in our place. In other words, the feeling of powerlessness in the face of overwhelming might, one of the feelings that Rudolph Otto associates with the holy. But only a hint. To my knowledge, no one was ever won over to God or the gods by looking at a wildflower, not even one that towers far above us.

The Meadow at Pelham Bay Park

Here is another meadow, quite open to the public and quite ignored by them, which makes it that much more interesting for me. It is accessed from the picnic area at Orchard Beach, but only if you know which path to take, since there are several false starts leading nowhere. After failing to find the right path and giving up on the Meadow several times, I finally learned to watch for a threesome of trees, two of them sycamores, and to get my bearings from the location of several distant buildings. Doing this, I then found the one right path and followed it into some underbrush, where it zigged and zagged over dry ground and then emerged in an open weedy area. From this point on, the noise of picnickers and the more distant bathers faded, and I had the whole place to myself, with the occasional exception of a nude male sunbather, another initiate whom I could easily avoid.

In the Meadow I found the hairy bright red fruit of the staghorn sumac, and early goldenrod and mountain mint and other wildflowers, and above all, silence. Sitting on a smooth outcropping of rock, watching puffy white clouds drift across a clean blue sky, I was immersed in silence, in the gentle fullness of summer, and maybe, just maybe, in God.

There's lots to ponder here. A public space found only by the knowing few. False starts, and then a secret path: seek, and ye shall find. Silence, calm, peace.

The Groin of Summer

This spot is a low, wet area on Staten Island's Red Trail that I have often visited on a hot, muggy day in August, and that I have rarely had to share, even briefly, with another hiker. There, thriving in the rich, moist soil, are a bunch of thirsty wildflowers. Boneset, once used for healing, thrusts its hairy stem with paired veiny leaves and clusters of white flowers, and Pennsylvania smartweed offers tight spikes of tiny pink flowers. Dominating the scene by rising to a height of seven feet, is a thick growth of New York ironweed that lures bumblebees and cabbage butterflies and swallowtails to its flat-topped clusters of flowers of a bold purple hue. I have christened this spot the Groin of Summer because it seems the very essence of the season, secret, fertile, moist, hot, and sensual. Before hiking on to higher, drier ground with different flowers, I have always lingered there, reluctant to leave a very special spot that I won't see for another year.

Yes, the Groin is profoundly sensual. Far from hinting of the spiritual and sacred, it seems to suggest the very opposite: the Slut of Sluts, Eve, Big Mama, the vegetation goddess whom so many pagan religions and primal societies have worshiped under many names. But these seeming opposites, the sensual and the spiritual, are strangely linked. As a Sister of Mercy of my acquaintance once told me, there is no sensuality without spirituality, and no spirituality without sensuality. Eve the Temptress was shunned and abhorred by the male-dominated early Christian Church, until pressure from below—from the people—forced the male hierarchy to acknowledge her, to accept and embrace her as the pure and compassionate Virgin, the spiritual face and persona of the many-faced, inevitable, and inescapable Great Mother. So the Temptress became the Pure One, Madonna, the Goddess who pleads for us all on the Day of Judgment. And boy, let's hope she'll do a good job of it because, if you go that route, most of us are going to need some help.

The Giant Stairs

The last of my special spots is the Giant Stairs, a huge jumble of rocks and boulders that over the centuries have fallen down from the Palisades, that towering wall of dark gray rock stretching for miles along the Jersey side of the Hudson River. The Shore Path of the Palisades brings you to this stretch, which I have clambered over several times, rarely meeting another hiker along the way. To hike this quarter-mile stretch always took me forty-five minutes, since you hike up, down, and around the fallen boulders, some of which teeter under your feet. Lizards, small mammals, venomous copperheads, and other creatures lurk in the dark tunnels and caves and crevices beneath the boulders, but you never encounter them, since your noisy clambering warns them to get out of the way. The thought of hidden creatures, some of them fanged and dangerous, lurking below your trudging boots adds a spicy thrill to the hike. The sun-bathed surfaces are ours; the dark recesses are theirs.

So what is there of the spiritual or sacred here? A reminder of the power—seemingly capricious and unpredictable—of Nature, or whatever force underlies or inspires Nature's doings. On May 12, 2012, a huge face of rock came crashing down from the cliffs, dumping a fresh layer of boulders onto the Stairs and sweeping a whole growth of trees into the river. Because the slide occurred in the evening, the Stairs were clear of hikers and no one was injured. But like any sudden and unexpected manifestation of Nature's power, it was alarming and humbling, worthy of the savage God, jealous and unpitying, of the Old Testament. Skeptics will scoff at the suggestion of a divine intervention, but deep down in most of us lurks the fear, irrational and unavowed, of just such a God-wrought calamity. Reason has its limits; even the most secular of us aren't always sober and sane.

My five spots are all gateways to silence, portals of dream. They invite quiet and reflection, provoke fantasies of Big Mama or Yahweh, an awe-inspiring Other that we aspire to or may want to avoid. *My* fantasies, of course, no one else's. Another hiker might get no hint of the sensual Eve in the Groin, no thought of a punishing God while scrambling over the Giant Stairs. Maybe we find what we already know and contain within us; maybe we seek because we have found.

The silence of my special spots points me back to another German scholar, Max Picard, and his work *The World of Silence* (*Die Welt des Schweigen,* 1948). Picard's silence, which is mine as well, is all around us, embracing our little universe of noise. We come from it, we in the end go back to it. It is a complete world in itself, uncreated and everlasting, distant, yet close. When we talk to one another, it is always there, listening. It reveals itself in the dawn, in the aspiration of trees toward the sky, in the descent of night, in the change of seasons, but above all in the silence of our inner selves. Art can convey it. Cathedrals were built around silence. Today the marble statues of Greek gods lie embedded like white islands of silence amid the noise of our world. The cities of that world are reservoirs of noise. As for the radio (Picard was writing before television), one can imagine what he thinks of its incessant babble. But in sleep, if it is deep and soothing, we can return to the great silence of the universe. And beyond that silence is Being, the Creator.

Even in the babble and bustle of New York, then, one can experience a silence that leads us back to the spiritual, the Other, the Creator. We can find it in a museum as well. In the South Asian galleries of the Metropolitan Museum of Art, I never fail to marvel at the sinuous, twisting body of a bejeweled, limbless, full-breasted dancer who seems the very embodiment of the sensual. Yet in that same hall I am awed by Shiva, delicately poised on one foot in his cosmic dance, and by the sublime calm of a nearby Jain seated in meditation.

These images, too, convey silence, rich, meaningful, profound. How can that silence, even when tinged with eroticism, not be spiritual as well? And in Shiva and the Jain, as in Buddhas anywhere, the sacred shines forth; how can we not acknowledge and revere it? Without some form of the sacred, our lives would be incomplete.

Chapter 20
Dying

D Ying is BY natUre soLitarY, yet we want someone there to see us out. When Sarah Bernhardt died, the person who mattered most was at her side—not any of her numerous lovers, but her son, who stayed with her to the end. And when André Gide died, he, too, had the person who mattered most to him at hand: the young man, now married and with a family, who as a boy had been his lover, and who came to him in spite of his family ties. Many such stories can be told.

But it isn't always that way in the city, where death can be sudden. There is death by fire, death by hit-and-run. Or you can be hit on the head and killed by a falling branch, which occurred in Central Park in February 2010, when a man was struck by a snow-laden branch weighing 100 pounds. Or you can be electrocuted when you step on an electrified metal plate installed in the street by Con Edison to cover wiring, as happened to a young woman while walking her dogs on East 11th Street in January 2004. Since the wiring was not properly insulated, Con Edison paid her family $7.2 million. Or you can be with your family watching Macy's Thanksgiving Day Parade, when high winds loosen a giant balloon that knocks a lamppost on your head and puts you in a month-long coma. This happened to a woman in 1997, but she recovered, only to come home to her high-rise apartment in 2006 and find that a plane had just crashed into her bedroom, setting it on fire and killing the pilot and his flight instructor.

And there are suicides. People jump off the George Washington Bridge, or this or that high-rise, hoping to keep clear of projecting balconies and ledges, so they can hit the ground with a smash. Or they choose death by water. In the spring of 2016 three bodies were discovered in Central Park: one in the reservoir; one in a pond in the southeast corner of the park at 59th Street and Fifth Avenue; and one in the Conservatory Pond near Fifth Avenue and East 74th Street. All were badly decomposed, having been in the water for weeks, if not months, and none showed signs of violence. Only one, a homeless man, was identified.

Some people kill themselves by way of protest. In February 2018 a taxi driver in his early 60s, desperate from his loss of business to competitors like Uber, went to City Hall in Lower Manhattan and there, in front of the building, killed himself with a shotgun. He left a post on Facebook explaining that he now had to work more than 100 hours a week to survive. whereas 40 a week had been typical in the 1980s. And in April 2018 a nationally known civil rights lawyer and environmentalist, depressed by the Trump administration's rollback of environmental regulations, went to Prospect Park toward dawn, and to make a statement about protecting the environment, set himself on fire.

These were unusual deaths. Far more common in the city is a quiet, solitary death from natural causes, often sudden. Such was the fate of my friend John, whom I had known for years. Neighbors and the super found him collapsed on the floor in his Manhattan apartment soon after his death. Probably he died of a stroke; I never learned for sure. There was no memorial service, and I never heard from his executor, an artist friend whom I had never met. Just like that, he was out of my life forever. John's death was solitary, but neighbors knew who he was, and his death was soon known to some of his friends. But in New York many deaths of people who live and die alone go unnoticed at first, and the body may not be discovered for days. If no one claims it, it is shipped off to Hart Island, a small island in Long Island Sound near City Island in the Bronx, where the anonymous, the indigent, and the forgotten are buried in plain pine coffins stacked three deep in a common grave dug by inmates from Riker's Island. Other visitors are rarely allowed on the island, because it is covered with the crumbling remains of abandoned buildings used by facilities long since gone, dilapidated structures where one risks one's life on entering. To die alone in the city and be buried on Hart Island is a thought to haunt us all: the saddest end conceivable. And Hart Island, open as a final resting place since 1869, holds 800,000 such coffins, with more arriving daily.

In October 2015 the *New York Times* surprised its readers by running on the front page of its Sunday edition a long article recounting in detail the lonely death of a man named George Bell: precisely the kind of death so many city residents dread. A neighbor in a Jackson Heights apartment building in Queens detected a fetid odor from the apartment and dialed 911. The tenant hadn't been seen for several days, and his car, parked on the wrong side of the street, had been ticketed. The firemen came, jimmied the door open, entered. The police followed, found an apartment crammed with things, a jumble of possessions strewn on the furniture and floor, heaps of litter, trash: the den of a hoarder. And collapsed on the living room floor was a puffy body, decomposed, unrecognizable. They assumed it was George Bell, the resident, though no one knew for sure.

Now began the complicated routine involving a combination of city agencies. An investigator from the Office of the Chief Medical Examiner came and quickly concluded that there was no evidence of crime. A Fire Department medic formally declared that the man was dead, and the body was taken to the morgue and placed in a refrigerated drawer. To locate the next of kin, detectives phoned some phone numbers found in the apartment but got nowhere, for the man presumed to be George Bell evidently had no wife or siblings. Fingerprints were taken at the morgue and sent to city, state, and federal databases, but without results.

After nine days the medical examiner reported the death to the Queens County Public Administrator, an obscure official whose office manages estates when there is no one else to do so. Twelve days after the body was discovered, two investigators from the administrator's office clad in white hazmat suits entered the cluttered apartment to search for clues that might identify the deceased and his heirs, found $241 in bills and $187.45 cents in coins, all duly noted. They returned twice, found an old passport, tax returns, and a will naming four heirs and specifying that the remains be cremated. Now at last the authorities had something tangible to work with.

Letters went out to the four heirs, but only one responded: a man who had not been in touch with George Bell for some time. The deceased's car was sent to an auctioneer, and an unverified death certificate was issued, stating the cause of death as hypertensive and arteriosclerotic cardiovascular disease, with obesity a significant factor. Though city law requires burial or cremation within four days of discovery, an exemption in this case was granted, pending conclusive identification. Months passed.

At last, a bit of luck: In response to queries sent out far and wide, a radiologist reported that he had X-rays of George Bell dating from 2004. Retrieved from a warehouse, they were compared to X-rays taken by the medical examiner's office and proved at last—four months after his death—that the body was indeed that of George Bell. A rented hearse took the remains to a funeral home, where they were placed in a wooden coffin and sent on to a crematory for cremation, with no mourners, no member of the clergy: the simplest, bleakest disposal conceivable. Workers from a junk removal service cleaned out the apartment and sent the contents to a dump in the Bronx that paid good rates. The heirs were traced via the Internet. Two had died; the others, long out of touch with him, were surprised at being named in his will. Distant cousins were found and included as heirs; one had never even heard of George Bell. The apartment, the last asset to be disposed of, was sold to a neighbor. The estate finally came to $540,000, which commissions, fees, and other expenses reduced to $264,000. Fourteen months after George Bell's death, checks to the heirs went out.

Interviews with people who had known George Bell filled in a few details of his life. He had been in the moving business and developed a close friendship with one of the heirs. In 1996 he had injured his shoulder during a moving job and had retired. By then his old friends had died or drifted away. His life became empty, but he had one good friend in the neighborhood with whom he went fishing and talked by the hour. Even that friend had no idea that George Bell had become a hoarder; he felt that George had died of sadness. "I miss him," he told his interviewer. "I would like to see George one more time. He was my friend. One more time." So ends the story, scant as it is, of George Bell, who died alone in the city.

Should the *Times* have pried into the life of this lonely man who in his last years kept to himself and concealed his hoarding? In spite of its length—8,000 words—over three million people read the story immediately, either in print or online. Many letters to the editor praised the *Times* for printing the story; a few called it a violation of privacy. But George Bell's surviving friend and his heirs all approved of the story's being published. It reports on a sad fact of city life: the lonely deaths of people who live alone. All of us who live in the city are potential George Bells. This story reminds me of a 1911 novel by the French author Jules Romains, *Mort de quelqu'un* (The Death of Someone), which recounts the life of a childless widower, a man so ordinary that when he dies, only his aged parents remember him for any length of time. When they die, the memory of him likewise dies, and it's as if he had never existed on this earth. Though I read the story long ago, it haunts me to this day.

My own brush with death, and all it entails in the city, was less problematic by far, for the body did not need to be identified by strangers.

My longtime partner Bob had been suffering from late-stage Parkinson's for at least five years. Parkinson's involves shaking hands, a slow physical deterioration, constipation and incontinence, hallucination, and finally, an utter dependence on others. Bob went from an early stage where, at first without a cane and then with one, he could get out for short forays and have lunch in a nearby restaurant. He would come back smiling and announce, "Here I am, Shaky, the eighth dwarf." Then he couldn't go out anymore, but ordered by phone for food to be delivered. Once he fell in the apartment, and I had to get a neighbor to help me get him back to bed. Soon we found we needed help, and Partners in Care sent a series of aides. Finally we found Jacques, a Haitian, who was totally capable and could do whatever was needed; he became one of the family. And a doctor was found as well who made weekly house calls.

Parkinson's, though slow, is relentless; mainstream medicine can treat it but cannot cure it. Bob was able to walk less and less, until finally, with me and Jacques helping him, he could do only a few steps with the walker, then one or two, then none.

Thursday, August 16, 2018, started out like any other day. Bob talked little, but ate a few bites for breakfast. He was sluggish and slept lots, his mouth open, but lately he had not slept well at night, and so slept much in the daytime. But by midafternoon Jacques and I became alarmed. His whole body was limp, his head drooping and his mouth agape, and we couldn't arouse him. Jacques called 911, and within eight minutes two Fire Department medics were there. They examined him briefly, found no pulse or other vital sign; his heart had stopped. They summoned help, and soon there were eight medics hovering over him, one of them rhythmically massaging his chest as he lay flat on the floor. They asked me to step out of the room for a few minutes, probably so they could appraise the case candidly, and then let me back in. For two long hours I watched from the doorway as they tried to resuscitate him, trying every trick they knew of. After one hour Jacques and I knew it was useless. After two hours, the medics gave up.

Two policemen had arrived by now, and when the medics left, they remained. A medical examiner was notified, but she couldn't come immediately, having many other calls to make. Then two men in suits arrived: a short, thin one and a tall, stocky one, both with a very deadpan, down-to-business look. The short one took a quick look at Bob, now replaced on his bed and wrapped up like a mummy, though with his face visible, mouth agape. The visitor then talked briefly and quietly with the two policemen, following which he and his companion left. "Detectives," said one of the cops, who then told us that, since Bob's death was in no way suspicious, the medical examiner wouldn't be coming.

There were now two possibilities: we could notify a funeral home to come collect the body, or Bob would be taken to the morgue at Bellevue.

They urged us to notify a funeral home, since getting the body to Bellevue would be long and complicated. Bob and I had long since made arrangements with the Neptune Society to be cremated, with the ashes to be scattered at sea. So I dialed Neptune, learned that it had morphed into the New York Atlantic Funeral Services, and informed them of the situation. Since they were out on Long Island, it would take the hearse an hour and a half to come. The two cops told us that they couldn't leave until Bob did, but Jacques was able to leave at 8:00 p.m. as usual. The cops and I settled in for a long wait.

While the two young cops waited, and I sat at my computer informing friends by e-mail of Bob's death, I could hear the cops' police radio reporting other situations: a man lying flat on his face in his apartment on 14th Street; a woman raging about in her apartment on 10th Street, probably delusional; and so on.

"Boy," I said, "our stuff here seems dull. You guys must get some pretty wild cases."

"In a city of nine million," said one of them, "we get anything that can happen."

I nodded. "That's exciting. For all its faults, I love this city."

"I love it, too," said the officer. "Our job is never dull."

I managed a quick snack in the kitchen, while one of the policemen went out to get both of them a bite to eat. An hour passed, then an hour and a half; still no hearse. Used to a bedtime at eight, I resigned myself to a long, sleepless night. A phone call: The driver of the hearse explained that a highway accident not involving him was causing delays; it would be more than an hour and a half. The cops asked if I would want a few minutes alone with Bob to say good-bye; I declined. That mummified thing on the bed wasn't Bob, just some pitiful remnant of the Bob I had known. Bob was somewhere else. Finally the hearse arrived, and two burly men strapped Bob to a stretcher and took him down the stairs.

"That's how I'll leave this place, when the time comes," I told the two cops. "Horizontally, not vertically." Four flights or not, who would give up a sun-drenched, rent-stabilized apartment with four rooms, especially in Greenwich Village?

The cops smiled, shook hands with me, gave me a sheet with their names and the number of the case, and left. They had been great; all honor to the Sixth Precinct. At 11:00 p.m., exhausted, I finally fell into bed.

So ended the day of Bob's passing. So how did I mourn? By going to my local library to see Mae West in *She Done Him Wrong,* a pre-Hays Office film with her starring opposite a very young Cary Grant. In the film she uttered her famous line, "Come up and see me sometime," and sang "Frankie and Johnny Were Lovers," an old song that has been echoing in my mind ever since. Bob, who loved Mae West, would have applauded my seeing the film. Then, that done, I began getting used to a quiet and seemingly empty apartment and initiated the endless tasks of being an executor.

Part 3

OUR THOROUGHFARES: FROM GOATS AND BUMS TO CONDOS AND TRUMP TOWER

Chapter 21

Broadway: From *Heere Straat* to The Great White Way

Who hasn't heard of Broadway, Fifth Avenue, the Bowery, and Wall Street? Each of them is more than a street, each has a history behind it. The chapters of this section are devoted to their history and lore, with West 14th Street thrown by way of contrast, as an example of a street devoid of history and lore.

If you ask most people what the word "Broadway" means to them, they would probably say splashy musicals whose tickets cost a helluva lot, the Empire State Building, and Times Square with costumed characters like Minnie Mouse and Elmo trying to get you to take their photo, so they can demand an outsized tip. And they wouldn't be so wrong. When I queried my friends, some of whom are New Yorkers and some not, they came up with "bright lights," "traffic," "theater," and "glitzy." But if I should add *Heere Straat*, Gentleman George, the Lime-Kiln man, Pocahontas Bitters, and the Arc de Triomphe, people might arch an eyebrow and ask, "What and who are they?" And, regarding the Arc de Triomphe, "That belongs in Paris. What does it have to do with Broadway?" Answering those questions is what this chapter is all about.

Broadway is arguably the most famous street in the world. It runs fifteen miles through Manhattan and the Bronx. It was once a trail used by the Lenape, the native people of the region, and then, with the coming of the Dutch, the main thoroughfare in the settlement of New Amsterdam. The Dutch named it the *Heere Straat* (the Gentlemen's Street or High Street) or *Breede Weg*, and when the English took over, they translated the latter as "Broadway." It still runs the length of Manhattan at an angle, defying the gridlock pattern of the city's streets decreed by the city fathers in 1811.

In New Amsterdam the *Heere Straat* went from the fort that gives the Battery its name up to a gate in the wall that gives Wall Street its name. Right from the first, it teemed with a mix of peoples, not just Dutch and English, but other Europeans too, as well as Africans both slave and free, and Native Americans. One visitor reported eighteen different languages in the settlement, and they would all have been heard on Broadway.

In the eighteenth century Broadway witnessed one of the most significant events in our history: George Washington's triumphal entry into the city on November 25, 1783, following the evacuation of the last British troops, and with them, some 28,000 Loyalist refugees and many former slaves whom the British had liberated. Washington and his officers entered from the north and proceeded down Broadway to the Battery, to the cheers and applause and waving hats and handkerchiefs of onlookers. Though ticker tape was absent, it could be considered the first of many parades of heroes on Broadway. For years afterward, November 25 was celebrated as Evacuation Day.

The city of circa 1830 was charmingly small, so small that the gentry knew, or knew of, almost everyone who mattered; for all its ongoing changes, their world was ordered and safe. Few people kept carriages, and those who did were known to everyone, and their carriages were seen on Broadway. One of these was Dandy Marx, a dashing young blade whose clothing defied the somber colors of the day as he drove four handsome chestnuts down Broadway, bearing with perfect nonchalance the sneers and jealousies of others. Another familiar sight was Dandy Cox, a mulatto driving a spirited horse to a light wagon where he sat perched high on his seat, his well-brushed beaver cocked at an angle, his green jockey coat displaying polished brass buttons, his leather gloves spotless. He was imitating, and perhaps even mocking, the fashionables of the day.

But in those times almost all the men worked, so that the fashionable promenade of Broadway, which went from the Battery to Canal Street, was mostly given over to belles and their mamas for shopping. One of the few male interlopers was Gentleman George, a neat, trim, tastefully dressed young man who drove a stately gray with aplomb. Where does his money come from? the men of the town wondered. Meanwhile the mothers eyed him with suspicion, well aware that their daughters were casting furtive glances his way, intrigued by this timid but respectful young man whom they so often met on their morning strolls. Gossip about him saved many a tea party from dullness. Was he gay? A question we would ask today, but unknown back then. George was seen and puzzled over for years, until at last he disappeared into the city's rapid growth and expansion, a mystery to the end.

The sidewalks of Broadway also offered a few eccentrics who stood out. The Gingerbread Man was a harmless lunatic in a swallowtail coat who jog-trotted up and down the avenue as if on a pressing errand, his only sustenance a seemingly endless supply of gingerbread stuffed in his pockets that he was constantly consuming. One day he failed to appear and was never seen again, another Broadway mystery.

Also seen on Broadway for some twenty-five years was the Lime-Kiln Man, a tall, gaunt figure, his unkempt hair and thin face smeared with lime, who took no notice of the looks of pity he garnered. Little was known of him, though it was later said that disappointment in love had unhinged his mind. In July 1855 he was found dead in a lime kiln where he had slept at night for years.

Yet another common sight was McDonald Clark, the Mad Poet of Broadway, in a tattered blue cloak and a red neckerchief, his unbuttoned "Byronic" shirt collar a sharp contrast to the primly buttoned shirts of most males. His melancholy gaze at the pavement and his soul-deep sighs seemed to make of him, in this city of bustling doers, a singed angel or gentle demon. Having in his younger days loved many a time and lost, he now penned odes to gravestones and melancholy, his reason slightly zigzag. Often penniless and homeless, he slept for months in a hearse, and when expelled from there, on tufts of grass among the headstones of Trinity Church. A host to fleas and angels, he proclaimed critics, landladies, and kings of cash pimples on the forehead of Creation. One evening in Trinity churchyard, shivering in the wind, he informed a querying watchman:

"McDonald Clarke is dead. Three nights ago on this very tombstone, he dashed his brains out. The storm that night was the tears Heaven shed for him. His body was revivified by God. Before you behold Afara, archangel of the Almighty!"

They lodged him in a cell in the Tombs, pending transfer to Bloomingdale Asylum. By morning he was dead—of brain fever, the prison doctor reported. Rumor had it that, having turned on a faucet in his cell and flooded it, smiling, he drowned. So ended, in 1842, a fragile denizen of Broadway described by those who knew him as "innocent as a child."

The society of those days, though conformist, tolerated a number of oddballs because they were familiar and posed no threat. What people were leery of was the blatant display of wealth. Elegance was allowed, and the women of New York were famous for dressing in the height of fashion, and even the black underclass could be surprisingly chic; but the elegance had to be quiet and discreet. All this was visible on Broadway.

By the 1860s everything had changed. Irish and German immigrants had flooded in since the 1840s, the city had become a metropolis, and Wall Street was now the money center of the nation. The Civil War permitted gold speculators and war contractors to amass a fortune, and New Money was blatantly in evidence everywhere. Ever since Central Park had opened in 1859, its Drive had become the preferred promenade of the affluent, who drove there in elegant equipages, so that Broadway was now essentially commercial.

And what did one see on Broadway? Red and yellow and blue-painted stages. Open and closed carriages with liveried footmen. Drays, hacks, wheelbarrows, milk carts with clattering cans, horsemen, and lager beer wagons. Express trucks rushing about stacked high with boxes labeled **ASTOR HOUSE** or **ST. NICHOLAS HOTEL**. More massive still at times was a wagon hauled by six straining horses and conveying, to the astonishment of visitors, the towering bulk of a safe as big as a house. This traffic emitted a deafening roar, as it sliced through the mud of the street, until it jammed up amid shouts, curses, and whinnyings, and maybe the shriek of a coachman being beaten by a truckman for not giving way. With no stoplights or stop signs, how was a pedestrian to get from one side of Broadway to the other? Without the help of a policeman, you were risking your life. And in wet weather the thoroughfare was ankle-deep in mire, while in dry weather it was caked with teeth-gritting, breath-choking dust. And always, being embellished with garbage and manure, it stank.

Lining Broadway were barbershops, liquor stores, lottery offices, daguerreotype galleries, artificial teeth manufacturers, sewing machine and pianoforte showrooms, plain and fancy jewelers, oyster cellars, bookstores, billiard table stores, ice cream parlors, and gambling dens. Elegant hairdressing establishments for gentlemen emitted whiffs of menthol, musk, and cologne. Uniformed doormen waved customers into fancy dry-goods stores, while sandwichmen advertised POCAHONTAS BITTERS and PHILIPOT'S INFALLIBLE EXTRACT, and visitors from the provinces gaped at displays of patent sarcophagi in rosewood, mahogany, and iron, satin-lined with silver mountings, and featuring glass-paneled lids to display the face of the dear departed. Along this crazy street one could find anything and everything except peace of mind and tranquility. To know Broadway was to know New York.

But what did the old-timers think of all this? Remembering the tranquil days of their childhood, by the 1860s they were dazed. The jam of people and vehicles on Broadway overwhelmed them, and if they stood at an entrance to Central Park and watched the showy equipages heading for the Drive, they had no idea who these promenaders were or where their money came from. Gone was the discretion of an earlier time; New Money paraded its wealth brazenly. Engulfed by this mass of strangers, these relics of a simpler age felt small, mere atoms lost in the city's never-ending flux.

Change, often radical, was the rule in the never-finished city. By the mid-1870s buildings were rising to eight, ten, and twelve stories high, provoking mixed reviews: a new dimension to space, said some; top-heavy horrors and "Towers of Babel," said others. Broadway had been the first New York City thoroughfare to get gaslight in the mid-1820s, and now it was the first to be lit with electricity. On December 20, 1880, the whole stretch from 14th to 26th Street was suddenly bathed in Mr. Edison's brilliant light; observers gaped and raved. And in 1879 the first telephone exchange opened, with the first phone directory listing all of 252 names. Businesses rushed to adopt the new gadget, but at first it was much too costly for use in private homes.

Telephone and telegraph wires now crisscrossed one another from the tops of buildings, darkening the sky over Broadway with what seemed like meshes of a net. Worse still, overburdened wires had a way of snapping and falling to the street, with potential peril to passersby. Then in 1889 a lineman working overhead was electrocuted on a wire gridiron in the heart of the business district; thousands watched as the body dangled for nearly an hour, its mouth spitting blue flame. The enraged public now demanded that the wires be put underground, and the relevant corporations finally, after long delays, complied.

The advent of the automobile in the 1890s marked another major change for Broadway. The first recorded motor vehicle fatality in the United States, and indeed in all the Americas, occurred in New York, though not on Broadway. On September 13, 1899, Henry H. Bliss, a New York real estate salesman, was getting off a streetcar at West 74th Street and Central Park West, when an electric-powered taxi struck him and inflicted fatal injuries. He died the next day, a mortality that soon ushered in the twentieth century. The first traffic light was not installed in New York but in London in 1868, but in 1916 New York installed the first three-color stoplight at its busiest intersection, Fifth Avenue and 42nd Street. That the location chosen was not Broadway shows that by now Broadway was no longer the city's most significant thoroughfare.

By the early twentieth century it was electricity that gave the midtown stretch of Broadway, the section from 42nd to 53rd Street also known as the Theater District, the name "The Great

White Way." The streetlights alone justified it, but the advent of neon signs in Times Square confirmed it. This is still the Theater District, though most of the theaters are on side streets nearby, and Times Square today, especially at night, is more astonishing than ever.

Broadway today on the Upper West Side is a wide avenue with a thin strip of park down the middle. Back in my student days I loved walking down from Columbia University to some restaurant or movie theater on Broadway, and traipsing it at night always lifted my spirits. This stretch of Broadway was not constricted by tall buildings as it was downtown; it was big, open, and free—New York at its best.

No longer is Broadway the single jammed artery of the city, for traffic flows, and far too often jams up, on other streets as well. But nowhere does traffic swirl with more intensity than at Columbus Circle, where it pours in from different directions and surges giddily around Columbus high atop his pedestal. And nowhere is the magic of New York at night more impressive than at Lincoln Center, close by Broadway between West 60th and 66th Streets, when all the buildings and the fountain in the plaza are illuminated. Jammed and noisy, Broadway can lead to marvels as well.

Far uptown on or near Broadway are sights that few tourists ever see, and that most New Yorkers are unaware of, for instance:

+ The Hamilton Grange at West 141st Street, the 1802 seat of Alexander Hamilton's 32-acre country estate, which is now a leafy park just east of Broadway.

+ A graffiti-scarred replica of the Arc de Triomphe, looming improbably behind some stores between West 215th and 218th Streets: the 1855 gateway to the now vanished country estate of an eccentric gentleman and his heiress wife.

✦ A steep flight of 110 steps at 215th Street, leading up to Inwood Hill Park, recommended only for the intrepid few.

And where does Broadway end? According to my Hagstrom map of Manhattan, at West 225th Street, where the northern tip of Manhattan meets the Harlem River, beyond which lies the Bronx. Some hardy souls boast of walking its entire thirteen-mile length, and this is where they stop. But Broadway goes on another two miles into the Bronx, and some even see Broadway continuing out of the city into Yonkers and beyond, maybe, like the old Albany Post Road, all the way to Albany.

But Broadway, famous as it is, is also a state of mind, a legend. The very word "Broadway" suggests theater, traffic, congestion, the spirit and bustle and frenzy of a great metropolis. As such, it has been celebrated in song: "Give my regards to Broadway / Remember me to Herald Square" (George M. Cohan), and "I'm just a Broadway Baby" (Stephen Sondheim). So maybe Broadway never ends. Maybe, like Ol' Man River, it just goes on and on.

Chapter 22

Fifth Avenue:
From Goats to Grandeur

Today the name "Fifth Avenue" suggests elegant and pricey stores and a whole mile of museums. But early in the nineteenth century Fifth Avenue was a muddy rutted road leading north from Washington Square, where the city's most distinguished bankers and merchants had just built handsome Greek Revival houses fronting three sides of the square. Optimistically, the city opened the avenue to 13th Street in 1824, then to 21st Street by 1830, and to distant 42nd Street by 1837. But the "avenue" was at first inhabited by only those few who, having little need of company, preferred a landscape with rock outcroppings grazed by goats, and clusters of squatters' ramshackle shanties.

This changed in 1834, when Henry J. Brevoort, Jr., was so adventurous as to build a Greek Revival mansion on the northwest corner of Fifth Avenue and Ninth Street. Indeed, from about 1830 on, the city's prosperous merchants grew increasingly discontented with their Federal-style row houses on Lower Broadway, and were motivated to move north partly by the intrusion of commerce and the lower orders, and partly by a desire for the greater space and splendor of a freestanding house. With Washington Square at its base to shield it from commercial inroads, the new Fifth Avenue enticed these migrants northward, and in time the wide thoroughfare, now tree-lined and paved with cobblestones, was built up well to the north. By the 1840s the avenue was lined with elegant residences all the way to 14th Street and beyond.

Then, in 1858, the six-story white marble Fifth Avenue Hotel opened on Fifth Avenue between 23rd and 24th Streets, offering accommodations for 800 guests and such unheard-of luxuries as sumptuously decorated public rooms, private bathrooms, and that startling new invention, the vertical railroad, later known as an elevator. "Too far uptown!" proclaimed skeptics, but once again they were proven wrong. The hotel prospered from the start, inaugurating an era when Madison Square at 23rd Street, where Fifth Avenue and Broadway intersect, became the center of the city's fashionable world.

Already, by the 1850s, a new style had come into fashion along Fifth Avenue and its parallel, Madison, and the cross streets between them: Italianate brownstone, which would characterize these and other thoroughfares for many years. Brownstone, obtained from quarries in New Jersey and Connecticut, was now viewed as more dignified than wood or brick, though it was used simply to cover over brick façades and give them a dark "Romantic" look. High stoops rose to a parlor floor above the street, giving the residents privacy. I know, because today when I walk past a brownstone and try to peek inside, all I see of the parlor is a bit of ceiling. And the stoop, so challenging to mount, also gave a feeling of superiority; to mount those stoops was to leave the grubby everyday world behind and enter a realm of elegance and gentility. Also, this soft stone allowed for elaborate façades with carved curlicues and foliage, in contrast with the elegant restraint of the Greek Revival style, now seen as plain and dowdy. (Though not by me; I love it.) So from now on, for exteriors and interiors alike, classical simplicity was out; Victorian clutter was in.

The residents of these brownstones were Knickerbockers, old Dutch families that could trace their lineage back to the days of New Amsterdam, but also old English families that had come to the city in colonial times. They lived quietly in homes where the somber gilt-framed portraits of their forebears, governors and mayors and their wives, stared down austerely from the walls. It was a world where everyone knew everyone, their forebears, and how they made their money. They socialized and married among themselves and were leery of the "new" people. A tight little world of Old Money, conformist, predictable, and dull, but its residents found the dullness reassuring, a bit of stability in a world of endless change.

For change was all about them, gnawing at the edges of their tidy little world. In 1858 William B. Astor, Jr., and his brother John Jacob Astor III, built adjoining townhouses on the north-east corner of 33rd Street and Fifth Avenue. John Jacob's house featured a mansard roof, a style fresh from Second Empire Paris that at once became all the rage. And who were these Astors? Grandsons of John Jacob Astor, the German immigrant who came to America and made a fortune in the fur trade before branching out into other fields of endeavor, a man remembered for sharp dealings and the ruthless accumulation of wealth. As usual in America, the grandchildren and great grandchildren were glad enough to put space between themselves and the gritty founder of the family fortune, who was so lacking in the social graces. Whatever the Knickerbockers might think of them, the Astors were now exemplars of Old New Money, as opposed to upstarts like the Vanderbilts, foremost in the mounting tide of New New Money.

Of concern to Old and New Money alike was the announcement in 1853 by Archbishop John Hughes, the leader of the city's Catholic minority, of plans to build an impressive cathedral far to the north of the settled parts of Fifth Avenue, on its east side between 50th and 51st Streets—a location so far to the north that the whole project was greeted once again by many with exclamations of "Up *there? Ridiculous!*" The cornerstone was laid in 1858, and slowly, very slowly, the white marble walls of the Gothic structure began to rise. The WASP majority, though leery of Romanist plots and the boozy doings of Hughes's mostly Irish parishioners, began to take note. The construction, however slow, of such an edifice seemed to confirm slick-tongued developers' predictions that Fifth Avenue, stretching on to the north, would be the city's axis of elegance.

In 1859 the new Central Park was opened, prompting a steady flow of shiny carriages north on the avenue to the park entrance at 59th Street and Fifth, en route to the park's pebbled Drive, where Fashion went to see and be seen by Fashion. Soon after, the outbreak of the Civil War halted construction, but by 1863 a whole new horde of parvenus had appeared, their fortunes fattened by war contracts and speculations. More fancy brownstones went up, residences of gold and cotton speculators, stockbrokers, factory owners, railroad and patent medicine men, and even the inspired inventor of a truss. In other words, the grossest New Money, inflicting horror on the genteel Old Money residents of the lower avenue, who labeled the newcomers "Avenoodles."

During the last several decades of the nineteenth century—the so-called Gilded Age—the arbiters of taste labeled brownstone mansions as dingy and drab. Supplanting them (the brownstones, not the arbiters) was the ornate French chateau style, as Old and

New Money alike migrated to the upper avenue, which came to be known as Millionaires Row. Reigning over Society with a capital *S* was Caroline Astor, the wife of a wealthy grandson of old John Jacob. Hailed by admirers as "the Mystic Rose," *the* Mrs. Astor invited to her annual Astor Ball the 400 people whom she deemed socially acceptable in New York, that being the number that her sumptuous ballroom could accommodate. For the socially ambitious, not to be invited was calamitous. But her nephew Waldorf Astor, annoyed by his aunt's pretensions, tore down his residence adjoining hers and in 1893 opened on the site the luxurious 13-story Waldorf Hotel, forerunner of today's fabled Waldorf Astoria on Park Avenue.

Miffed by this intrusion of commerce, the Mystic Rose then joined the exodus northward, establishing herself in a magnificent French chateau-style mansion at Fifth Avenue and 65th Street. There she continued to hold her annual ball, but the relevance of such affairs, and the whole concept of the Four Hundred, was now being questioned by public opinion, following the publication in 1890 of Jacob Riis's *How the Other Half Lives*, whose photographs documented the squalid living conditions of the city's poor. The Astor Balls slowly faded from the scene, but Caroline Astor, now an aging victim of dementia, at times still stood at the entrance to her empty ballroom, a spectral presence greeting throngs of imagined guests. She died in 1906.

With the coming of the Twentieth Century commercial enterprises moved in, and both Old and New Money moved out. The Avenue was still an axis of elegance, but renowned now for fancy hotels and stores. A guarantee of elegance and cultural eminence was the completion in 1911, between 40th and 42nd Streets, of the New York Public Library, a magnificent Beaux Arts structure fronted by two stalwart marble lions that are still much photographed and reproduced in art.

Meanwhile fashionable upscale stores were coming in, among them Lord & Taylor, Saks Fifth Avenue, Bergdorf Goodman, and Bonwit Teller, all of them clothing retailers catering to an elite clientele. By the 1930s they were enticing shoppers with lavish window displays, and in 1939 one memorable incident resulted. When the artist Salvador Dalí discovered that Bonwit Teller had altered a window display that he had done for them featuring a bathtub lined with Persian lamb, he was furious. Entering the store, he went to the window and wrenched the bathtub free of its moorings. As he did so, the tub slipped from his grasp and crashed through the window onto the sidewalk, along with the artist himself. This impromptu Surrealist happening astonished onlookers and led to Dalí's arrest for malicious mischief, but the judge let him off, making allowances for artistic temperament.

By the late 1920s Art Deco skyscrapers were also going up in Manhattan, marking a sharp break with the Beaux Arts style and anything smacking of the Old World and the nineteenth century. Prominent among them was the 102-story Empire State Building at 34th and Fifth. Completed in 1931, for the next forty-two years it was the tallest building in the world. To make room for this, the world's most famous skyscraper and a magnet for would-be suicides (whom the building staff take elaborate measures to forestall), the original Waldorf Astoria was demolished, to be replaced by the current one on Park Avenue.

Meanwhile John D. Rockefeller, Jr., son and heir of the Standard Oil magnate and philanthropist, was at his own expense building Rockefeller Center, a complex of fourteen commercial buildings in Art Deco style bounded by 48th and 51st Streets and by Fifth and Sixth Avenues, a project of breathtaking magnitude that was begun in 1930, pursued through the worst of the Depression, and completed in 1939, with further subsequent additions.

A must-see for visitors, Rockefeller Center's cluster of sky-scrapers screams BIG BIG BIG, but then, so does the city. I take the Center in small bites, one feature at a time. At ground level, there are flags of many nations. On the Fifth Avenue side just across from St. Patrick's Cathedral, looms a seven-ton bronze sculpture of Atlas bearing the heavens on his shoulders. A sunken plaza becomes an ice-skating rink in winter, and dominating that sunken plaza is another huge bronze statue representing Prometheus bearing stolen fire to mortals, though to my eye he looks like he's trying to swim. The installation of a giant Christmas tree towering above Prometheus and the rink is an annual event widely hailed throughout the city, its lighting witnessed by thousands, while thousands more watch on TV.

The pricey retailers of Fifth Avenue were never quite my thing, least of all in my budget-conscious student days, but regarding Bonwit Teller I have a story to tell. Back in the summer of 1954, when I was a graduate student living on campus at Columbia, I got to know a good-looking young gay man named Jim, very personable, who had a teaching job in his home community, a small town in the South, and had come to Columbia for courses at Columbia Teachers College. Ours was a social friendship, nothing more, and the second week I knew him he had a tale to tell.

A young woman from a wealthy family in his hometown had arrived in New York for a shopping tour and asked him, an old friend, to escort her to Bonwit Teller at Fifth Avenue and 56th Street, which he was glad to do. When they entered, she immediately asked for a consultant. This set the tone for their visit, for it said *money*, and knowledgeable *money* at that. A well-dressed older woman was summoned, and the girl announced that she and Jim were engaged, and she needed a whole new wardrobe.

The engagement was news to Jim, but he played along. "From then on," he told me, "the shit was flying all over the place. 'What a lovely young couple!' the staff kept murmuring." Over the next two hours the consultant, having learned the presumed fiancée's needs and tastes, showed her a vast array of fashionable outfits, from which she made a large selection; money was clearly no object. "Would the gentleman also like to see some clothing?" the consultant then asked. "No," said the girl, "he already has his things."

When the girl was given the bill, she wrote a check that was accepted without question. How the store had verified her credit was a mystery to both Jim and me, but she left with a load of high-priced outfits, having arranged to have the rest shipped home. So ended Jim's tale, my only glimpse into the world of high fashion and its workings. The girl obviously had her eye on Jim, but I never saw him again in later years, so I don't know how the story ended. Being a young gay man in a small Southern town posed problems enough; as he got older, they would only increase. Maybe he ended up marrying her and, like many married men, lived a double life. I think he could have pulled it off.

I set foot in Saks Fifth Avenue just once, when relatives from Indiana were visiting and chose to go there. We weren't there for long, but I have two vivid memories. First, a salesgirl sprayed the women with a perfume—just a dash of it, done courteously with a warm smile—so as to give them a sample. Second, the men's room on the second floor had wood paneling and, at eye level just above the urinals, original art. Which struck me as the ultimate in—in what? Elegance? Sophisticated interior design? Pretension? Take your choice. How the artists would feel about it, if they knew, I hesitate to say.

Fancy stores, a magnificent library, tall buildings, and an over-whelming cluster of Art Deco structures aren't the Avenue's only distinction, since Upper Fifth Avenue from 82nd to 110th Street is lined with museums both old and new, now ten in all, earning it the name of Museum Mile. The granddaddy of them all is the Metropolitan Museum of Art at 82nd Street, presenting a Beaux Arts façade with neoclassical features. Through its labyrinthine halls I have often wandered, and in its ornate reading room I have often perused old books from long ago by the hour. By way of contrast, a distinctly modernist note is provided by the Solomon R. Guggenheim Museum at 88th Street, a strikingly original spiral-shaped affair designed by Frank Lloyd Wright. When I go there I take an elevator to the top and then descend the gently sloping ramp all the way to the ground floor, view-ing the displays en route, which, I have since learned, is exactly what Wright intended.

One could end here, but that would omit one further devel-opment: the fifty-eight-floor Trump Tower on Fifth Avenue between 56th and 57th Streets. Completed in 1983, it houses forty high-end stores, 263 luxury condominiums, the headquar-ters of the Trump Organization, and the three-story penthouse condominium of the owner. In this edifice Donald Trump's suc-cessful 2016 presidential campaign was planned. His periodic visits to "White House North" cause no end of turmoil in the street below, where security is strict and anti-Trump protests rage. And what was demolished to make room for the Tower? The Bonwit Teller building, and with it some Art Deco sculptures and a decorative grille that art lovers had hoped to have donated to the Metropolitan Museum of Art. Trump had them destroyed, insisting they were "garbage."

The history of Fifth Avenue goes from a muddy country lane to Millionaires Row to Museum Mile to Trump Tower, an amazing trajectory accomplished in a mere century and a half. The Avenue is absolutely essential to the city's image as a center of fashion and culture; who could think of New York without it? As for real estate values, in 2016 *Forbes* magazine ranked it as the most expensive street in the world, surpassing even Hong Kong's pricey Causeway Bay area and Paris's Champs-Élysées.

One last note. Since 2002, Fifth Avenue at 27th Street has featured yet another museum: the Museum of Sex. Sculpted animals humping each other, provocative paintings, nude photographs, naughty diaries, the history of the condom, and sculpted outsized penises are displayed inside. What surprises me is that it took so long to appear. Maybe feisty New Yorkers preferred to gather data firsthand, rather than absorbing it in an institution. And the folks from Kansas City and Peoria? All I know is, multitudes flock.

Chapter 23

The Bowery: From B'hoys to Bums to Condos

W hen i grew Up in the 1930s and 1940s, the word
"Bowery" meant just one thing: bums and drunks, and
the cheap saloons and flophouses that catered to them, and the
missions trying to rescue them. Even as late as the 1960s an
acquaintance of mine recorded an interview with a literate and
somewhat sober Bowery denizen who, when not interrupted by
spasms of coughing, gave him a brief tour of the locale, stressing
that "these men have given up." The interview was then played
on a local radio station, but so far as I know, nothing more came
of it. But in those days the Bowery was the refuge of the lost, the
drunk, and the damned. You couldn't sink lower; your next home
was the morgue. But the history of the neighborhood known
as the Bowery involves much more than this. Let's have a look.

The street known as the Bowery runs from Chatham Square,
at Park Row in Lower Manhattan, north to Cooper Square at
East 4th Street, though it once was considered to end at Union
Square, where it and Broadway converged. Originally it was a

path of the Lenape people that traversed the entire length of the island of Manhattan. When the Dutch came and founded New Amsterdam, they named this path the *Bouwerij,* an old Dutch word for "farm," because it connected farms and estates outside the city wall to the settlement at the southern tip of Manhattan. In 1651 Peter Stuyvesant, the last Dutch governor, bought a large farm that in time came to 300 acres bounded by what is now 17th Street on the north, the East River on the east, Fifth Street on the south, and Fourth Avenue on the west. When, over his objections, the colony surrendered to the British in 1664, he retired to this estate, died there in 1672, and was buried in the floor of his private chapel.

But that's not the end of Old Silver Leg, a name he acquired because he wrapped his wooden leg in silver bands to strengthen it. His descendants lived on in the area, and in 1778 his great-grandson sold the crumbling chapel and graveyard to the Episcopal Church. St. Mark's Church-in-the-Bowery was built on this site in 1799, with the family vault holding the governor's remains under its east wall. From then on there were reports of a one-legged ghost stalking about, its peg leg going *clop clop clop* on the floor, and of the church bell being rung by unseen hands. Old Silver Leg was evidently still angry about the colony's surrender and resented as well the disturbance of his remains. These reports continued into the twentieth century and beyond. In 2002 the *clop clop clop* of his wooden leg was once again allegedly heard in the church.

In the eighteenth century the dusty road known as Bowery Lane ran past gentlemen's estates and farms, several of the farms owned by the old governor's descendants. A small community named Bowery Village sprang up with a few houses, a blacksmith, a wagon shop, a general store, and a tavern. By the early 1800s, as the city expanded northward, the village attracted more wagon stands, shops, groggeries, and an oyster house where post riders could leave mail. There was also a brothel, in spite of which respectable residences were also built in the neighborhood. Clearly, change was coming, as evidenced in 1812, when Third Avenue was cut through Stuyvesant property, and old roads were closed and the houses on them removed or demolished. The Stuyvesants resisted bitterly and managed to save a few homes, but the neighborhood, no longer rural, was subjected to the commissioners' rigid grid plan designed for all the island of Manhattan.

As the years passed, the Bowery, sometimes paved with cobblestones and sometimes with gravel, became a broad avenue paralleling and rivaling Broadway. In spite of a few fine residences, the street soon became a commercial and entertainment center for the working classes, a poor man's Broadway. In 1836 the Bowery Savings Bank was established at 130 Bowery to serve the workers in the area, where there was no other bank. Lining the avenue by the 1840s were saddleries, druggists, jewelers, pawnshops and junk shops, taverns, and livery stables, and shopkeepers who spread their wares out on the sidewalk. Working class and gutsy, the street was hailed by some as the most democratic scene in the city, and even the most Christian. If a fellow who had seen better days showed up in a torn coat and battered hat, no one thought the worse of him, since they or their friends had all been through the same.

Prominent among the Bowery denizens was the Bowery B'hoy, known at a glance by his loud clothes, often the red flannel of his volunteer fire company, and by a lingo strewn with *dese, dose,* and *dat.* His soap-greased sidelocks were topped by a stovepipe hat set at a rakish angle, and gracing his mouth was a cigar or a chew of tobacco. A butcher or mechanic, or a shipbuilder or carpenter or unskilled laborer by day, at night and on holidays he swaggered down the Bowery as if he owned it, which in a sense he did. Everything about him proclaimed his rowdy independence, his hate of pretense, his disdain for bourgeois sobriety. Good-humored, loyal to his pals, and fiercely protective of his girl, he believed in fair play, and was always ready for a fire, a fight, or a frolic. Hearing a fire alarm, he rushed to join his volunteer fire company and help haul their engine to the scene of the fire, clashing with any rival company that got in the way. Mounting a ladder, he often plucked terrified occupants from the upper stories of houses consumed by flames.

Matching him in independence was the Bowery Gal, a working girl who in her off hours sashayed along the Bowery with a swinging gait. Her gaudy bonnet was trimmed with flowers, feathers, outsized bows, and ribbons. The clashing colors of her clothing, and her short skirt revealing a well-turned ankle, proclaimed her the very opposite of the well-mannered young middle-class lady schooled to be proper, modest, tasteful, and demure. More than one journalist of the time discerned in the Bowery Gal and her male counterpart a unique species of human nature possible only in a New World society. And today feminists clasp the Bowery Gal to their collective bosom and exalt her to the stratosphere.

Catering to the rowdy working-class denizens of the Bowery was the Bowery Theatre, which opened at the corner of Canal Street and the Bowery in 1826 and survived numerous fires, being rebuilt each time and lasting well into the twentieth century. Women and children and the less hardy patrons took refuge in the gallery, leaving the pit to the boisterous males who, when the doors opened, rushed in like a horde of unchained demons. If any stranger was so misguided as to claim the seat of a regular, the B'hoys lifted the offender bodily over the heads of the crowd and passed him to the rear of the theater.

The fare offered at the Bowery was primarily melodrama, with heroes rescuing damsels in distress from the clutches of villains who died wretchedly, with jerks, spasms, and groans, to the cheers and hisses of the audience. If the curtain failed to go up on time, whistles and stomps erupted, and shouts of "H'ist dat rag!" But if the play ended satisfactorily, no audience ever produced such thunderous applause.

By the 1850s a great influx of Irish and German immigrants added new colors to the Bowery, with half the signs in German, since Germans settled in large numbers on the Lower East Side. On Sundays German families flocked into the beer gardens for a day of entertainment, singing, dancing, and feasting. By way of contrast, the Irish saloons had a strictly male clientele, some married and some not, who met there for conviviality. Then, rarely sober, the married ones trudged homeward to a demanding wife ready to pocket for groceries and other essentials whatever pay her bibulous husband had managed not to spend.

But to really know the Bowery one had to see it on Saturday night, when it was ablaze with gaslight, while horsecars passed with colored lights and jingling bells, and working-class males surged along the sidewalks looking for fun and entertainment. Music and laughter issued from the dance halls, and the crackle of rifle fire from shooting galleries. On the sidewalk small German bands played waltzes, organ grinders presented their gaudily clad monkeys, and black quartets sang spirituals, while dime museums enticed passersby with mechanical contrivances, flea circuses, and wax figures representing vividly the most lurid crimes. Whatever distractions a young workingman might desire on his night off were available here, and cheap. Yes, there were abundant drunks and whores, occasional gang fights, and now and then even a riot, but the Bowery had a life all its own, unmatched by any other scene in the city. Raw, undisciplined, and free, it was intensely and defiantly *alive*.

Nineteenth-century New York was perennially in flux. In 1878 the Third Avenue El began operation, running from Chatham Square north over the Bowery and then over Third Avenue all the way to 129th Street. Not only did it darken the street, but it also made a screeching noise and showered pedestrians with oil drippings, soot, and hot cinders. A year later the Bowery Mission was founded at 14 Bowery, seeking to provide food and shelter to the homeless men of the neighborhood. The Mission, still in operation today, continued at various addresses on the Bowery, which was becoming more and more the haunt of down-and-outers, with flophouses and cheap restaurants and clothing stores catering to them, as well as cheap saloons. By the 1890s prostitutes abounded, as well as bars and dance halls for "degenerates" and "fairies," who found a working-class neighborhood more tolerant than middle-class localities elsewhere. But if Bowery residents scorned middle-class gentility, that gentility began pursuing them. "Souselumming" became fashionable, as respectable fun-seeking citizens made forays into this realm of outcasts and the damned.

By the early twentieth century the Bowery had become what I and my generation perceived: the Skid Row of New York, and the most famous one in the nation. In 1907 the population of its flophouses, missions, and cheap hotels was estimated at twenty-five thousand. The Depression of the 1930s only made matters worse. And yet, by way of contrast, the Bowery from Houston to Delancey Street became the city's chief market for lighting fixtures and lamps, and from Delancey to Grand Street its chief market for bar and restaurant equipment, markets that are still there today.

In the late 1960s a friend took me to Sammy's Bowery Follies, a unique joint at 267 Bowery that was part dive, part tourist trap. What I chiefly remember is feisty women in garish outfits singing feisty songs; it was fun. Sammy's was past its prime by then, having been founded in 1934 by Sammy Fuchs first as a run-of-the-mill saloon, but then, in a spurt of inspiration, as a cabaret that he proclaimed "the Stork Club of the Bowery." In its heyday Sammy's, with its packed sawdust floor and Gay Nineties pictures and photos of prize fighters on the walls, drew drunks and celebrities alike, skylarking sailors and local down-and-outers, the rich and the forgotten, all of them rubbing elbows in a Gay Nineties-style bar while reborn vaudeville has-beens belted out songs. It got so famous that tour buses rolled up and sent their occupants thronging in for a brief taste of how the other half lived. But in time its glory faded, and in 1970, a year after Sammy Fuchs died, it closed its doors. Sitting at the bar on that last night were Prune Juice Jenny, Box Car Gussie, Juke Box Katie, and Tug Boat Ethel, all mourning the loss of a beloved hangout.

Another sign of change was the demise of the Third Avenue El. The Depression had brought decreased ridership for all the elevated lines, and Mayor La Guardia decided to eliminate them so as to raise property values. The Third Avenue El ceased service on May 12, 1955. My partner Bob was a longtime fan of the line, which he rode sometimes for the sheer fun of it. With many like-minded veterans of the El, most of them casting mournful looks and some of them swigging champagne, he rode on the very last train from Chatham Square to 34th Street, where he got off because of the crowds now jamming the train. Property values may well have soared, but a bit of colorful old New York was gone forever.

The Bowery never quite dies. In 1964 Anthony Amato established his Amato Opera at 319 Bowery, near East 4th Street, where it flourished for thirty-five years, presenting mostly French and Italian operas on a postage-stamp stage; in recent years Bob and I attended many. And in 1973 the music club CBGB moved into 315 Bowery, just a few doors away, to offer hard-core punk, then rock, folk, and jazz to enthusiastic audiences. Meanwhile the Bowery's vagrant population was declining, partly because of the city's effort to disperse it. Decidedly, the Bowery was on an upswing, leaving its Skid Row image behind.

Today high-rise condominiums are appearing, plus an upscale food market and the New Museum of Contemporary Art. There are curio shops, art galleries, a poetry club, celebrity lounges, and the luxurious Bowery Hotel, offering 24-hour room service, valet parking, a fitness room, spa services, and many other amenities. The elite no longer come on quickie slumming tours; they come to stay. So the boisterous turf of Old Silver Leg and the Bowery B'hoy and his Gal, and Box Car Gussie and Juke Box Katie and a multitude of down-and-outers, has succumbed to that most humiliating and dismaying of fates: gentrification.

Chapter 24
Wall Street:
From a Buttonwood Tree
to Credit Default Swaps

I t's sUrprising hoW names enshrine forgotten bits of history. Canal Street: there once was a canal. The Battery: there once was a fort. The Bowery: there once was a farm. And Wall Street: there once was a wall.

Yes, long before stocks and bonds were heard of, and short sales and derivatives and leveraged buyouts, there was a wall. A twelve-foot-high stockade, it marked the northern limit of the old Dutch settlement of New Amsterdam, with one gate in it for the street that became Broadway. The wall was a defense against the native peoples whom the Dutch had come to trade with and on occasion to cheat and kill. New Amsterdam became New York with the arrival of the English in 1664, and in 1685 surveyors laid out Wall Street along the lines of the original wall. Even in these early days merchants and traders were meeting there in the open to buy and sell stocks and bonds, and in 1711 the Common Council made Wall Street the city's first official market for the buying and selling of slaves.

By the late eighteenth century, traders were gathering under a buttonwood tree at the foot of Wall Street to buy and sell securities. In 1792 twenty-four of them got together to sign the Buttonwood Agreement, whereby the signatories agreed to charge each other a standard commission, while charging others a higher rate. This was the origin of the New York Stock Exchange, which to this day is a private entity with its own rules and regulations. And from the very first, a monopoly.

Doing business outdoors had its inconveniences, since snow and rain might dampen the spirit of traders, so in 1794 the Tontine Coffee House, a four-story brick building, was built at the northwest corner of Wall and Water Streets to function as a merchants' exchange for brokers, merchants, insurers, and others. In those days before the telephone and telegraph, a merchant went "on 'change" daily to see others on business, and to make himself available to those who might wish to see him. At the Tontine, while some drank coffee, others traded securities, auctioned goods, read or discussed the latest news, and argued politics. It was also used for banquets and balls, and on occasion witnessed gambling and slave trading, and fistfights and other minor mayhem sparked by political differences.

In time the trading of stocks required more space, so in 1817 traders formally organized the New York Stock & Exchange Board and rented rooms at 40 Wall Street. The street was still partly residential, but residents were soon fleeing its noise and bustle for calmer scenes uptown. A disastrous fire in 1835, and another in 1845, devastated the business district, but by the very next day workers were clearing away the smoking debris and hot rubble to rebuild.

Mid-century Wall Street was still a simple and rather narrow cobblestoned street frequented by dogs and grunting pigs in the early morning, when it had a small-town air. Beginning at the west on Broadway, where the Gothic grace of Trinity Church loomed reverently and chimed the hours and quarter hours, the street ran east for less than half a mile to South Street and the anchored sailing vessels of the East River docks. Regardless of pious chimes and grunting pigs, its rows of temple-fronted banks and brokerage offices were now the financial capital of the nation, where money gushed in good times, looking for investments, then in bad times shrank to a trickle, until recovery let the money spigot dribble, then flow, then gush and splash again. Throughout the century boom followed bust followed boom, each bust wiping out the fortunes of many, and each boom sprouting a new crop of richies.

If newcomers to the city visited Wall Street in the 1860s during the Civil War, what would they have seen? A cobbled lane lined by Greek temples of banks and brokerage houses. Outside on the street, men in silk hats babbled, newsboys shrieked news from battlefields, peddlers hawked cakes and balloons, and street orators ranted against mammon and intemperance. Sweating messengers toted bags of coins, and if one was jostled and coins spilled out on the pavement, bystanders would form a circle around the scene, permitting the messenger to retrieve the spilled treasure safely. In William Street, just off Wall, brokers screamed amid upraised arms in an ill-lit den called the Coal Hole, watched by a horde of onlookers, some frayed and seedy-looking, others top-hatted in wild stripes and rich satin vests: the losers and winners in the feverish wartime speculation in gold, which soon would be transferred to a massive exchange known as the Gold Room, in whose cavernous murk brokers shrieked and gesticulated.

Here and there along Wall Street and the side streets, silken ladies reclining on cushions in fancy carriages waited anxiously, while servants fetched quotations from brokers' offices. And thronging those offices were pink-cheeked youths from the provinces, feisty steamboat skippers, and hefty merchants and lawyers, all of them thrusting at clerks across a glossy black walnut counter their banknotes and checks, to be deposited in hard iron safes. Among the speculators there were Westerners in broad-brimmed hats, displaced soft-voiced Southerners, and threadbare ministers hoping with one day's scoop in the market to top their salary for a year. Incongruously, the whole scene was blessed on the hour by a chime in the Gothic steeple of Trinity.

Such was Wall Street at the height of the wartime speculation of the 1860s, soon to subside with the end of the war. The next boom, fed by feverish construction of railroads into a Western wilderness that as yet had no need of railroads, turned to bust with the Panic of 1873, heralding a bleak six-year depression. As always, more booms and busts would follow, each bust wiping out a generation of speculators and ill-timed investors, and each boom hatching a new wave of moneyed speculators spurred by hope and greed.

In 1907 an attempt to corner a stock on the New York Stock Exchange led to the failure of a brokerage house and a bank, which triggered runs on other banks and precipitated the Panic of 1907. At this point, with chaos impending, enter J.P. Morgan, the most prestigious banker of the day, a massive man with piercing eyes, and a nose rendered purple by a skin condition that prompted him to lunge with upraised cane at photographers. He was also equipped with a fierce mustache, a thundering voice, and so overwhelming a presence that one man said a visit from Morgan left him feeling "as if a gale had blown through the house." Top-hatted, frock-coated, and ponderous, he was Wall Street and moneybags incarnate, fitting perfectly our stereotypical image of the fat-cat banker, the tycoon. As for power, he had plenty of it, controlling 70 percent of the steel industry, one fifth of all the corporations on the New York Stock Exchange, the three biggest U.S. insurance companies, and several banks. If he liked big deals, he also liked big boats and loved cruising about on his yacht with a passel of guests, especially (with his wife tucked away elsewhere) handsome women.

Hearing of the panic while attending an Episcopal Church convention in Virginia, this phenomenon rushed back to New York by train to redeem the situation. Conferring with other bankers, he talked and blustered and bullied them into putting up huge sums to keep threatened banks afloat. Crisis after crisis followed, and Morgan finally locked his fellow bankers in a room in his library until they forked over the sums needed to stem the panic. You didn't say no to J.P. Values on the stock exchange fell by 50 percent, but an even greater panic was averted.

Only Morgan had the resources and prestige to pull off this desperate act of redemption. At first he was hailed as a hero, but then his role was scrutinized by Congress, and doubts were raised about the wisdom (or lack of it) of having one man wield such power. As a result, in 1913 Congress created the Federal Reserve System to regulate banks and maintain the stability of the financial system. It took a complex system of twelve regional banks, with a seven-member governing board appointed by the president, to replace old J.P.

Earlier that same year Morgan died, marking the end of an era; on Wall Street flags were flown at half-mast. He was smart to check out when he did, since in that same year the Sixteenth Amendment was passed, permitting Congress to enact a progressive income tax. Some see the end of the Gilded Age as 1914, with the beginning of World War I, or 1900, with the coming of a new century. Personally, I suggest 1913, marking the enactment of the income tax. How Wall Street must have groaned! A tax on, of all things, one's income! Worse still, the more you earned, the more you paid. From now on, amassing millions wouldn't be quite as much fun. But it wasn't just those pesky Democrats who did it; the Republicans went along with it, too. Back then Republicans did all kinds of progressive things, such as busting trusts and creating the National Park System. Ah, those were the days!

In the twentieth and twenty-first centuries, Wall Street has had its ups and downs—bubbles and busts, attempts at regulation, the Great Depression and the Great Recession—but in the long run it has mostly seen ups. Its image as a citadel of wealth and privilege persists, provoking attacks and challenges. Prominent among them:

✦ In 1920 an anarchists' bomb exploded at the corner of Wall and Broad Streets, killing 38 and injuring 143.

✦ In 1967 Yippie leader Abbie Hoffman and a band of merry pranksters invaded the visitors' gallery of the Stock Exchange to hurl real and fake dollars down on the hectic trading floor below. Traders booed and laughed and scrambled for the windfall. The invaders were promptly expelled, and the Exchange spent $20,000 to enclose the gallery with bulletproof glass.

✦ In 2011 Occupy Wall Street protested inequality, greed, corruption, and the undue influence of Wall Street by occupying Zuccotti Park. Their slogan, chanted with fervor: "We ... are ... the 99 percent" (as opposed to the top 1 percent). Expelled, they slowly faded from the scene.

What motivates a Wall Street trader? In an article in the *New York Times* entitled "For the Love of Money," former hedge-fund trader Sam Polk tells how thrilled he was by his first bonus of $40,000, until one week later a trader four years his senior was hired away by another firm for $900,000, twenty-two times the size of his bonus. Four years later, at age twenty-five, he was making $1.75 million a year, yet he would wake up in the middle of the night, terrified by the thought of running out of money. Realizing that he was addicted to greed, and that he was doing nothing useful or necessary for society, he got out. With effort he shook off his addiction and began providing services for the underprivileged.

Addicted or not to greed, the Wall Street of today is not the Wall Street of yore. In the age of computers and the Internet, there is no need for the financial industry to be concentrated in one district, so as to facilitate the delivery of securities. Some big banks have migrated to midtown, and others have deserted New York and its high costs for the charms of New Jersey. Wall Street itself is now dominated by soaring high-rises. Empty office buildings have been converted to lofts and apartments, and recently there has been a trend toward luxury apartments and upscale retailers, alleviating the deathlike stillness that used to characterize the area at night and on weekends and holidays.

But the Wall Street that remains is ever changing. Today, even on days of tumultuous action, with the market soaring or plunging, frenzied trading floors have given way to small groups of people in front of computer screens monitoring their firm's passive investments. "Passive" says it all. Instead of actively managing their investments, giant investment firms rely on sophisticated computer programs to funnel their investors' money into the stocks and bonds that make up indexes throughout the world. And hedge funds let indexes measuring sharp market swings tell them when to buy and sell, convinced that computer models do a better job of creating stock portfolios than humans do. When stocks rise or fall, managers watch their computer screens with confidence and calm, letting their computers do all the work. Passive, indeed.

One survivor from an earlier time is the New York Stock Exchange at 18 Broad Street, a pillared Beaux Arts Parthenon that opened in 1903 and is now a National Historic Monument. Topping its noble façade is a marble pediment with high-relief sculptures showing Integrity Protecting the Works of Man. Integrity, a classically robed female, stretches her arms outward in a protective gesture toward figures symbolizing Agriculture and Mining on one side, and Science, Industry, and Realizing Intelligence (whatever that is) on the other. How relevant this is to the Wall Street of today, enamored of credit default swaps, structured investment vehicles, and collateralized debt obligations, I leave it to the reader to decide.

Today's Wall Street is also a tourist destination. High points for visitors include the Stock Exchange itself, and the Federal Reserve Bank on Liberty Street whose gold vaults, eighty feet below street level, house $415 billion in gold bullion behind a 90-ton steel door. And from May to September there is a weekly "Scoundrels of Wall Street Tour" featuring robber barons of the Gilded Age, and more recent financiers like Bernie Madoff, who made off with his clients' investments totaling in the billions. But if today's miscreants who operate within the law get fat bonuses, they have to pay federal, state, and city income taxes, and the city can sure use the money.

Chapter 25

14th Street:
Auntie Guan, ezPawn,
BLOOD AND FIRE, Macs

I have oFten taken a bus or walked along West 14th Street, a busy east-west cross street that separates the West Village from Chelsea, and that refuses to be gentrified. It is determinedly commercial, not big-time commercial, but small. As one store's sign put it,

KEEP 14TH STREET GREEN
BRING MONEY

West 14th is a poor relation of the other thoroughfares in this section, lacking their history and significance. I include it here—specifically, the stretch between Ninth Avenue and Union Square—as an example of the city's many cross streets, unglamorous and basic. But the rich variety of small shops lining it produce juxtapositions that catch and charm the eye. Consider:

1. Chelsea Bagel & Café next to Bunga's Den next to Gemini 14 next to Satori Laser next to Desco Vacuum.

2. Edible Arrangements next to Smoke Shop next to Yo Yo Spa next to Pharmacy.

3. Bling Lash above Auntie Guan's Kitchen next to Urgent Medical Care ("open 7 days").

4. Brick Oven Pizza next to We Buy Gold and Diamonds/ We Pawn.

5. El Paraíso Spanish/Chinese Food above City Eyebrows Threading Salon next to Framing, and over Framing, Defensive.

6. ezPawn Corp next to Jupioca, a "vibrant outpost for blended fruit juices, protein shakes, tapioca drinks, smoothies & more."

7. Toosh next to Electronics.

8. Dragon Tattoos over Cigarville next to 24 hr. Parking (clearance 6'8").

9. Potbelly Sandwich Shop next to Sprint next to Wigs Plus next to Lighting and Beyond.

Some of these are clear, some are baffling. Let's take a look.

1. Desco Vacuum is known to me, since I have bought vacuum parts there, and Satori Laser offers laser hair removal But Bunga and Gemini escaped me until I consulted the Internet. Bunga's Den is a "relaxed, funky neighborhood joint offering a number of beers on tap, plus pub eats & comedy nights." Fine, but who Bunga is remains for me a mystery. And Gemini 14? It proves to be "a color bar salon dedicated to perfection." It dyes and styles your hair, even to the point of "magic wand" hair

extensions "personally crafted to your needs." One good
session here and you're bound to make a hit at Bunga's.

2. Clear enough.

3. Auntie Guan's is, as I assumed, a Chinese restaurant,
no doubt presided over by a motherly Chinese lady in
love with food and her customers. It offers northern
Chinese food, including "braised beef noodle soup and
dried tofu noodles "with pepper lunch special." Sounds
good, I'll admit. And Bling Lash claims to be "NYC's
Best Eyelash Extensions and Nail Art Spa." So here, too,
a session should set you up for a glamorous entrance in
Auntie Guan's. And if northern Chinese cuisine doesn't
suit your system, Urgent Medical Care is right nearby.

4. No mystery here.

5. Defensive is a driving school.

6. Clear enough.

7. What, oh what, is Toosh? A shoe store, it turns out.

8. No problem.

9. Lighting and Beyond offers lamps and electrical appliances, but Sprint baffled me at first. Now, thanks again
to the Internet, I know that it is a "provider of wireless
plans, cell phones, accessories & more." Wigs Plus,
predictably, offers a collection of "gorgeous wigs, extensions and hair pieces ... something for every occasion.
Shop today!"

On 14th Street you can satisfy every conceivable need—not
luxury needs, but basics. You can spruce up your appearance,
pawn something, and buy cigars, smoothies, wigs, pizza, cell
phones, and vacuum cleaners. You can have a good meal at Auntie
Guan's and a beer at Bunga's. And if these material delights aren't

enough, and Urgent Medical Care can't help, there's always the Salvation Army right nearby.

But West 14th Street has more than small shops and eateries. On the northwest corner of Ninth Avenue and 14th Street the Apple Store looms, a three-story edifice usually topped by a display of giant computer screens. I have trekked there several times, lugging my desktop on a cart to consult computer "geniuses" on the top floor about smoothing out computer kinks and exploring computer possibilities. This Apple Store—so trendy, so twenty-first century—opened here in 2007, but previously this was the gateway to the Meatpacking District, which stretched from here west to the river. The building itself was an outlet for Western Beef, with open barrels of pig ears and snouts in brine, jugs of pork bellies, and carpet-sized rolls of tripe. So 14th Street, like the rest of the city, is in constant flux. From pig ears to Macs—quite a change!

At 330 West 14th Street, dominating the south side of the block between Ninth and Eighth Avenues, is Our Lady of Guadalupe at St. Bernard's Church, a Victorian Gothic edifice built in 1873–1876 for the area's growing Irish population. Its pointed Gothic arches and twin square towers contrast vividly with the commercial buildings lining the street. But "Our Lady of Guadalupe" hardly sounds Irish. Indeed, by 2003 St. Bernard's parish had dwindled, while the numbers of Latinos worshiping down the street at Our Lady of Guadalupe had grown, so the two parishes merged.

Now let's move east. At no. 219 is We the People, a self-styled debt-relief agency that proclaims in bold letters

DIVORCE $499
INCORPORATIONS $399
BANKRUPTCY $499
WILLS $199

To which their card adds in fancy lettering, "Rest in Peace."

On the southwest corner of 14th and Seventh Avenue is a five-story red-brick building built in 1888-1889, its front entrance flanked by caryatids and topped by a balcony guarded by griffins. For years I went by it without noticing the entrance, much less the white stone statue above it, which stands out in sharp relief against the dark red brick and the brownstone trim. The statue is Joan of Arc, for the building was once known as the Jeanne d'Arc. It was a good example of that novelty from Paris, the multifamily building offering French flats, or what we today call "apartments." Apartments caught on with middle-class New Yorkers who, because of soaring real estate values, could no longer afford a single-family home. Such homes, brownstones and Greek Revival houses, still line the street at intervals, but have long since been converted to commercial uses.

Modern grandeur presents itself at 120-130 West 14th Street, where the Salvation Army's Territorial Headquarters rises massively, an Art Deco masterpiece completed in 1930. I confess to having walked or ridden past it countless times without giving it a wisp of attention, until my growing interest in New York architecture sparked an awareness of it as perhaps the most hugely magnificent structure on West 14th Street. The most arresting feature of the asymmetrical three-building complex is the deep grotto-like entrance with a stepped concrete façade with curtain-like folds.

Guarding the entrance are great gilt metal gates that seem always to be locked tight shut, sometimes with several homeless people sprawled or huddled in front of them. Peering through the gates, one gets only a glimpse of monumental stairs mounting to the left and right, leading to a spacious interior. Clearly visible

on the wall in back of the grotto are the words of the Army's
English founder, William Booth:

> While women weep, as they do now,
>   I'll fight.
> While men go to prison, in and out,
> In and out, as they do now,
>   I'll fight.
> While there is a drunkard left,
> While there is a poor lost girl upon the streets,
> While there remains one dark soul without the light of God,
> I'll fight—I'll fight to the very end.

Impressive, I admit. And on the wall high above those words is
the Army's crest, a circular rising-sun motif topped with a crown
and containing the Army's motto, *Blood And Fire,* signifying the
blood of Jesus and the fire of the Holy Spirit.

On the southeast corner of Fifth Avenue and 14th Street is a building I love to hate: the New School University Center, a sixteen-
story boxy monstrosity with a skin of horizontal brass bands
artificially aged to acquire a "dark golden-brown hue" (they look
gray to me). It boasts of its "innovative stair system" providing
a "grand avenue," glass-encased, that creeps up the sides of the
building, its space meant to provide students with "informal
interaction." I don't know which I hate more—those horizontal
strips or the exposed staircases, the brass or the glass. But I'm
sure that the students, without architectural stimulus, will manage plenty of informal interaction on their own. Granted, the
building is innovative and eye-catching, and far from dull. But

I still detest it, and it's good to have something to detest, since it keeps you from getting bland. And hating a building is fun; it can't hate you back.

Finally, at 14th Street and Fourth Avenue we come to Union Square, whose greenmarket I have patronized in all seasons for many years. Here too, in the granddaddy of all the greenmarkets throughout the country, one encounters an array of signs:

✦ Holy Schmidt's Horseradish / 7 Hot Flavors

✦ DRINK LOCAL / Orange County Distillery

✦ Lavender by the Bay

✦ Hudson Valley Duck Farm / duck prosciutto

✦ Body and Soul / Vegan

✦ OSTRICH EGGS

✦ Bourbon chix liver paté / YUM

✦ BISON MEAT

✦ Andrew's NYC Honey

✦ Feisty Acres / pickled quail eggs

✦ If thou tastest a crust of bread, thou tastest all the stars and all the heavens. Robert Browning

I've tried the honey and the lavender, and swear by the bread, though I'm not sure I ever tasted stars or heavens, usually only olives or raisins or cranberry. And I've never sampled the horseradish, the outsized ostrich eggs, the pickled quail eggs, or the bison meat. But maybe someday, in an adventurous mood, I will.

Every time I ride the bus or walk along West 14th Street, I say thank God it's there. Still commercial and ungenteel, basic, blunt, and fun.

Part 4

ARTSY FARTSY: MUSEUM WARS, A FIGHTING MOM, AND A WHISKEY-TASTING CEMETERY

Chapter 26
Museums and Museum Wars

N ew Yorkers are much involved with the arts. They care about their museums and monuments, their statues in public places, and even their landscaped cemeteries. And they argue about them, endlessly. That's what this section is all about.

It was glitter, it was power, it was chic. And of course it was money, lots of it. All the biggies of the art world were there—museum directors, the socialites and billionaire financiers who pay hefty secret fees to sit on museum boards, the owners of trendy galleries masking their mutual ill feelings and contempt, prominent European and American collectors, and the "in" artists of the moment whose works command stratospheric prices. It was a stellar social event, a black-tie dinner in 2014 at the Metropolitan Museum of Art, celebrating philanthropist Leonard Lauder's $1 billion gift of 81 Cubist paintings to the Met.

The Met? Picasso and Braque and Gris going to the Met? Going to that storehouse of the eternal that in the past had turned its patrician nose up at the petty doings of modern art? Why not to the Museum of Modern Art, which from the day of its founding has given its heart and soul and facilities to the promotion and display of modern artists? MOMA's honorary chairman, Ronald Lauder, the brother of the donor, was present, along with other MOMA biggies, all doing their best to smile and celebrate this stunning gift of art to the venerable and monumental, if slightly stodgy, Met, when it might logically have gone to sleek, young, sexy MOMA.

Yes, there are museum wars in New York, wars fought gently and furtively, and sometimes savagely, among the museum directors and curators and board members and donors and critics. These prestigious institutions are constantly vying for preeminence and gifts of art and money—vast, eye-popping amounts of money—so as to maintain and expand their operations. Who is number one? Who is number two? Are they planning to expand, and if so, is the expansion brilliant or ill-advised? Will it please or irritate the public? Will it cost them some donors? Are they rolling in money, or secretly desperate to meet their needs? Such are the questions that those involved in museum politics are constantly asking, whether discreetly over cocktails at a social gathering, or publicly in articles and columns in the press.

For me, a layman, these matters are distant and enigmatic. Over the years I have many times visited both the Met and MOMA, paying MOMA the hefty admittance required, and giving the Met whatever my thrifty little heart deems appropriate, since they claim that admission is voluntary. (But offer them a truly paltry amount, and see the look of utter contempt you will reap.) Looming in Beaux Arts majesty on Fifth Avenue, fronted with imposing Greek columns and accessed by wide-ranging steps, the Met, built in the 1870s, is vast and labyrinthine. Vast to the point of intimidating; it overwhelms. Many a time, seeking a particular exhibit, I have wandered down long halls celebrating ancient cultures I have never even heard of, before reaching my destination. Of course I have my favorites. One is the South Asian collection, where benignly serene Buddhas appear in close proximity to a voluptuous Hindu dancer whose lack of arms in no way impairs her haunting sensuality. Of the old masters, I am always drawn to El Greco's view of Toledo, and next to it, his portrait of a magnificently robed cardinal. With Cézanne's *Card Players*, the Met is edging toward the modern, and with Picasso's portrait of Gertrude Stein in the American Wing, it has jumped smack into it. I have always allowed the Met some Cézannes and other Impressionists and Post-Impressionists, but a Picasso is definitely transgressing on the turf of the Modern. Long before the Lauder gift of 81 Cubists, I could detect the Met's tentacles reaching out insidiously toward the modern art it had once dismissed with scorn. Still, Cézanne and Picasso and the Cubists are now widely acclaimed and "safe." The Met doesn't take real risks, doesn't plunge into unknown hinterlands of art, doesn't discover, doesn't *dare*.

MOMA, by way of contrast, is trendy, with-it, and chic. Dating from 1929, it had several midtown homes before moving into its present location on West 53rd Street in 1939. A big hunk of steel and glass in the "International Style," it has always struck me as plain-fronted, massive, and cold, making the palatial Met look like a nest of warmth. But the interior is another matter. Visiting it often before the 2002–2004 renovations, I marveled at the permanent collection. Van Gogh's *Starry Night* always enchanted me, even if it had appeared on too many Christmas cards. Matisse's *Piano Lesson* was intriguing and complex, showing a boy sitting at a piano while a maternal figure sits stiffly at a distance, countered on the other side by an enticingly voluptuous nude. Also arresting were Picasso's *Boy Leading a Horse,* and any number of German Expressionists, a school I highly esteem and never can find enough of.

A victim of its own success, MOMA found that it needed more space to house its huge collection, pursue educational and research activities, and accommodate the ever-growing throngs of visitors. Which wasn't easy, since the museum is situated in the heart of midtown Manhattan, squeezed in by other buildings on all sides. So what did it do? Expand in the only direction possible: upward. In 1983, as part of its expansion it built the 52-story Museum Tower at 15 West 53rd Street, a soaring high-rise providing six floors of museum space and, above that, 248 condominium apartments with high ceilings, huge rooms, and floor-to-ceiling windows offering views to the north of Central Park and the city skyline and, for some apartments, the museum's sculpture garden. The Tower's amenities include doormen, a concierge, a fitness center with a sauna, a steam room and a meditation room, a business conference room, and housekeeping and laundry services, and more. What, indeed, does it not offer? But these attractions aren't for just anyone. A one-bedroom apartment currently starts at $1.4 million, and a two-bedroom at $2.7 million. So bigger is better for those who can afford it, and for the finances of the museum, which sold the tower's air rights to a private developer for $17 million. But who lives in the tower remains a mystery, since real estate agents promote the amenities offered but not who takes advantage of them.

For MOMA, the 1983 tower was just the beginning. In 1997 the Japanese architect Yoshio Taniguchi beat out ten other international architects to win the competition to redesign the museum once again. The museum was closed from May 21, 2002, until November 20, 2004, while Mr. Taniguchi worked his miracles, imposing a long fast on those tens of thousands, myself included, eager to feast on MOMA's splendors. Still, for a modest taste of those splendors, you could undertake a perilous journey into the wilds of Queens, where a few treasures were displayed in a former staple factory in Long Island City. So what wonders did the museum now offer, at a cost of $858 million? Yet more space for exhibitions and other activities. But more than that, Mr. Taniguchi promised to make the architecture disappear. Did he? I can hazard an opinion on the public spaces, since I have set foot there, an adventure denied me for the 1983 tower. And what have I found? Plunging perspectives that make me feel distinctly uneasy, even though I have no particular fear of heights. And glass walls that make it seem like there are no walls at all, which likewise makes me uneasy. Having survived these challenges, I'm always glad to enter exhibition rooms that have four solid walls, a ceiling, and a floor, with no such menacing perspectives. When it comes to Mr. Taniguchi's innovations, I confess to being a hopeless old fogey.

Museum wars don't just pit museums against each other; they also pit museums against critics and the public. So what did the critics say of the new MOMA? Roberta Smith of the *New York Times* decried a "big, bleak, irrevocably formal lobby atrium," hard-to-find escalators and elevators (true), and too-narrow glass-sided bridges (also true) in a "beautiful building that plainly doesn't work." Author John Updike in the *New Yorker* cited the "enchantment of a bank after hours, of a honeycomb emptied of honey and flooded with a soft glow." The prevailing criticism seemed to be coldness and a want of charm. Granted, New York critics have a talent for savaging, but in this case I agree. For the ever-expanding MOMA, bigger is not better. Better in terms of new space acquired, but at the cost of less intimacy, less warmth, less comfort and ease for visitors.

But MOMA's plans for the future didn't stop there. In 2007 the museum sold a lot on its west side at 53 West 53rd Street to Hines Development, an international real estate developer, for $125 million. Hines announced grandiose plans to build Tower Verre, an 88-story high-rise designed by French architect Jean Nouvel that would be almost as tall as the Empire State Building, with a faceted exterior with crisscrossing beams, its sleek form tapering to a set of crystalline peaks at the very top, where glass walls with tilting trusses will give a sense of being simultaneously both enclosed and exposed. "Tower Verre," or the Glass Tower: The very name has magic. A design that shocks some but excites many, myself included, which redeems me from the charge of old fogeyism. The Tower Verre is an exciting leap into the stratosphere. Bland it ain't.

The Department of City Planning insisted that the structure's height be cut by 200 feet on aesthetic grounds, but many welcomed the Tower Verre as an enterprise that would finally let New York compete with the startling initiatives of Dubai and Singapore and Beijing. The tower will house three floors of exhibition space for MOMA, a 5-star hotel, and—you guessed it—171 luxury apartments. But the economic crisis of 2008 hit architecture hard, and Hines's soaring residential tower was delayed indefinitely until, in October 2013, the needed $1.3 billion was reported to have been found, thanks to loans from a consortium of Asian banks and from billionaire investors in Singapore, with an assist from that local stalwart, Goldman Sachs. In September 2014 the investors bought the air rights from MOMA, and Tower Verre was renamed 53W53—as drab a name as I could imagine. Construction of what is now to be an 82-story building is well underway, much of it already clad in glass, and condos are being sold to the public.

So what do I think of the projected Glass Tower, not meant to be the tallest building in the world, but one that narrows, stabs, and needles upward to celestial heights? The English art critic Ruskin said of Gothic architecture, "It not only dared, but delighted in, the infringement of every servile principle." If New York is to rival the architectural daring of Asia, what better place for it to happen than at MOMA and its midtown neighbors? So can New York still dare and astonish? Does the dark eros of the city—the force that drives New York—still exist? Nouvel's surging tower suggests that it does. If foreigners have faith in the city, surely New Yorkers can, too.

Meanwhile the Met, likewise burdened with an embarrassment of cultural riches, has also been expanding, but its expansion won't disturb the skyline. In what some hail as a brilliant move, it has taken an eight-year lease on the Breuer (pronounced BROY-er) Building, the former site of the Whitney Museum of American Art, while the Met's modern and contemporary wing undergoes renovation. The Whitney, which owes its existence to the Met's rejection of Gertrude Vanderbilt Whitney's 1929 offer of 500 works of American art, has moved into a new home in the West Village's Meatpacking District, right smack next to the High Line. There its unsettling new structure—which to my eye looks like a pile of huge unaligned cartons—contributes to the gentrification of a displaced gay S&M bar scene featuring such now vanished cultural joys as the Mineshaft and the Toilet. Here at last it can display its riches uncluttered. In 2016 the new Met Breuer opened to the public, promising to offer the Met's growing collection of contemporary and modern art. A sort of upside-down ziggurat dating from 1966, the Breuer was the controversial work of architect Marcel Breuer, himself a product of the fiercely modernist Bauhaus. It looms at Madison Avenue and East 75th Street as a top-heavy hunk of dispiriting brown granite relieved only by a few—very few—rectangular windows and, on the side facing the avenue, two skinny bright red banners. Which is all right by me, if there are wonders within.

And what about the Guggenheim Museum, that other champion of modern art? What is it doing, as these other icons of modernity scramble and scheme and struggle for more space? Since the 1992 addition of a rectangular tower that overtops it, not much, except for a necessary renovation of the exterior. It just sits there at Fifth Avenue and East 89th Street, a coil of a building designed by Frank Lloyd Wright, whose mother must have been frightened by snails during pregnancy, given her genius son's obsession with spiral architectural shapes. I have been there many times, and learned to cope with its layout by taking an elevator to the top and then gently descending the spiral, admiring startling works of modernity along the way. Which, as I noted earlier, was precisely the approach that Wright himself intended.

But these are the biggies that everyone has heard of. New York has a plethora of museums, some of them known only to the few. Who has heard of the Museum of Contemporary African Diasporan Arts, or the Gallery Korea, or the Living Torah Museum, or the Ukrainian Museum, or the Toy Museum of New York, or the Museum of Mathematics, or the Museum of American Finance, or the Museum of Reclaimed Urban Space? One that does get attention is the Museum of Sex, denounced by some as a Museum of Smut; visitors flock. Popular or obscure, all these museums exist, and for a reason. Someone wanted them, and someone financed them. More power to them all.

There is little doubt that the New York City's museum wars, pitting museums against museums, and museums against critics and donors and the public, will continue indefinitely. New Yorkers think they own the arts, and when it comes to the Met and MOMA, not to mention a host of other museums in the city, they aren't too wrong. And about the arts they will always voice, and sometimes shriek, opinions.

Chapter 27

Statues and Statue Wars

T he hUge BronZe BULL, head lowered with flaring nostrils, pawing the ground and ready to charge, dwarfs the mere humans who come to stare at him. Onlookers snap photos, children crawl over him, and adults touch his nose, horns, and testicles for luck. A symbol of the city, even compared by some to the Statue of Liberty, he stands facing uptown at one end of a small park near Bowling Green.

Charging Bull is the work of sculptor Arturo Di Modica, who on December 15, 1989, planted it without permission in front of the New York Stock Exchange on Broad Street, a Christmas gift to the city. Just getting its three and a half tons there must have been a job, but he did it. Hundreds of people saw and admired it, before the police arrived to haul it away. Howls of protest immediately erupted, so the chastened authorities relocated the statue to nearby Bowling Green, where tourists from all over the world have flocked ever since to see this bold image of dynamism and virility, of massive and perhaps dangerous power. Mr. Di Modica says that it conveys his feelings following the 1987 stock market crash: a salute to a resurgent (i.e., bullish) stock market and nation. And if a visitor has his picture taken while he rubs the bull's testicles, it is said, the visitor will be lucky financially. One thing is certain: from all that rubbing, the testicles shine.

There the bull stood, in solitary glory, for twenty-eight years. Then, on March 7, 2017, the night before International Women's Day, another bronze statue was placed directly in front of the bull: *Fearless Girl,* a four-foot-tall girl, chin up, feet apart, hands on hips, standing defiantly as if confronting the bull. Once again, a surprise installation without a city permit, and once again an instant hit with the public, who flocked to see, admire, and photograph the girl, and celebrate her feminine, indeed feminist, challenge to the snorting maleness of the bull. Designed by artist Kristen Visbal, the work was commissioned by State Street Global Advisors and the advertising firm McCann as part of a marketing campaign for SSGA's index fund investing in companies with women in senior positions. A plaque below the statue reads, "Know the power of women in leadership. SHE makes a difference." (SHE is the fund's NASDAQ ticker symbol.) Yielding again to popular opinion, the city granted *Fearless Girl* a permit to stay on the site until the next International Women's Day in March 2018.

But this is New York, where nothing comes easy and controversies rage. At a news conference in midtown Manhattan on April 12, 2017, Mr. Di Modica denounced *Fearless Girl* as an insult to his bull, whose message, he insisted, was not male power and domination, but "freedom in the world, peace, strength, power, and love." Confronted by *Fearless Girl,* he said, the bull was transformed into "a negative force and a threat." While insisting that he was in no way hostile to gender equality, he wanted the girl moved elsewhere. He and his lawyers then sent letters to this effect to the mayor and to SSGA, McCann, and other relevant parties. But Mayor Bill de Blasio had already hailed *Fearless Girl* as a symbol of "standing up to fear, standing up to power, being able to find in yourself the strength to do what's right." And he saw the statue as especially relevant in the light of Donald Trump's election, and the women's rights marches that followed his inauguration. Which is a lot of relevance for a four-foot statue of a little girl facing down a massive bull about to charge. Meanwhile the whole brouhaha brought more gawking tourists to Bowling Green and its bronze antagonists.

Then, a month later, artist Alex Gardega installed *Pissing Pug,* a small statue of a urinating dog, next to *Fearless Girl,* in support of Mr. Di Modica. The girl, he insisted, was "corporate nonsense" and "advertising/promotion" masquerading as art. Feminists reacted furiously online, one of them calling the pug "disgusting," and Mr. Gardega a "misogynistic, pathetic bastard." After three hours the artist removed his pug, not wanting it to be removed by someone else.

Next, in October 2017, it was reported that State Street Corporation, the parent company of State Street Global Advisors, had paid $5 million to settle a lawsuit alleging that 300 women and 15 black employees were paid less than their white and male peers. SSGA's sponsoring of *Fearless Girl* was now suspect, and critics labeled the girl an opportunistic publicity stunt capitalizing on the success of the bull.

Fearless Girl continued to confront *Charging Bull* until April 2018, when Mayor de Blasio announced that she would be moved to a spot facing the New York Stock Exchange. For years, visitors had posed for photos with the bull, but *Fearless Girl* had attracted even larger crowds that spilled out into the street, creating a safety hazard and maybe even a tempting target for motorized terrorists. Being heavily restricted to traffic, the Stock Exchange location accommodates large pedestrian crowds but little traffic. And maybe the bull would go there too, though its creator still resents their juxtaposition.

Personally, I think that *Charging Bull* is a remarkable work, massive and epic, and that Mr. Di Modica's wishes should be respected, and *Fearless Girl* installed at another location. So why not the Stock Exchange, even though that was the site originally chosen by Mr. Di Modica for his bull? The whole brouhaha shows how New Yorkers love to argue, and how they argue artistic matters with the fervor that other parts of the country devote to sports. Wherever the two statues end up, separately or together, they will draw crowds and spark controversy, because that's how it is in New York.

But there are other statue wars as well. By 2018 it was all the rage in the nation, when not denouncing male sexual predators, to remove statues from public places, if they reminded us of an objectionable or embarrassing part of our past. Especially vulnerable in the South were statues of Robert E. Lee, Stonewall Jackson, Jefferson Davis, and Nathan Bedford Forrest, Confederate leaders in our Civil War. So Mayor de Blasio named a commission to review all possible "symbols of hate" in public places. Since New York has a dire shortage of statues celebrating the Confederacy, the commission had to go after other suspect sites and finally, after due deliberation, made its report. To the surprise and dismay of many, it targeted just four sites.

In Central Park at Fifth Avenue and 103rd Street stood a statue of Dr. J. Marion Sims (1813–1883), a South Carolina slave owner and physician who did pioneer work in gynecological surgery. So far, so good. But he did many experiments on female slaves, often without anesthesia. So the city, having decided not to destroy objectionable statues but to banish them, banished Dr. Sims to Green-Wood Cemetery in Brooklyn, whose president had offered him sanctuary, since the cemetery hosted his mortal remains. So out he went, to the cheers of onlookers. But the other suspect sites posed problems. In appraising statues or any work of art, it's useful to consider when they were created, by whom, and why. Down near Wall Street there is a plaque, not a statue, honoring Marshal Philippe Pétain, who following the French defeat in 1940 headed the collaborationist Vichy government, helping to send thousands of French Jews to German concentration camps and death. How could such a man merit even a lowly plaque? But the plaque dates from 1931 and is one of more than 200 honoring those celebrated in ticker-tape parades in the so-called Canyon of Heroes in Lower Manhattan. In 1931 Pétain was remembered as the heroic French leader in the 1916 battle of Verdun, when German troops commanded by the Crown Prince tried to crack the French defenses and failed. Such considerations must have swayed the mayor, for he decided that the plaque should remain, stripped of its Canyon of Heroes title.

But what about the statue of Christopher Columbus, perched loftily on a pedestal overlooking the traffic-clogged circle at 59th Street that bears his name? Admittedly, when New Yorkers, in vehicles or on foot, negotiate Columbus Circle and its swirling mass of traffic, they have no time or inclination to eye the distant statue or ponder the fact that the circle bears his name. Yet Columbus, in his first report to Ferdinand and Isabella of Spain, informed their Catholic Majesties that the inhabitants of the New World seemed docile and ripe for bondage. In light of what followed, he could justifiably be accused of the genocide of the native peoples of America.

A problem: Columbus has long been hailed as a hero by Italian Americans, who march in celebration on Columbus Day, just as Irish Americans march on St. Patrick's Day. And there are lots of Italian Americans in New York, and yes, they do vote in elections. Proud of his heritage, Governor Andrew Cuomo announced that as long as he was governor, the statue would stand "tall and proud in the City of New York." (Though both were Democrats, the governor and the mayor nursed for each other a keen antipathy.) So Columbus would not be banished—a decision bitterly resented by Native American groups. Columbus was also a hero, it can be argued, for it took plain old-fashioned guts to sail westward day after day into the unknown, hoping to sight land somewhere in the offing. He risked his life and that of his crew in so doing, but it did in the end pay off, though not for the native peoples. History is messy.

Finally, there was the towering ten-foot bronze equestrian statue of Theodore Roosevelt, dating from 1939, that looms heroically in front of the Museum of Natural History. The rough-riding, game-hunting Roosevelt, the very essence of macho, sits astride a horse, flanked by two stalwart half-nude flunkeys on foot, one "African" and one "American Indian," carrying his rifles. Never has white dominance and WASP superiority been more flagrantly proclaimed. And if Roosevelt was a fervent trust-buster and the founder of our national park system, he was also an imperialist ("Speak softly but carry a big stick") and a racist who dismissed the non-white peoples of the world as inherently inferior to whites. So what to do?

In effect, nothing. Roosevelt too was a complicated figure, opined the commission, since he was both an environmentalist and a devotee of eugenics. "Cop-out!" cried some. Their criticism has some validity, but the hesitation to judge can also be defended. How are we to know if today's mood will be that of tomorrow? Roosevelt was once hailed as a rough-riding hero and progressive whose trust-busting was cheered, his imperialist views approved, and his racism either approved or at least tolerated. Tomorrow our readiness to condemn may look a bit hasty and one-sided; who is to say? So the statue remains.

The first statue war probably dates back to 1776 when, as soon as the Declaration of Independence was known in the city, a bunch of patriots, some of them sober, tore down an equestrian statue of King George III at Bowling (yes, that place again) Green. The lead statue was later melted down to make musket balls for use in the war, but the disfigured head was rescued by the British and sent back to England.

Not all the city's statues have caused controversy. The most famous one of all, Lady Liberty, is universally hailed and merits a chapter all her own. Two statues popular with visitors and residents alike are the two marble lions flanking the entrance to the New York Public Library on Fifth Avenue at 42nd Street. Christened Patience and Fortitude by Mayor LaGuardia, they have been decorated with holly wreaths in winter and with floral wreaths in spring. People have crowned them with top hats, graduation caps, and Mets and Yankees caps. Tourists have been photographed beside them, and the two lions have appeared in cartoons and children's books, and have been replicated in bookends. Throughout it all, and the blare of parades down the avenue, they have indeed shown patience and fortitude.

Less celebrated than the lions, but dynamically heroic, is the equestrian statue of Wladyslaw Jagiello, King of Poland and Grand Duke of Lithuania, commemorating his victory over the Teutonic Knights, a German military order, in 1410. Located at the east end of the Turtle Pond, where I first discovered it while birdwatching in the area, it shows the king holding two crossed swords over his head in celebration of victory. It was created by the Polish sculptor Stanislaw Ostrowski for the Polish pavilion in the 1939 New York World's Fair, a replica of a monument in Warsaw that would be melted down and converted into bullets by the Germans, after they invaded Poland in September 1939.

Caught here by the outbreak of war, the statue was presented by Polish authorities to the city of New York and installed at its present location in the park. In 1939 the Poles had good reason to celebrate a victory over Germans, even if they had to go back centuries to do it. Some might find the statue a bit overdone, but I find it dramatic and inspiring, and I'm not even Polish.

For Art Deco heroic, we have *Atlas* and *Prometheus* in Rockefeller Center. Again, let's consider not just when and by whom they were created, but also why. John D. Rockefeller, Jr., created the center named for him, and he and his wife wanted its artwork to express the intellectual and spiritual progress of the human race. Admittedly, an uplifting but rather vague idea. *Atlas*, the work of sculptor Lee Lawrie, was unveiled in 1937. A bronze muscleman with very stylized features, he bears on his shoulders a bunch of concentric hoops representing the vault of heaven. In Greek mythology Atlas instructed humans in astronomy, which is why the tilted axis of the sphere on his shoulders points to the North Star, as seen from New York City.

Placed at the Fifth Avenue end of Rockefeller Center, right from the start the huge seven-ton statue was controversial. Some Catholics thought it inappropriate to place a statue of a half-naked male right across the street from St. Patrick's Cathedral. And some critics thought that Atlas looked like the Italian dictator Benito Mussolini or, as one artist put it, like Mussolini thought he looked. And later it became associated with Ayn Rand's novel *Atlas Shrugged,* published in 1957 with the statue pictured on the cover, which made it a symbol of her controversial views. More recently, a blogger has called it creepy, because it's a huge pagan nude just across from a church, but I dismiss his objection, since he likens it to a "cereal killer" (I kid you not) moving in across from a police station.

Less controversial is *Prometheus*, a gilded eight-ton statue created in 1934 by Paul Manship. Placed in the lower plaza in the middle of Rockefeller Center, it shows an airborne Prometheus stealing fire from the Chariot of the Sun and bringing it down to humans. Upon first viewing it, one observer declared that Prometheus looked like he had just sprung from a bowl of soup. Another said he looks like he's doing a sidestroke, while others have described him as recumbent. I'm inclined to agree that he lacks energy, look a bit like he's trying to swim. But in December every year he becomes memorable, being complemented by a huge lighted Christmas tree above him, and below him, the gliding and whirling skaters on the sunken rink. Then, surely, he is worthy of the dynamic city of New York.

Chapter 28
Lady Liberty and How She Almost Didn't Happen

She Looms there in the harbor, holding her torch aloft. Visitors from home and abroad hurry to the side of the Staten Island ferry to snap photos of her, and some even go to Liberty Island to see her up close, though the view from a distance is better. It seems like she was always there, but she wasn't, and it wasn't easy getting her set up in the harbor to greet incoming vessels back before travel by air.

The idea for the statue was the inspiration of a French legal scholar and author, Edouard René de Laboulaye, who admired the American Constitution and wanted to commemorate the federal government's abolition of slavery. In 1865, when our Civil War ended, he established a committee to raise funds to assist the slaves in their transition to freedom, and hoped that France and America might collaborate in building a bronze colossus honoring this act of liberation. This was under the Second Empire, which collapsed in 1870 in the revolution that created the Third Republic. These developments encouraged Laboulaye and his friends to revive their somewhat neglected project, offering to design, build, and pay for the statue, if Americans would provide a suitable pedestal and location. In a time of monarchy, it would be a joint effort in the name of liberty by the two republics. The projected statue's official name was *Liberté Eclairant le Monde,* or "Liberty Enlightening the World."

When Laboulaye's associate, the French sculptor Frédéric Bartholdi, came to this country to promote the idea, he decided that the ideal location would be Bedloe's (now Liberty) Island, recently ceded by New York State to the federal government for military purposes. Installed there, it would greet every ship arriving in the harbor of this, the nation's busiest port. Both President Ulysses S. Grant and his successor, Rutherford B. Hayes, authorized the construction of a monument on the island.

A done deal? Not at all. Tired of sectional strife and overwhelmed by a severe depression brought on by the Panic of 1873, white Americans didn't want to be reminded of the issues that had so recently and so disastrously divided them. Worse still, the North was choosing to ignore the proliferation of Jim Crow laws in the South. Also, other states were reluctant to help finance a giant bronze female that would grace the harbor of distant, imperious New York, while New Yorkers felt too pinched by hard times to spare the needed funds for the massive granite base.

With this in mind, advocates now promoted the statue as a memorial of the hundredth anniversary of American independence, and the time-honored alliance of the French and American people. Never underestimate the energy of a bunch of American boosters eager to promote a project they fervently believe in. The fund-raising committee published articles in the press, arranged benefit performances of popular plays, and persuaded wealthy citizens to exhibit their art collections and charge admission, the proceeds going to the committee. Bartholdi sent over the statue's giant right hand and uplifted torch, so it could be displayed at the Centennial Exhibition in Philadelphia in 1876. This honor the Empire City grudgingly ceded to its perennial rival, the City of Brotherly Love, since that was where the Declaration of Independence had been written and approved. At the exhibition, competing with Alexander Graham Bell's telephone, the Remington Typographic Machine, Heinz Ketchup, Hires Root Beer, and other earth-shattering innovations, this fragment of Bartholdi's colossus towered above the mere mortals who were allowed, for fifty cents each (proceeds going to the committee), to ascend a ladder to the observation platform just under the torch.

Even so, the campaign to raise the needed funds was still dragging on, when Laboulaye died in 1883. In December of that year the statue's promoters held an auction for which they solicited artwork and literary manuscripts that would be assembled in a portfolio with a letter from President Chester A. Arthur and other items. Among those asked to submit a poem was thirty-four-year-old Emma Lazarus, a writer who, though from a wealthy Jewish family, had done volunteer work to help the Jewish immigrants now flocking to the U.S. from eastern Europe. The result was a sonnet entitled "The New Colossus," the closing lines of which would in time become famous:

Not like the brazen giant of Greek fame,
With conquering limbs astride from land to land;
Here at our sea-washed, sunset gates shall stand
A mighty woman with a torch, whose flame
Is the imprisoned lightning, and her name
Mother of Exiles. From her beacon-hand
Glows world-wide welcome; her mild eyes command
The air-bridged harbor that twin cities frame.
"Keep, ancient lands, your storied pomp!" cries she
With silent lips. "Give me your tired, your poor,
Your huddled masses yearning to breathe free,

The wretched refuse of your teeming shore.
Send these, the homeless, tempest-tost to me,
I lift my lamp beside the golden door!"

The auction brought in only half the hoped-for amount, and the poem was soon forgotten. Political partisanship caused further delays, with Republicans at both state and federal level allocating funds for the pedestal, only to be blocked by Democrats. Packed away in over 200 crates in a European warehouse, the statue gathered dust. The French people, having paid to have it cast, grew bitter, and Boston and Philadelphia, New York's perennial rivals, promised to build a pedestal at once, should the statue come to them. New York's finest hour it was not.

The last-minute savior of the project proved to be Joseph Pulitzer, the Hungarian-born publisher of one of New York City's yellow-press dailies, the *New York World.* Nothing pleased him more—or boosted circulation more—than a crusade in print against monopolies, corruption, and the misdeeds of the rich. Seeing the statue as a gift from the common people of France to the common people of America, he announced that what high-society fundraisers had failed to do in a decade, he and the read-ers of the *World* would accomplish in a matter of months. "The *World* is the people's paper," he declared, "and it now appeals to the people to come forward and raise this money."

Pulitzer's journalistic instincts were sound. Money poured in—pennies, dimes, and quarters—and circulation soared. Organizers ordered work on the pedestal to resume, and when the crates with the statue arrived in New York harbor on June 17, 1885, the yet-to-be-assembled statue was greeted with the great-est excitement. On August 11 Pulitzer announced that the donations totaled an astonishing $100,000. It took four months to assemble the 300 pieces of the statue, which was reinforced by an interior support structure of iron designed by Gustave

Eiffel, who would later design the Eiffel Tower. When the Lady was dedicated by President Grover Cleveland and unveiled by Bartholdi on October 28, 1886, none of the speeches by dignitaries mentioned immigrants. But from then on, incoming vessels crammed with immigrants fleeing inequality and oppression in Europe began viewing the Lady as a symbol of the liberty they hoped to enjoy in America.

Viewing the statue from a distance, as most of us do, we may miss some significant details. The pedestal, a truncated pyramid, has classical touches, including Doric portals. But it's the statue *on* the pedestal that catches the eye. The right hand holds aloft a torch that lights the world, while the left hand clasps a tablet inscribed in Roman numerals with the date July 4, 1776. Covered with a thin coat of copper, the Lady has turned light green from exposure to the elements. Troubled by this, Congress in 1906 voted to have her repainted, but the public protested, having come to love her blue-green look, and that look persists to this day.

Invisible unless seen close up, at the statue's feet lies a broken chain half hidden by her robe—a discreet allusion to emancipation. And those seven spikes radiating from her head? Rays from her crown, representing the sun, the seven seas, and the seven continents. Modeled on the Roman goddess Libertas, the Lady radiates classical gravity and dignity, and not the fury and violence of the French Revolution, as shown in Delacroix's painting *Liberty Leading the People,* dating from 1830, another year of revolution. Delacroix's bare-breasted Liberty leads an armed mob over the bodies of the fallen—just the kind of violence that prompted Tennyson, a good English conservative, to deplore "the red fool-fury of the Seine." Bartholdi and his friends believed in freedom and democracy, but not in revolution and violence.

To be seen from a distance, Lady Liberty had to be big, and big she is, with a 35-foot waistline, and her face more than 6 feet high. Her index finger is 8 feet long, her nose 4 feet 6 inches, her mouth 3 feet wide. Her sandal is 25 feet long, meaning a woman's shoe size of 879. So it's better to see her from a distance. It's not easy admiring a lady with a three-foot mouth. There was a time when, to have a marvelous view of the harbor, visitors could climb up into the statue's torch. But when German spies blew up a munitions depot on a Jersey City pier in 1916—a year before we entered World War I—the statue's arm and torch were damaged by flying debris, and the torch was closed to visitors forever. Only in 1984 was the arm satisfactorily repaired, using techniques not hitherto available. The torch was then replaced with a new one made of copper and covered with gold leaf. Today the torch is still closed to visitors, but they can visit the crown if they make a reservation in advance. The only problem: to go from the statue's feet to the crown means climbing 377 steps, and there's no restroom en route. Those with heart conditions, respiratory problems, claustrophobia, or acrophobia—not to mention a small bladder—are discouraged from attempting it.

Bartholdi's Lady has worn well, surviving the political partisanship that might have dethroned a more controversial figure. But her symbolic value has attracted protesters. In 1971 the Vietnam Veterans Against the War occupied her for three days to protest the Vietnam War. In 1977 Puerto Rican nationalists wanting independence for Puerto Rico draped her forehead with the Puerto Rican flag. And in 1980 a time-delayed bomb exploded in her base; no one was injured, but the FBI suspected Croatian nationalists wanting Croatia's independence from Yugoslavia.

The elements, too, have assailed her. In 2012 Hurricane Sandy flooded much of Liberty Island and knocked out all power, causing a nine-month closing for repairs. But today the Lady still stands proudly, a symbol of both the city and the nation and what, at their best, they stand for. The torch emits light not from a flame, but from light bulbs. One employee for thirty years had the task of keeping the statue's 800 light bulbs lit, which made him the keeper of the flame.

Sadly, Emma Lazarus did not live to see the triumph of the statue and recognition of her sonnet, for she died of cancer in 1887. Americans who were not recent immigrants were slow in seeing the statue as welcoming immigrants to the land of freedom. Only in 1903 did they place a bronze tablet inside the entrance to the statue's pedestal bearing her now-famous lines.

Lady Liberty might seem immune to controversy, but jealous little New Jersey, always resentful of the Empire State, has presumed to lay claim to Liberty Island and, by extension, to the Statue of Liberty. But those incoming hordes of immigrants didn't dream of New Jersey as their goal; did they even know it existed? No, they dreamed of New York City as the gateway to the land of liberty. And so, New Jersey, hands off our colossus! Send us your mosquitoes, if you must, but leave our Lady alone.

Chapter 29
Cemetery Wars:
Green-Wood vs. Woodlawn

Ashes to ashes, dust to dust,
If Green-Wood don't get you, Woodlawn must.

I n miD-nineteenth-CentUrY New York it was the dream of
every dowager, and the dream of not a few elegant gentlemen
as well, to be "buried by Brown from Grace." "Grace" was Grace
Church, the fashionable Episcopal church that still lifts its Gothic
spire skyward at Broadway and East 10th Street in Manhattan,
and "Brown" was Isaac H. Brown, the sexton of Grace Church,
and the city's definitive arbiter of taste. He and he alone decided
what the "in" thing was for funerals in a given year, what the
flower arrangements should be, how the casket (not coffin)
should be decorated, how the dear one should be laid out, and
whether or not the casket should include a plate-glass panel to
allow the deceased to be visible. His knowledge was vast, and
his decree, absolute—until the following year, when his dictate
might change drastically.

To the phrase "buried by Brown from Grace" one should add "in Green-Wood," for Green-Wood Cemetery in Brooklyn, founded in 1838, was the desired final resting place of the elite of Gotham. Embodying a new concept of the cemetery as a landscaped work of art, its spacious park contained tombs and mausoleums of granite or marble adorned with sculpted weeping willows, winged cherubs, pensive female figures, draped urns, and broken lutes. Gone were the simple gravestones of an earlier age, and the crowded graveyards of congested Manhattan, most of them displaced to the outer boroughs for reasons of health. Gone too were the plain pine coffins from a carpenter's shop, replaced by polished rosewood and mahogany caskets displayed on the sidewalks of Broadway in front of the elegant shops that offered them, caskets provoking astonished stares and wonderment from visitors from the nation's distant provinces. By mid-century, burials of citizens of the better sort had to be done in style. Let's see how a dowager of that time might have departed this earth.

Mourning is duly performed in a draped parlor steeped in romantic gloom, the mourners in the bleakest mourning, dabbing their eyes and sniffling, while visitors sign a guest book to record the dear one's dearest friends. Hovering in the near-distance is Isaac H. Brown himself, red-faced, ample, bald, in elegant black, and lucky they were to get him (at a price). His eye vigilantly surveys the furniture, the flowers, and the casket with silver-plated handles and a calla lily cross at the foot, and at the head, a bed of moss and evergreen with the word MOTHER in violets. When the mourners finish their viewing, at a nod from Brown the attendants close the casket's lid, with the dear one elegantly visible through the panel of glass, and cushioned comfortably in velvet and lace, a hint of a smile on her face, suggesting, after this world's tribulations, the deepest sleep and peace.

Six sturdy pallbearers in gray kid gloves bear the casket down the steep brownstone stoop to a black-plumed plate-glass hearse, with the dear departed visible to all and sundry, showing bystanders the status and elegance of the family. Following the hearse are a series of shiny black carriages (most of them rented), bearing the dear one's family in solemn procession through the streets to the waterfront. There, accompanied by only the closest, dearest kin, who are determined to see the dear departed through to the end, the hearse is put aboard a ferry and borne across the East River to Brooklyn.

On that alien shore the retinue disembark and proceed through unfamiliar wilds to Green-Wood, whose Gothic gates loom large, topped with spiky spires, and adorned with panels showing appropriate funereal scenes, the whole effect suggestive of a medieval cathedral. Beyond those gates is a pleasing vista of hillocks and ponds and fountains and planted trees, and scattered discreetly among them, noble monuments dedicated to other loved ones of like status and elegance. Awaiting the deceased is a mausoleum of the finest marble, bearing the family's engraved name. Here she can rest in peace with other dear departeds close about her, and all around her the soothing presence of Mother Nature, offering tranquility and ease after a lifetime of struggle and strife amid the urban turbulence of New York.

Less happy, perhaps, are the prospects for the feminine bereaved, who by the rigid dictates of society must cease to be seen in public for a matter of weeks, if not months. During that time they remain sequestered at their domiciles, garbed in black that will gradually yield to a dash or two of purple. As for the males, somber clothes and a band of black crepe on the topper suffice, and no confinement at home, since they must see to the humdrum daily needs of society.

By 1880 the funeral director was being invited, even urged, to take charge of the entire operation. Services were now held at a funeral home or church, with sermons eschewing the old fire-and-brimstone rants designed to scare mourners into virtue and compliance, replaced now by shorter spiels meant to console the bereaved and assuage their grief. As for the deceased, to get to heaven now, they had only to die—a condition that still holds today. Clearly, this transformation of the funeral and mourning reflected the transition of the final resting place from crowded urban graveyard to the vast and soothing expanses of the landscaped cemetery. The whole sad business of seeing off the dead had become, if not pleasant, at least less challenging, albeit at greater cost.

Ah yes, the cost. According to James D. McCabe's *New York by Gaslight,* published in 1880, a first-class New York funeral could cost $2,191, the biggest items being flowers, $100; rosewood coffin, $300; Green-Wood lot, $600; and granite monument, $900. The smallest item was gravedigger, $5, and I'm sure the poor fellow, who did the meanest physical work, deserved more. (In pondering these figures, bear in mind that an 1880 dollar would be worth $24.61 today.) McCabe's comment: "As only the rich can afford to live in New York society, so only the rich can afford to die in it." And die they did, with ceremony.

The preeminence of Green-Wood as a final resting place was unchallenged throughout the nineteen century, and visitors flocked to it as well to stroll about and picnic. By the 1860s it was one of the most popular tourist attractions in the country, second only to Niagara Falls. Its buried residents included such stellar names as editor Horace Greeley, jeweler Charles Lewis Tiffany, and assorted fat cats of the time. To which might be added another name of dubious repute. Once, when I was traipsing Green-Wood's vast domain while doing research for a biography, I was amazed to come across a plot bearing the name TWEED and, within it in a commanding position, the grave of the Boss himself. Though hounded from office by reformers and fated to die in prison, the ex-boss was still deemed by his family to be deserving of a distinguished last resort.

Managing funerals is a business, and successful businesses invite competition. By the early twentieth century a tidal wave of Gilded Age arrivistes were forsaking Green-Wood for its brazen rival, Woodlawn. Founded in the farther reaches of the Bronx in 1863, this Johnny-come-lately of cemeteries was almost as vast as its rival (400 acres vs. 478) and just as lovingly landscaped, but it had been number two for decades. In an 1866 guide to New York City that I have in facsimile, Green-Wood rates almost a full page, with mention of its fifteen miles of avenues, its views of the city and harbor, and its costly monuments; Woodlawn, just three years old at the time, isn't even briefly described. But right from the start Woodlawn was enticing notables of the day, and sprouting elegant mausoleums to house them.

Was Green-Wood worried? You bet! What followed, and continues to this day, is a sort of Harvard-Yale rivalry, or should one say Home Depot vs. Walmart? Green-Wood got Henry Ward Beecher, the nineteenth-century's most famous preacher (and sinner), while Woodlawn buried author Herman Melville. Woodlawn got publisher Joseph Pulitzer, but Green-Wood already had *New York Times* founder Henry James Raymond. Green-Wood buried stained-glass artist Louis Comfort Tiffany, but Woodlawn had snagged his father, Charles Lewis Tiffany, founder of Tiffany & Company. Woodlawn got ballroom dancer Irene Castle, who with her husband pioneered the fox-trot, but Green-Wood had the notorious actress Lola Montez, onetime mistress of King Ludwig I of Bavaria (Bavaria didn't want her). And if Green-Wood got both Nathaniel Currier & James Merritt Ives, Woodlawn had department store mogul J.C. Penney. In addition, interred in both are assorted Civil War generals and CEOs famous in their own time and lost to oblivion today.

"I've had to cede all the jazz musicians to Woodlawn," Green-Wood's president, Richard Moylan, lamented to a *New York Times* interviewer in 2015, having lost Duke Ellington, Miles Davis, and others. Himself a fan of classic rock, Mr. Moylan was cut to the quick when he lost a stellar musician to his rival. But Leonard Bernstein was buried in Green-Wood in 1990, and subsequently, with Brooklyn in the forefront culturally, Mr. Moylan had a wish list of prominent Brooklynites whom he hoped to snag. Not prominent in his list of secured notables is mobster Albert Anastasia, master of organized crime's Murder, Incorporated, who was cut down in a hail of bullets in the barbershop of the elegant Park Sheraton Hotel in 1957. To my knowledge, this Green-Wood guest has no match among the residents of Woodlawn.

The Green-Wood/Woodlawn rivalry parallels in many ways the rivalry of MOMA and the Met. Woodlawn today describes itself as more than a cemetery, and as a place of rest in a city famous for its restless energy. It boasts of being an outdoor museum visited by more than 10,000 visitors a year who tour the "breathtaking beauty" of its grounds. Its monuments, including over 1,300 mausoleums, were designed by legendary American architects, landscape designers, and sculptors. There are also concerts, book talks, nature walks, and an arboretum, as well as adult education programs, tours, and events, and even summer camps and field trips for children. Clearly, a formidable rival for Green-Wood.

Meanwhile Mr. Moylan hosts an annual benefit gala to raise money for the maintenance of Green-Wood's historic grounds. Cocktails are sipped genteelly in an area bordered by the entombed remains of the cremated, whose proximity seems not to dismay the patrician imbibers, old-school richies who view anything trendy with disgust. One gala brought in $80,000, which followed a gift of $1 million for the restoration of a greenhouse that will become a visitor center. So after a long decline in prestige, Green-Wood is becoming again a place of aspirational burial, the desired last resting place of the city's socially prominent, especially the newly arrived of Brooklyn's bohemian elite. Visitors still stroll there, and wreath-making classes are offered, as well as trolley tours, scavenger hunts, and whiskey tastings. (Yes, that's right, whiskey tastings. This is, remember, a city where anything goes.) Meanwhile, mourners have been known to bedeck gravestones with flowers, bracelets, pinwheels, teddy bears, Barbie dolls, and tiny bottles of liquor. So watch out, Woodlawn. Green-Wood has risen like the Phoenix from its ashes, and I don't mean those of the cremated. Its spiky Gothic gates are wide open; they beckon, they entice. And you can have a single-burial plot there for only $19,000.

Needless to say, Green-Wood and Woodlawn aren't the only cemeteries in New York City, where burial grounds range in size from a tiny snippet of an old Jewish cemetery on West 11th Street in Manhattan, to Calvary Cemetery in Queens, which with three million burials boasts the largest number of interments of any cemetery in the country. But Green-Wood and Woodlawn are special; they have *class.* Galas with cocktails, concerts, nature walks, whiskey tastings, an arboretum, hillocks, ponds, and fountains in beautiful landscapes with breathtaking views—in these two marvels one can almost forget the fact of death. Green-Wood and Woodlawn are inspired by a deeply ingrained American optimism, an addiction to sunshine and joy, a determination to avoid the darkness, the ugliness, the sheer inconvenience of death. And of course they make money doing it.

Chapter 30
Landmarks: Saving the Old from the New

Nineteenth-Century New York was too drunk on the idea of Progress (usually capitalized) to worry about preserving anything. It was Young America, it was Go Ahead, breaking free from the old and embracing wholeheartedly the new. Obsessed with Bigger, Better, Faster, it didn't need the ideas of the Marquis de Condorcet, the eighteenth-century *philosophe* whose buoyant optimism saw humanity as marching ever onward and upward. (Alas, the marquis was imprisoned by the Revolution and died there in 1794, either murdered or a suicide.)

In New York, no need of philosophy, for New Yorkers had proof of Progress right there before their eyes. Almost daily, as the city's growth exploded, they learned of or attended a cornerstone laying, a bridge opening, a ship launching, or the laying out of yet another street. These events were marked with ceremonies, speeches, cheers, drunken huzzahs, and sometimes even the booming of cannon. One amazing change after another transformed their lives: the steamboat, the railroad, indoor plumbing (no more chamber pots!), the telegraph, the elevator (so buildings could go to twelve, then fifteen stories high!), electricity, the telephone (at first, for the moneyed few), and by the end of the century, the automobile. New Yorkers were fiercely convinced that their city was the locomotive pulling the rest of the nation faster and faster into the dazzling vistas of tomorrow.

Spreading northward on the narrow, cigar-shaped island of Manhattan, the city was in constant flux, tearing down and building up. In the name of Progress old cemeteries were dug up and their bones scattered, so the property could be developed, and pious congregations joined the general migration northward, their abandoned churches becoming warehouses, stables, markets, tenements, and even, alas, houses of prostitution. And when the Great Fire of 1835 destroyed the whole Wall Street area, including the Merchants' Exchange, an elegant marble-faced building topped by a soaring rotunda, the fever to rebuild was such that work immediately began on lots still warm from the fire. On the site of the old Merchants' Exchange, where everything from steamboats to whale oil and molasses had been sold, a new exchange rose in Greek Revival style, even more massive and impressive. As for the loss in the fire of the last old Dutch houses in Manhattan, not a tear was shed for those hopelessly quaint, hopelessly old-fogey brick structures. The very notion of landmark preservation would have struck the citizens as needless, alien, and outlandish; it would have to wait a century or more.

The cult of Progress continued well into the twentieth century and took on a very American air with the appearance in the 1920s and 1930s of that distinctly American phenomenon, the skyscraper. The Chrysler Building and the Empire State Building were hailed as New World wonders, and Rockefeller Center, built in the very depths of the Depression, seemed dazzlingly grandiose and daring. The Art Deco style characterizing all three was a sharp break with the Beaux Arts style of Grand Central Station and the New York Public Library, adorned as they were with naked and half-naked gods whose relevance was not always evident. Creating marvels free of anything that smacked of the Old World, New York was still the locomotive chugging the rest of the nation into the world of tomorrow.

The World of Tomorrow, indeed, was the theme of the New York World's Fair of 1939, and industrial designer Norman Bel Geddes' popular Futurama exhibit presented a model of the world twenty years into the future, with sprawling suburbs, and lane-divided highways allowing a free flow of traffic and pedestrians. An 18-minute ride on a conveyor system gave spectators a simulated aerial view of the panorama.

The prime New York developer of the twentieth century was Robert Moses (1888–1981), who pursued public works—and pursued them ruthlessly—under six New York State governors and five New York City mayors. In the city he transformed Pelham Bay Park and Riverside Park, completed the Triborough Bridge, built the West Side Highway, and helped create Lincoln Center, the United Nations Headquarters, Co-op City, Stuyvesant Town and Peter Cooper Village, and the New York Coliseum. And that is only a partial list of his accomplishments. New York City has always dreamed big, and Moses dreamed bigger than anyone. But he wasn't just a dreamer, he built. And to build his grandiose projects he flattered, schemed, pressured, and lied, and so became, in the words of his biographer, "the world's biggest builder since the pharaohs of ancient Egypt." But to realize his dreams, he thought nothing of invading old neighborhoods, tearing them apart, destroying them, and displacing thousands of residents, all for the sake of the New.

In 1952 Moses announced a plan to have two streets flank the Washington Square Arch and run on south through Washington Square Park, obliterating the fountain. But he hadn't counted on a local resident and mom by the name of Jane Jacobs. Moses' assault on a beloved green space in Greenwich Village aroused the fierce opposition of local residents, who were well educated and savvy in the ways of protest, and Jane Jacobs was in the lead. She had plenty at stake, since she and her husband owned a three-story house at 555 Hudson Street, but a short walk from where I live. Long active in urban renewal, her efforts now and later earned her the scorn of the entrenched male power structure, who tried to dismiss her as a housewife, an amateur, and a "crazy dame." An anti-modernist, she believed in "micro-villages," urban neighborhoods where residents knew one another and helped and protected each other and the neighborhood. Moses and Jacobs met only once, and then just barely. It was at a hearing about the Washington Square Park project where officials were to speak first, and only after them, the public. Furious at the opposition his plan had encountered, Moses declared that nobody was against his project, nobody, except "a bunch of mothers!" And he stomped out before his opponents could speak.

In America it's risky putting down Motherhood, especially if it's a fighting mom like Jane Jacobs. A woman in her forties with outsized glasses and unkempt, straggly blonde bangs, no beauty and not the least bit chic, Jane Jacobs had a keen mind, supreme self-confidence, and a focused sense of purpose. She enlisted support from everyone, including local children and former First Lady Eleanor Roosevelt. People were encouraged to write letters, attend meetings, sign petitions. Carmine DeSapio, the Tammany leader and a local resident, supported her, as did the newly launched and very radical *Village Voice,* though not the mainstream *New York Times.* Public opinion is often a huge, heavy mass that sits there, immobile, until activists poke and pry and push. Jane Jacobs poked and pried and pushed, and the huge mass stirred, gained momentum, moved. A long and complicated legal fight followed with many ups and downs, but David finally triumphed over Goliath, or rather, Jane Jacobs over Pharaoh Moses. In 1958 the park was saved and all vehicles were banned from it forever. For Moses it was a rare defeat, and an indication that the era of grandiose urban projects was coming to an end.

In 1961 Jane Jacobs's book *The Death and Life of Great American Cities* was published, denouncing urban planning for destroying organic city neighborhoods and replacing them with sterile urban spaces. When Bennett Cerf of Random House, the publisher, sent a copy to Robert Moses, he returned the book with a note calling it intemperate, inaccurate, and libelous. "Sell this junk to someone else," he said. Which is about as much of an acknowledgment of Jane Jacobs as he ever deigned to give.

Yet even as Jacobs and her fellow Villagers fought off the attack by Moses, developers were demolishing old buildings in the Village and replacing them with big new apartment buildings with fancy lobbies and uniformed doormen, and names that reeked high culture: the Van Gogh on Horatio Street, and the Cézanne and the Rembrandt on Jane Street, the very street where I was living. Passing these unlovely but well-scrubbed behemoths as I often did, I wondered when a Puvis de Chavannes or a Whistler might appear, or perhaps a Bouguereau, though this last would be ill-advised, since Americans might pronounce it "Bugger." Only with the creation of the Greenwich Village Historic District in 1969 did these depredations stop, and even then the district's borders zigged and zagged capriciously, stopping just south of 14th Street on the north and short of the Hudson River on the west, while reaching only to Washington Square on the south and east. The heart of the Village was preserved, but not all of it.

What finally triggered a widespread movement to protect city landmarks was the demolition in 1963 of the old Penn Station, a 1910 Beaux Arts masterpiece built by the celebrated firm of McKim, Mead & White. The pink granite façade on Seventh Avenue between 31st and 33rd Streets featured a colonnade of Tuscan columns. The high-vaulted waiting room inside, patterned on the Baths of Caracalla in ancient Rome, was the largest enclosed space in the city and one of the largest in the world. Adjoining the waiting room was a concourse of glass and wrought iron, equally vast and imposing. Photographs of the exterior and interior give breathtaking views, and aerial photographs of the ensemble, which occupied two whole city blocks, are awesome.

Demolished? one asks in wonderment. A monument as magnificent as it was colossal—destroyed? There were protests at the time, but the Pennsylvania Railroad, faced with dwindling revenues and the expense of maintaining the existing structure, had sold the air rights to a developer who planned to build a new Madison Square Garden on the site. Of course there would be a new Penn Station, and air-conditioned. Much smaller in size, it was built below street level—the cramped mediocrity of a station that travelers, myself included, are stuck with today. Comparing the old and new stations, an architectural historian remarked, "One entered the station like a god; one scuttles in now like a rat." Expedience and cost effectiveness had triumphed over magnificence, and with a touch of irony as well. Stanford White, the famous architect whose firm had created the old Penn Station, had been shot to death in an earlier Madison Square Garden that he had also built. Now the construction of yet another Madison Square Garden, the fourth of that name, was the pretext for demolishing his masterpiece.

The full significance of the city's loss registered with me only when I saw a *New York Times* photograph showing some of the station's huge columns lying abandoned in a field in New Jersey, soon to be used in a Meadowlands landfill. One wanted to denounce the railroad management and the developer, but weren't we all to some extent guilty? Hurrying through those remarkable vaulted spaces, we were too preoccupied with catching our train to pause and absorb the splendor all around us.

If enough New Yorkers get together to yell and argue and sign petitions and raise genteel, or not so genteel, hell, things happen. A firestorm of protest led to the creation, in 1965, of the New York Landmarks Preservation Commission, an agency charged with protecting all buildings and districts deemed architecturally and historically significant. To be declared a landmark, a building must be at least thirty years old. A property owner can continue to use a landmarked building, but cannot demolish it or alter its exterior without the commission's approval. As a result, many an old building stands with its façade intact, though the interior has been gutted and renovated. One of the commission's greatest accomplishments was the preservation of Grand Central Terminal, when Penn Central tried to alter the structure and top it with an office tower. But the commission's decisions are often controversial—in feisty New York, how could they not be?—and they can be appealed.

Was the commission's founding enough? If you think so, you don't know New Yorkers. In 1973 a small group of architects, lawyers, planners, writers, and preservationists joined together to found the New York Landmarks Conservancy, which works to preserve and reuse the city's architecturally significant buildings. Financed mostly by donations from the public, the Conservancy works closely with owners and community groups in all five boroughs to safeguard landmarked buildings, and campaigns to get landmark status for buildings not yet designated as such.

For Village residents this still wasn't enough, so in 1970 another bunch of concerned citizens (of whom New York has an endless supply) founded the Greenwich Village Society for Historic Preservation (GVSHP) to protect the cultural and architectural heritage of the Village and adjoining neighborhoods. The Village had been declared a historic district in 1969, but many sites deserving preservation lay outside the district's boundaries. And just as Robert Moses was the *bête noire* of preservationists in the 1960s, so New York University, with its perennial plans for expansion, has become GVSHP's no. 1 opponent, with the Real Estate Board of New York a close no. 2.

And just as some concerned citizens felt the need of an organization focused exclusively on Greenwich Village, more of these good folk have joined together to maintain city parks: the Central Park Conservancy, the Brooklyn Bridge Park Conservancy, the Battery Conservancy, the Staten Island Greenbelt Conservancy, the Washington Square Park Conservancy, and many more. Rare indeed is the park or historical site in this city that doesn't have a clutch of residents organized in a nonprofit to care for it.

All these organizations win some battles and lose some, but grandiose projects like the ones that Robert Moses sponsored are probably a thing of the past. In the constant battle between the Old and the New, the Old appears to be finally holding its own.

With the Vietnam War raging and two of her three sons threatened by the draft, and tired of fighting the New York City authorities, Jane Jacobs left the U.S. in 1968 and settled her family in Toronto, where she became a Canadian citizen and remained for the rest of her life. Her accomplishments were significant, but she risks being idealized, even sanctified as the Saint Joan of the old neighborhoods and small-scale projects beloved of preservationists. Focused so intensely on the small—the urban neighborhoods that she loved—she lost sight of the Big. As a resident of the West Village I want it preserved, but I am dazzled by Lincoln Center at night, and by certain soaring high-rises that taper into glass pinnacles radiant with light. New York is a mix of Big and Small, and that's the way I want it.

Part 5

GLORIES AND HORRORS OF THE PAST: CHOLERA, THE BEATLES, AND THE MIRACLE OF LIGHT

Chapter 31

Light: The Conquering of Darkness

"Let there Be Light," said God in Genesis 1:3, "and there was light." In myths worldwide, light is associated with life and good, whereas darkness suggests death and evil. Lucifer, the Light Bearer, rebelled against God and was cast down into hell to become the Prince of Darkness. In many cosmic myths the forces of light and darkness are at war, nor is the victory of light guaranteed. Prehistoric humans huddled around their fire at night, or used fire as a barrier at the entrance to their cave. For them, darkness meant risk and danger and prowling wild beasts, whereas light brought at least relative security. And without light there could be no life, so they worshiped the sun, the source of life and light.

The story of lighting in the city of New York, like that of all cities, replicates these cosmic myths and beliefs, for it is the story of

287

light versus darkness, of pushing back the night. In our well-lit cities today we have little experience of the night sky, the starry infinitudes of space—an experience both humbling and inspiring. But back in the eighteenth century, darkness was a part of people's lives, something to wonder at, yet also something to be reckoned with, to be fought. And what means of illumination could they use, to fight back the darkness of night? Outside, torches; in their homes, the fire on the hearth, candles, and lamps. The torch, dating from prehistoric times, has been called the first portable lamp. The fabled lighthouse of Alexandria, one of Herodotus's Seven Wonders of the World, was simply a soaring tower with a torchlike fire at the top, visible for miles at sea. In this country and especially in this city, well into the nineteenth century torchlight parades served to honor visiting dignitaries like the Prince of Wales in 1860, and to rally supporters during political campaigns.

Inside homes, the wood fire on the hearth was a source of light and warmth, and in the kitchen, the means for cooking meals. Lamps too existed from prehistoric times: a small open or covered bowl containing some kind of inflammable liquid, and a porous wick that sucked up the liquid and could be lighted. In the 1700s the American colonists discovered that spermaceti, a semiliquid, waxy substance obtained from the head of the sperm whale, burned with a bright glow without any disagreeable odor. It was therefore used more and more in both lamps and candles, and in streetlamps as well, creating a profitable market that sent whalers out in great numbers to search the North Atlantic and later, in the nineteenth century, as the Atlantic sperm whale population declined, on voyages of several years into the far Pacific, as described in Melville's *Moby Dick*. Lacking the means to buy candles using sperm, ordinary people still used candles made of tallow, a mixture of refined animal fats. But tallow candles were smelly and smoky, dripped, and gave a feeble light, so from the eighteenth century on, Americans who could afford them bought candles using sperm oil.

But what about the interiors of large buildings? The theaters of ancient Greece and Rome relied on daylight; night performances were unheard of. During the Renaissance, theater moved into the great halls of the nobles, and then into theaters as such, which were lit from overhead by chandeliers with candles. This was not the ideal lighting, since they dripped hot grease on actors and audience alike, but the best that the times could do. So let's count our blessings today. In our theater seats we're quite safe from drippy candles, and risk only a crashing chandelier, if a Phantom of the Opera is lurking overhead.

So eighteenth-century New Yorkers fought the night with means of illumination that had been used for millennia: torches, hearth fires, lamps, and that more recent invention, the candle. All these involved flame and, when used inside, had serious drawbacks. They had to burn right side up, be supplied with air, be distanced from inflammable objects, and be protected from drafts. Such lighting affected the most ordinary tasks; people sat hunched over a book or their sewing at night, straining their eyes to read or sew.

Another problem: these fires were hard to start. What, no matches? Not until 1827, when the first friction matches, called lucifers (that name again!), were invented in England; soon afterward they appeared in New York. But before that, how did people light candles and lamps? From other candles and lamps, if available, otherwise from fire struck with flint and steel. And yes, there's the old joke about doing it by rubbing two Boy Scouts together, inspired by the Scouts' practice of rubbing two dry sticks together to produce the friction that creates a flame. But however it was done, it was work.

The nineteenth century brought changes that revolutionized lighting. Candlemaking by machine made mass production of candles possible, so that cheap candles became available to everyone. And with the introduction of paraffin wax in the mid-1850s, candles were made that burned cleanly without the smell of tallow candles. But by the second half of the century candles were on their way out, replaced by competing illuminants. First introduced in London in 1814, gaslight came soon afterward to New York, where the Common Council granted charters to competing companies to lay pipes in different sections of the city, replacing the whale oil lamps then in use. In 1824 a banker's residence on Cherry Street became the first house in the city to receive gaslight. (Bankers and their pals have a way of getting the latest improvements first.) In the 1820s and 1830s gaslight lit more and more of the streets, with lamplighters snuffing the lamps at dawn.

But gaslight was not for every community, as it had several requirements. First, a plentiful supply of coal, from which the gas was manufactured, and the means of transporting it. New York City's coal was mined in the mountains of Pennsylvania and shipped by barge via the Delaware and Hudson Canal to the Hudson River and then on to the city. Gas works were also needed: clusters of red-hot retorts where the coal was burned to create gas, and gas containers, big bulblike structures of iron where the gas was held, before being sent by underground pipes to the streetlamps, fancy hotels and stores, and well-appointed homes of the affluent. Gas works were ugly and smelly, and therefore confined to the Hudson and East River waterfronts, well out of sight—and smell—of the fashionable sections of the city.

Big money and a lot of effort were needed to put up all those smelly gas works, so gaslight was confined to the big cities; small towns and rural communities were stuck with candles and lamps. But gaslight transformed New York, providing lighting such as had never before been possible. Hotel lobbies glowed, and the front windows of Fifth Avenue brownstones blazed with light as arriving guests mounted the steep front stoops, while theaters offered Spanish dancers, waterfalls, and naughty cancans in a stellar glare. Pickpockets worked overtime in the evening, though second-story men lamented the illumination, so detrimental to their operations.

In 1859 oil was discovered in a farming district of northwestern Pennsylvania, ending abruptly that region's rural tranquility. Oil rigs began drilling intensively, and kerosene, a petroleum derivative, became readily available and cheap enough to be widely used in lamps. As an illuminant it quickly replaced whale oil, which could only be obtained in far distant seas. Characteristic of the kerosene lamp was a glass chimney that protected the flame and controlled the flow of air to it, and a knob that adjusted the size of the wick, and thus the size and brightness of the flame. Kerosene lamps didn't require the infrastructure of gaslight and so could be used anywhere. My first awareness of these lamps came in the shoddy Westerns, often Saturday afternoon serials, that afflicted my childhood. These were the "Meanwhile back at the ranch …" species, humdrum black-and-whites meant to entice their young victims back a week later for the next installment, which they rarely did. Viewing them, I always knew that at some point a fight would erupt in the ranch house, a kerosene lamp would be knocked over, curtains would catch fire, and the whole place go up in flames. I was rarely disappointed.

Later I encountered the lamps in real life. In the 1960s, when I first went to Monhegan Island off midcoast Maine, kerosene lamps were still in use there. I learned how to refill them and light them, and how to trim the wicks of these cumbersome contraptions. Schooled by those dreary old Westerns, I was careful to keep them away from curtains. Alas, even two placed side by side gave a light too dim for comfortable reading. Only with the creation of a local company some years later to supply electricity to the island—first for only a few hours, then for more, and finally all day and night—were the kerosene lamps supplanted, thus repeating the progress of mid-nineteenth-century New York. Progress may be long in coming, but come it does … finally.

By the late 1870s gaslight, so wondrous at first, and hailed as a clean source of light, had worn out its welcome in the city. Gas jets emitted headache-inducing fumes of ammonia, sulfur, and carbon dioxide, turned ceilings black, and defiled the parlor, that sanctuary of middle-class gentility, with soot. In the land of Go Ahead, in this progress-giddy age, surely something better could be devised.

It was. On December 20, 1880, all of Broadway between Union and Madison Square was suddenly bathed in light. New Yorkers were dazzled, amazed. Projecting the light were a series of twenty-foot-tall cast-iron posts, one per block, each with an arc light that cast a brilliant glow. Arc lights, powered by steam engines and electric generators, were cheaper to install than hundreds of lampposts, so they were soon spreading illumination along the avenues and over outdoor markets, factories, railroad stations, and wharves. But arc lights were too intense for use in homes, and they too gave off noxious fumes, and created power failures when assailed by storms. (Sound familiar?) Something still better was needed.

In 1878 Thomas Edison, a young inventor already known for numerous inventions that included the phonograph, informed the press that he was going to develop an incandescent lamp suitable for homes. Canny investors on both sides of the Atlantic perked up their ears, opened their wallets, and helped create the Edison Electric Light Company, over which Edison himself, savvy in the ways of Wall Street, retained significant control. Vast sums and great hopes were invested in this ingenious experimenter, who so far had produced only promises.

Supremely confident, he got to work in his research laboratory in Menlo Park, New Jersey.

Months passed, progress was made. Aldermen and councilmen were invited to Menlo Park for a gala demonstration of the new lights. Then, having established his power station on Pearl Street, Edison had armies of workmen dig trenches to lay subterranean wires in massive insulated power mains, and in the power station installed powerful generators. Finally, on September 4, 1882, it happened: With a flick of a switch, fifty square downtown blocks housing the city's key financial, commercial, and manufacturing establishments were suddenly illuminated. If gaslight had been a wonder, and arc lights magic, this was a miracle.

J.P. Morgan and the Vanderbilts (those bankers and their pals again!) immediately installed incandescent lights in their mansions, and within a year over five hundred wealthy homes were electrified. The stock exchange followed, then office buildings, machine shops, piano factories, sugar refineries, department stores, and theaters, and middle-class homes as well, though tallow candles were still used in tenements. People in New York, and then the world over, marveled: at the flick of a switch—light! No lamp to fill, no wick to trim, no fumes, no flickering, just bright, steady light.

Nightlife intensified, as hotels, restaurants, and shops, and brothels and gambling parlors too, became radiant with light, and customers flocked. By the mid-1890s people were beginning to call a stretch of Broadway blazing with illuminated signs "The Great White Way." The New York of today was coming into being, to be further enhanced in the 1920s and 1930s by the advent of neon lights, first developed commercially by the French engineer and inventor Georges Claude. It was thanks to neon signs that Times Square became the dazzling nighttime spectacle that it is. Today, if in our cities awareness of the night sky has all but vanished, no one seems to care, since there is so much to do at night down here. Yes, darkness has been vanquished. Light: We take it so for granted.

Chapter 32
Catastrophes: 1832 and 1888

W e aLL moan anD groan when a bad cold or the flu afflicts us, and complain when a winter snowstorm hits the city. But be glad you weren't in the city in the summer of 1832 or March of 1888. This chapter tells you why.

1832

June 15, 1832: A steamboat from Albany brings word that cholera has leaped the Atlantic to bring devastation to Quebec and Montreal. *Cholera:* The very word spreads fear. The mayor immediately proclaims a quarantine; no ship is to come closer to the city than 300 yards, and no land-based vehicle within a mile and a half. Then, on the night of June 26, an Irish immigrant named Fitzgerald becomes violently ill with cramps. He recovers, but two of his children likewise get cramps and die. The city fathers pressure the Board of Health to declare them victims of diarrhea, a common summer complaint, but many physicians know better. Word spreads that, in spite of the quarantine and the prayers of the pious, cholera has come to New York. Other residents begin experiencing a sudden attack of diarrhea and vomiting, followed by abdominal cramps and then acute shock and the collapse of the circulating system. Panic follows.

New York City was used to yellow fever epidemics in the summer months, but not this; it was sudden, it was messy, it was fatal. Still, not all New York was affected. The white middle-class neighborhoods suffered less, while the slums were stricken. Especially hard hit was the notorious Five Points slum just east of City Hall, where Irish immigrants and African Americans were packed together in filthy housing. Soon horse-drawn ambulances were rattling through the streets, hospitals were jammed, mortalities soared.

The city's Sanitary Committee, under the sanction of medical counsel, published a pamphlet that was widely circulated, urging citizens to be moderate in eating and drinking, to abstain from ardent spirits, to avoid raw vegetables and unripe fruit, and to avoid getting wet, most of which was irrelevant. The science of the day had no accurate knowledge of the disease, didn't connect cholera with contaminated water. There was no modern water supply system, no adequate sewage disposal. Even the finest homes lacked running water, got their water from wells or cisterns, or from carts that peddled "tea water" (water to use when making tea) from a spring deemed safe. Doctors didn't think the disease was contagious, and attributed it to "miasmas"—noxious vapors from decaying organic matter. Recommended remedies included laudanum and calomel, and camphor as an anesthetic; high doses often did more harm than good. Other treatments included poultices combining mustard, cayenne pepper, and hot vinegar, and opium suppositories and tobacco enemas.

By early July the white middle class was fleeing the city. Roads in all directions were jammed with crowded stages, livery coaches, private vehicles, mounted fugitives, and trudging pedestrians with packs on their backs. Normal steamboat service was almost nonexistent, for other communities refused to let steamboats with passengers from New York approach the landings. Travelers had to disembark far from their destination and trek long distances through fields with their luggage before even finding a road. Farms and country houses within thirty miles of the city were filled with lodgers.

Back in the city, business was suspended and Broadway was deserted. Even churches closed down, though doctors, undertakers, and coffin-makers had plenty to do. Carts loaded with coffins rumbled through the streets to the Dead House. Unburied bodies lay rotting in the gutters, and putrefying corpses were taken to the potters' field and dumped in shallow graves to provide a feast to rats.

Many poor people blocked efforts to remove their sick to the hospitals, regarding them as charnel houses, and assaulted doctors or city officials who insisted. And of those who were admitted, many died within a day, which only stoked the public's fear. When private hospitals began turning away patients, the city established emergency public hospitals in schools and other buildings. One on Rivington Street was overwhelmed, and sketches made of patients there are haunting, their eyes wild, their faces contorted in the throes of death. The sketches appeared in a pamphlet published a year later by Horatio Bartley, an apothecary, with notes identifying the patients by initials only and tersely describing their suffering and the futile treatments attempted:

> H.W. aged 56. Born in Barbados. Admitted 6th August, 6 o'clock P.M. Was attacked with purging and cramps in the night ... prostration of strength ... hands corrugated.... Ordered dry frictions, and afterward rubbed with a liniment.... Was put under medical treatment, until 6 P.M. and died after an illness of 4 hours.

Surprisingly, a few were deemed cured and sent to a convalescent hospital. But the ravaged features of the sketches are haunting, for they dramatize the victims and their suffering as printed words cannot; you are seeing the face of death.

Removing themselves from the reach of cholera didn't keep well-scrubbed middle-class citizens from evincing strong opinions about who got the disease, and why. John Pintard, a prominent citizen and founder of the New York Historical Society, remained in the city and wrote one of his daughters that the epidemic "is almost exclusively confined to the lower classes of intemperate dissolute & filthy people huddled together like swine in their polluted habitations." And in another letter he declared, "Those sickened must be cured or die off, & being chiefly of the very scum of the city, the quicker [their] dispatch the sooner the malady will cease." This opinion was common among the better off. Never was there a more blatant case of blame the victims. Contrasting with such attitudes was the devotion of the Catholic nuns and priests who stayed in the city to tend the victims, many of whom were Irish immigrants. The Sisters of Charity performed valiantly, and some of them died as a result. The Protestant majority took notice and grudgingly—for a while—acknowledged their heroism.

By August the number of victims was declining. On August 22 the Board of Health announced that the city could be visited safely. The streets began to come alive, stores reopened, the rattle of wagons was heard again, and private carriages were seen. Normal service by steamboats and stages resumed, and the city was linked again to the outside world. But out of 250,000 residents, 3,515 had died, the equivalent, for today's population of eight million, of over 100,000 victims. "The hand of God," said some.

Fearing a recurrence, middle-class residents continued to move north to Greenwich Village, where numerous Greek Revival houses dating from 1832 to 1836 reflect this exodus.

Even though the link between cholera and contaminated water was not yet understood, the epidemic impelled the city to create a modern water-supply system that brought water from the Croton River to the city by aqueduct. This was completed in 1842, prompting a great citywide celebration, and from then on the gush of running water and the splatter of showers brought joy to the houses of the well-to-do, who could afford to pay the water tax. But the habitations of the poor knew no such amenities, and their residents still depended on water from wells often contaminated with human and animal waste.

Cholera returned to the city in 1848, claiming over five thousand victims, many of them Irish immigrants, and again in 1866, though only 1,137 died. Slowly there developed a growing awareness that cholera was more a social problem than a moral one. But middle-class prejudice dies hard. The lawyer George Templeton Strong wrote in his diary entry of August 6, 1866, "The epidemic is God's judgment on the poor for neglecting His sanitary laws." Not that he had to worry; his family were safe off on vacation in Vermont.

Science in time solved the mystery of cholera. In 1854 a London physician, Dr. John Snow, established the connection between the disease and contaminated water, when he discovered that most of the cholera victims of that year drew water from the same public well, and that a baby's infected diapers had been dumped in a cesspool nearby. As for the discovery of the bacillus that caused cholera, it was at first attributed to the German physician Robert Koch in 1883. But we now know that the Italian physician Filippo Pacini had discovered and reported it in 1854, though his work was long ignored by the scientific community. Finally, in 1965, the scientific name of the organism was officially changed to *Vibrio cholera Pacini 1854*. Better late than never.

1888

And now for a change of season and catastrophe. New York has experienced severe snowstorms in recent years, but when people complain, history buffs smile knowingly and say, "This is nothing compared to '88." Meaning not 1988, but 1888.

It seemed to come out of nowhere. On March 10, 1888, the temperature hovered in the mid-50s, and the weather forecast was for cooler but generally fair weather. New Yorkers thought spring was imminent. But the next day Arctic air from Canada collided with warm air from the south, and temperatures plunged. In no time rain turned to snow, and by midnight winds were blowing at 85 miles per hour. Overnight the snow kept falling, blanketing the whole Northeast and Canada, until by the morning of Monday, March 12, the city was buried under forty inches of snow, with drifts reaching the second story of some buildings.

Waking to this spectacle, New Yorkers were astonished. Blizzards, they thought, were something that happened on the Great Plains and in the Far West, but now a "Dakota blizzard" was happening here. Householders who tried to leave the house often found the front door and even the ground-floor windows blocked by snow. They had to fetch a coal shovel from the basement and exit by a side door that didn't face the storm head on, so that, with stiffening fingers and wind-stung faces, they could dig a path to the street. But of those who then departed, many soon turned back.

The municipal government was shut down, the stock exchange closed. A few trucks were seen on the streets, but they were soon stalled in drifts.

Some valiant citizens managed to trudge out to take the elevated trains to work, only to find the tracks soon blocked with snowdrifts. Some 15,000 passengers were stranded on snowbound trains, prompting some enterprising fellow citizens to appear with ladders and offer to rescue them ... for a fee.

By evening the streets were littered with blown-down signs, and abandoned horsecars lying on their sides, their horses having been unhitched and led away to shelter. Jammed with stranded commuters, hotels installed cots in their lobbies. That night well-dressed gentlemen who couldn't get a hotel room were glad to apply at a station house, usually the refuge of tramps and street kids, where they settled for an ill-smelling cot. Being located aboveground, telegraph and telephone lines, water mains, and gas lines were frozen, and violent winds prevented repair crews from reaching them. The electric streetlights were out, and lighting the gas lamps was impossible, so at night the city was plunged in darkness. Hospitals were overwhelmed with cases of frozen hands and feet, fractured limbs, broken skulls. Firemen, their teams trapped in heavy drifts, watched helplessly as fires raged in the distance. Transportation was at a standstill; cut off from the rest of the world, the city was paralyzed.

Walking the streets was perilous. The roaring, whistling wind stung your face, snow blinded you, exhaustion threatened. Policemen rubbed the numbed ears of pedestrians with snow to keep their ears from freezing, but at times encountered white, frozen hands protruding from giant wind-whipped drifts. A rigid corpse was discovered in Central Park, and another, that of a prominent merchant, on Seventh Avenue. Two *Herald* reporters wading through drifts on Broadway found an unconscious policeman half buried in snow at 23rd Street and half-carried, half-dragged him to the *Herald* office, where he revived. Braving the wind and cold, Senator Roscoe Conkling, one of the most powerful Republicans of the time, tried to walk the three miles from his Wall Street law office to his home on 25th Street near Madison Square. He made it as far as Union Square, collapsed; contracting pneumonia, several weeks later he died.

Brooklyn, then a separate city, was also isolated. The howling wind made a walk across the Brooklyn Bridge dangerous; the police advised against it. But when a great ice floe was pushed into the East River and jammed there, the ice provided a bridge that let people walk from Brooklyn to New York. But not without risk, for hours later the tide changed and the ice began breaking up. Some of those attempting the crossing suddenly found themselves drifting downriver on cakes of ice and shouted and waved their hands wildly for help. All the vessels on the river gave the alarm by blowing their whistles, and crowds ran frantically along both riverfronts shouting and screaming. Fortunately, several steam tugs quickly pulled out into the river and effected a rescue.

By dawn of March 13 the snow stopped falling, but the temperature was still below zero and the wind roared on for another two days, whipping the snow into weird, fantastic shapes. Huge mounds of snow blocked the streets, and between them were narrow paths where people trudged, sometimes seeing nothing but mountains of white on either side, and the sky above. Those who went out in snowshoes walked over the tops of trees. Their tracks covered, horsecars couldn't operate, but sleighs with jingling bells appeared, and people hired them for $30 or $50 a day. Caps and thick woolen gloves were hawked on the streets, and newspapers were sold for exorbitant prices that people gladly paid, partly out of sympathy for the half-frozen newsboys.

The price of coal doubled, and with their wives housebound and delivery of milk, bread, and other items suspended, many husbands lugged homeward whatever groceries they could buy in stores whose supplies were fast dwindling. A grocer on 8th Street who raised the price of a pail of coal from ten cents to a dollar found the wheels of his wagon stolen and replaced with shabby ones and a message in chalk: "Fair exchange is no robbery." State legislators trapped in the city feared that legislation might be passed in Albany in their absence. Sounds of revelry issued from saloons, where men were downing whiskey to ward off the effects of the cold. Some of the imbibers then staggered out into the wilderness of snow, often as not collapsing in a drift and ending up with injuries in a hospital. And on the city's outskirts exhausted survivors staggered in with tales of whole trainloads of passengers imprisoned in the snow without food or means of escape, following which rescue parties in sleighs were dispatched to rescue them.

When the wind at last subsided, travel on the streets was feasible, and the city tried to return to normal, but normal was still far off. Coal and foodstuffs were in short supply, and rail transportation remained suspended. For days there was no garbage collection, so people dumped their garbage in the streets. Huge piles of snow lined every sidewalk.

Snowplows drawn by a dozen horses began clearing the streets, and gangs of workers shoveled snow onto carts that hauled it to the docks and dumped it in the river. The main thoroughfares were the first to be cleared, but in other neighborhoods the lingering snow turned black and stubbornly persisted, until melted by the warm sun of spring; the last pile of it is said to have disappeared only in July. In all, some two hundred New Yorkers had died in the storm. But here, too, something positive resulted: a renewed determination to move all elevated trains and power lines underground, so they would be less vulnerable.

Everyone who experienced the Great White Hurricane treasured the memory. Forty years later a club of aging veterans was formed that met annually on March 12 to share their experiences of the worst snowstorm to ever hit the city. Younger citizens scoffed, insisting that the old codgers' tales were exaggerated and grew more so every year, but the old codgers knew better. The storm they had survived was unique.

Chapter 33
Brownstones

When i First Came to New York, I knew nothing of the architectural styles found in the city. But over the years I learned to recognize them and tell them apart. For instance:

+ If it's a skinny row house with a steep roof sloping toward the street and sprouting two cutesy dormer windows, it's Federal style.

+ If it's a bank or church or public building trying to look like the Parthenon, or a row house with an entrance flanked by pilasters (flat columns that never made it into the round), it's Greek Revival.

+ If it's dirty chocolate in color, with a steep stoop and tall front windows, it's a brownstone.

+ If it's lopsided with many spires and turrets and pointed windows, or looks like a haunted house, it's Victorian Gothic.

✦ If it's monumental and very symmetrical and trying to look grandiose and noble, with naked or half-naked gods lolling around, it's Beaux Arts.

✦ If it's streamlined and big and sleek and geometrical and monolithic, and trying like hell to look "modern," it's Art Deco.

Of all these styles, the one that has probably affected the lives of ordinary New Yorkers the most, both today and in the past, is brownstones. When foreigners, and even Americans new to the East Coast, come to New York City, they hear the word "brownstones" and wonder what it refers to. You can't understand nineteenth-century New York without understanding them, and they are still with us today. So let's take a look at brownstones.

First, the material. What was it?

A soft sandstone quarried in northern New Jersey and Connecticut and shipped by barge to New York City to be used in the construction of row houses. It served chiefly to cover the houses' brick façades. Brownstone residences, like the Greek Revival houses before them, were basically built with bricks.

When were brownstones built?

In Manhattan, in the 1850s and 1860s, when the Italianate style was in vogue. By the 1880s brownstones were being built on the Upper West Side of Manhattan, where Queen Anne and Renaissance styles replaced the earlier and simpler Italianate. And throughout the rest of the century brownstones were being built in various neighborhoods of Brooklyn, their façades adorned with bay windows and balconies.

Why were they built?

The growing affluent middle class wanted residences in a substance more impressive in appearance than brick, and more durable than wood. Brownstone, being softer than brick, could be shaped and sculpted so as to provide decorative detail on the façades. People fell in love with brownstone, which took on a deep chocolate color with time. They thought it was elegant, distinctive, genteel, and "Romantic." (Romanticism and broody moodiness were "in.") The brownstone residence became a symbol of bourgeois comfort and status.

Italianate style

The popular Italianate-style brownstone, first developed in Great Britain, included these features:

+ A steep front stoop, thought to be stately and elegant, though it took energy to negotiate it. Ascending, one supposedly left the hurly-burly of street and sidewalk life behind and accessed something nobler and more genteel.

+ An impressive front doorway with double doors topped by a rounded arch and a projecting hood and flanked by pilasters, informing all who managed to get up the stoop—formal callers, ministers, doctors, lawyers, and such—that this was a residence of wealth and refinement.

+ A basement door under the stoop to accommodate deliverymen, tradesmen, servants, and other social inferiors.

+ Tall first-floor windows.

+ Handsome cast-iron railings for stoops and area fences.

+ A flat roof with a boldly protruding cornice (the horizontal projection at the top of the building), providing a sharp limit to the structure's monumental rise.

+ By the 1860s, a steeply sloping mansard roof installed above the cornice, a hot new architectural feature from Second Empire France, adding a fifth story with dormer windows.

+ A parlor floor with three parlors, each one with sliding doors opening into the next, the first two often serving as a single deep parlor and the last as a dining room, the food coming up from the kitchen below by that marvelous new invention, the dumbwaiter.

What amenities did they have?

+ Heat. A coal-burning furnace in the cellar, generating hot air that was conducted in pipes to the lower floors, and coal-burning fireplaces for the top floors where servants resided. Coal provided a steady heat far superior to what wood-burning fireplaces had once provided.

+ Lighting. Gaslight for the lower floors, kerosene lamps for the upper floors with the servants' rooms.

+ Running water. Since 1842, when the city began getting clean water by aqueduct from the Croton River, anyone who paid the water tax could have running water in their homes.

As regards the last, indoor plumbing provided plentiful water for cooking and dishwashing, for shower baths and tub baths whenever you liked, and for that miracle of modern miracles, the flush toilet, replacing primitive improvisations that I don't have the heart to describe.

What was a brownstone parlor like?

Volumes could be written ... and have been. The Victorian parlor was the shrine and sanctuary of the affluent middle class, its best stab at propriety, calm, and culture, its chance to put its best foot forward. Plush and velvet abounded, with Brussels carpets from wall to wall. Elegant little spindle chairs dared intruding males to risk their bulk upon them, and antimacassars pinned to the backs of overstuffed sofas and armchairs protected the sacred upholstery from masculine locks reeking of macassar oil. More ornamental now than essential, white marble fireplaces gave off a lustrous sheen, and over them the mantel featured a large bronze or marble clock backed by a gilt-framed mirror rising five or six feet, or even all the way to the ceiling.

From the walls ancestors in gilt frames stared dourly down, or perhaps, more benignly but grandly, the master and mistress of the house. Displayed prominently was that inevitable symbol of bourgeois refinement, the pianoforte, its gleaming ivory keys awaiting the deft fingerings, at family gatherings, of the young ladies of the household, nervously anxious to reveal their accomplishments. Cluttered on whatnots were assorted bibelots, framed locks of the dear departed, and stuffed birds under glass. A cool gloom prevailed, and by day shades or drapes were drawn, and shutters closed, lest sunlight smite the damask. Here, the mistress of the house presided. Children were to be seen but not heard, and males of all ages were on their best behavior, never quite at ease. Loud talk was discouraged, arguments banished, smoking forbidden; gentility reigned supreme.

And the other rooms?

The dining room, usually the back parlor on the parlor floor, matched the front parlor in elegance and refinement. On the second floor the front room was often a sitting room or library where the family could gather casually and relax, without the formality required by the parlor; it was the forerunner of today's living room. (The parlor has no equivalent today; it disappeared with the Victorian mores that created it.) The back room on the second floor was the parents' bedroom, featuring an imposing four-poster and having access to a bathroom that, in some instances, was regal in splendor. The third and fourth floors had bedrooms for the children. At the very top, often including a fifth floor under a mansard roof, there were bleak and skimpy rooms for the servants.

Who maintained a brownstone?

Not the master and mistress, no way. Yes, they paid bills, but the real work was done by the servants, sometimes black, more often Irish. Ordinary middle-class families had three, a cook, waiter, and maid, while the more affluent had six or seven. The servants cooked, washed, scrubbed, dusted, polished, stoked the furnace, and toted the trash out to the curb for collection. They lived in those skimpy rooms at the top, but if there was a coachman, he would be lodged separately, usually upstairs in the coach house, a small two-story structure on a nearby side street where coach and horses were lodged. (Ironically, coach houses today are sought after by tenants willing to pay a high rent.)

What became of brownstones?

In Manhattan, taste changed. What looked fashionably dark and "Romantic" in the 1850s came to look like cold chocolate, dingy and depressing. When the Vanderbilts and Astors and other moneyed clans built their mansions on the Upper Fifth Avenue from 1880 on, they preferred brighter limestone residences in the French chateau style. But brownstones continued to be built on the Upper West Side in Manhattan, and in many neighborhoods in Brooklyn, where they sprouted balconies and porches and bay windows alien to the formal and rather severe earlier Italianate style. By the end of the nineteenth century, however, people were complaining about soft brownstone crumbling and cracking and flaking, which further doomed brownstone construction. But the second half of the twentieth century saw a brownstone renovation movement take hold in older cities throughout the East, often with impressive results.

So that's what brownstones were all about. Today, subdivided into apartments, they have a distinct advantage. Those thick walls muffle the infant screams and riotous music and shrieking arguments of the folks next door.

Chapter 34
Along the Docks in the 1870s

This Chapter WiLL take Us on an imaginary tour of the North River (Hudson River) and East River docks on a summer day in the 1870s. Our waterfront today has been prettified with parks and bike paths and dog runs and tennis courts. Now we'll see what it looked like back then. We'll start on the North River at 34th Street and stroll south along West Street to the Battery.

34th Street, North River. Moored beside a pier we see the offal boat, a small sloop piled high with the smelly carcasses of horses, cows, pigs, dogs, and cats that died on the city's streets. Scattered on the pier are barrels, tubs, and hogsheads of blood and entrails from the slaughterhouses. The offal boat will take this smelly cargo upriver to a bone-boiling plant that will turn it into leather, manure, soap, and fat, and bone for soup and buttons. So 1870s New York was recycling already. But it's rather smelly here, so let's move along.

Below 34th Street brigs are unloading bushels of potatoes. Workers take loads of cabbages from canal boats and toss them into wagons. Everywhere, unloaded heaps of fruit. Hungry street kids snatch a peach or two and flee.

Soon, a mammoth grain elevator dwarfs every other building in sight. Its steam-driven belt with buckets scoops up loose grain from the hold of a canal boat and hoists it up into the grain elevator's cavernous interior. Stored there in bins, the grain will be delivered through spouts into the hold of an ocean-going steamer bound for England, Holland, and Germany. So grain from distant Ohio and Illinois finds its way to New York by barge via the Erie Canal and is hauled down the Hudson River by tugs to New York, where it is transshipped and sent to Europe to feed hungry populations no longer able to feed themselves. We marvel: New York is feeding the world.

Next, in the hold of a canal boat, men smirched with coal dust shovel coal into buckets that are raised mechanically to the dock. Brought from the mountains of Pennsylvania via the Delaware and Hudson Canal, the coal will be carted off and dumped in cellars, then fetched up in buckets and pails to burn in fireplaces, giving heat. Or shoveled into furnaces to heat the boilers that make steam to drive the pistons of steamboats and locomotives, becoming power and speed. This country is drunk on power and speed: the more of them, the better.

An iron works. From the outside we see flames leaping in a dark interior, and hear giant machines screech and groan and pound. Iron from western Pennsylvania is being shaped into shafts to reinforce the buildings going up along Broadway. Or made into boilers and propellers and sugar mills and lathes, or steel rails for railroads. Or melted and poured from vats into molds for marine engines with a white-hot hiss and glare.

A lumberyard with whining steam-powered saws. A monster of a cotton press, its giant jaws clamping on a bale of cotton, compressing it to one foot thick. It does seventy bales of Southern cotton an hour, cotton that will then be shipped to the mills of Manchester and Leeds and turned into muslins and calicoes that will be shipped back to New York and sent by rail to the rest of the nation. We need English mills to process our cotton? Alas, yes; this country has yet to fully industrialize.

Sugar refineries towering twelve stories high, refining raw sugar brought to the city by brig and schooner from the slave plantations of Cuba. Piles of brownstone and brick hauled in by sloop from the nearby counties, to be used in the elegant houses of the affluent. And distilleries producing tiger's milk, diddle, or the oil of joy (any number of names for it) to sate the lusty gullets of Americans. The tiger's milk and bricks are fine, but we're refining sugar from the slave plantations of Cuba. Does this make us complicit? An unpleasant thought; we dismiss it.

Near 20th Street, the "Hotel de Flaherty," a tin-roofed shed patched together with wood, stone, mud, and plaster, offering over-ripe apples, dusty candy, and smoked sausages at two cents each, while hogs grovel outside by the door. Untempted, we move on.

Ice wagons load ice from barges at a dock. Harvested the previous winter from the upper Hudson by men with handsaws who cut it into chunks 12 inches thick, the ice has been stored in sawdust-insulated huge dark riverside barns. Now, tugged down-river on hundreds of barges, it will be hooked into wagons and hustled off through the steaming summer streets, to be tonged into homes or slid down ramps into cellars of fancy restaurants and hotels. Even without refrigeration New Yorkers will have their frothy cold schooners of beer in beer gardens, their fine white wines at Delmonico's, the prince of restaurants, and the chilled lemonades and tinted sherbets that they sip and nibble genteelly in ice cream parlors on Broadway.

18th Street: the smelly retorts and gas holders of the Manhattan Gas Company. Here, coal is scooped into red-hot retorts and burned, and its vapors carried off to be stored in gas holders, giant bulb-shaped bellies of iron. From there the gas is conveyed through underground pipes to hotels and restaurants and the bibelot-crammed homes of the rich. It becomes light, glowing from globed chandeliers, or from polished glass boxes of streetlamps along Fifth Avenue and Broadway and other thoroughfares where lamplighters light the lamps at twilight and snuff them at dawn. Thanks to gaslight, pickpockets work in the evening and hotel lobbies glow.

Offshore, a towering floating derrick with cables and pulleys. Using only one horsepower and five men, it lifts a sunken boat laden with 300 tons of coal. Progress! A few years ago, such an operation would have been impossible. Progress!

You think you've experienced noise and bustle so far? Hardly. At 11th Street we leave the quieter docks—yes, *quieter*—dealing with grain, lumber, sugar, iron, and ice, and come to the docks of the shipping lines linking New York to Boston, New Orleans, San Francisco, Liverpool, Le Havre, Hamburg, Canton, Jakarta, and Bombay. Surging across West Street come arriving and departing travelers, porters carrying baggage, and clerks with letter bundles scurrying after captains toting mailbags. All of them fight past wagons blocking horsecars blocking stages. Shouts and curses of drivers, lumber spilling from a cart, mountains of barrels and bales, and a black-garbed minister distributing tracts and Bibles to whoever will take them, amid smells of fish, brine, tar, and molasses. We dodge the crowd, move on.

The oyster market: rows of anchored oyster boats where men pry open oyster shells with knives, and toss the oysters in pails of water. Wagons take on loads of baskets of oysters that will be consumed by New Yorkers everywhere, in fine and not-so-fine restaurants, in oyster cellars, and even at stands in the street. New Yorkers love, absolutely *love*, oysters.

Next we come to slips where Coney Island sand is stored, so housewives can scour their pans and kettles and keep them bright. Sand too for the floors of saloons, where untutored males of the lower classes, and even some tutored males of the upper classes, still have a habit of spitting. Attuned to gentility, we don't approve.

10th Street: winches rattle, tackles run, and foremen whistle and gesticulate and halloo, as a gang of workers in a hold strain to hoist a huge mahogany log out with tackle. Mahogany from the steaming jungles of Honduras will be used in the fine furnishings of the palace steamboats of the People's Line, where ordinary Americans can revel in luxuries reserved for the wealthy and titled in Europe. Ah, democracy! Here, the common man is king. (And the common woman? Hmm, we hadn't thought about that.)

Under the piers of these docks are dense forests of pilings that only the smallest skiff can negotiate, a hidden world shadowy even by daytime where harbor thieves hide stolen goods that they hope to sell to licensed junkmen in boats who ask no questions. From time to time policemen search under the piers and clean out the stashes of stolen goods, but more goods will be stashed, and the game goes on. Here, we count on the maritime police.

Below Canal Street: a garbage dump where a long line of carts on a high pier dump refuse onto a lighter moored below. Crawling over the huge mound of trash like a horde of maggots are men, women, and children scavenging bones, coal, rags, and old metal to sell to peddlers, and even scraps of food that they devour greedily. Smells of burnt wood, ashes, shit. We hurry on.

At the Albany boat landing fashionables leaving for Saratoga scramble aboard amid the hubbub of cart drivers, cabs, baggage men, vendors, and the roar of escaping steam from the boats. Everyone who is anyone is fleeing the heat of the city, leaving behind their budget-strapped neighbors who can only pull their front curtains shut and avoid being seen on the street. Air-conditioning? Never heard of it.

The Washington Market, between Vesey and Fulton Streets: a sprawling old structure topped by a belfry, where gray-smocked vendors hawk their wares. Dangling from hooks are carcasses of beef, deer, ducks, turkeys, rabbits, and even the huge shaggy bulk of a bear. Glistening heaps of silver-gray fish, huge yellow mountains of cheese, and baskets of peaches, plums, and pota-toes attended by ruddy-faced market women in broad-brimmed hats. While buyers from the best restaurants scrutinize the soft velvet plumage of a heap of fowl, barefoot boys and old women pick at garbage sweepings that even dogs reject.

An island of silence, a plenitude of calm: the Battery, offer-ing a fine view of the river and harbor, where smoke-belching steamboats mingle with three-masted sailing vessels and smaller schooners and sloops, and ferries plying to and from Brooklyn and Jersey and Staten Island, and even rowboats here and there. But did I say peace and quiet? An old woman tending a peanut and pineapple stand suddenly erupts at some visitors: "Get out wid ye, spittin' all over me pineapples! Do yees think I've got nothin' to do but be washin' me slices all day after yees?" We move on.

From here we'll continue our imagined walk up South Street along the East River and see what today's South Street Seaport, a historic district with renovated commercial buildings and sailing ships, can only give a hint of.

North of Market Street, bowsprits of anchored sailing ves-sels jut high in the air overhead, while stevedores hustle huge bales and barrels and crates onto wagons and off of them, and iron-wheeled drays clatter on cobblestones amid smells of whale oil and sawn wood and brine. Facing the docks are rows of old brick buildings housing sparmakers and riggers, and sailmak-ers' lofts over the offices of shipping lines, and ship chandleries with everything needed for a ship: barometers, sextants, cordage, paint, canvas, windlasses, bilge pumps, and even cutlasses, axes, and knives. A reminder that this is the biggest and busiest port in the nation, and probably in all North America.

Along South Street forges glow in ship smith shops where hammers clang on anvils, and saws whine in spar yards, as shipwrights shape long timbers into spars. A crowd of ragged boys watch, wide-eyed, as an aproned figurehead carver with a hammer and chisel hews out the shape of a bare-breasted sea nymph to adorn the bow of a ship.

Above Wall Street, a brig from the Guinea Coast of Africa, having survived the deaths of a mate and two crewmen from yellow fever, unloads palm oil to be used in soaps and as a lubricant, and ivory needed for billiard balls, fancy buttons, jewelry, and the keys of pianofortes, fingering which young ladies in hushed parlors demonstrate their genteel accomplishments to guests.

Pike Street: huge dry docks, side by side. Using a steam engine, four men jerk a ship up out of the water for repairs. In the next dock over, two hundred workers peg away at a steamer's bottom, scraping off barnacles, cleaning and repairing it.

Pier 54, at the foot of Grand Street: huge blocks of Italian marble are hoisted from the holds of vessels by creaking windlasses, to be taken by cart to the marble cutters, who will saw and hew them into smaller blocks and slabs that will become ornamental fronts of houses, baptismal fonts for churches, and monuments to the dear departed. This noisy, grimy city aspires to elegance.

Near 12th Street, a sudden hush. The coffin of a skipper dead of a fever at sea is being borne down the gangplank of a ship. Stevedores stand silent, hats off, until a hearse bears the coffin off. Then, just as suddenly, the noise and bustle resume.

More shipyards, iron foundries, and gas works lie ahead, but it's late in the day and we're tired, so here we'll end our tour.

Day's end: sunset on the East River docks. We linger a moment in the fading ruddy glow, as piers grow dim and anchored ships loom with darkened hulls and rigging, and water shines with the blackness of night. Straggling teams pass with the last loads of the day, then silence. Soon, watchmen will make their rounds, yawning. Suspicious shadows will skulk, while ragged street kids fall deep asleep on cotton bales, and harbor thieves in small boats glide noiselessly, on the lookout for unguarded spoils. There will be a brief repose for the docks until, in the wee morning hours, the first market wagons lurch and grate and creak.

Such were the docks circa 1870, when machines were taking on more and more tasks once performed by men and horses and mules. Today the waterfront has dog walkers, joggers, cyclists, and sunbathers, but no grain elevators, sugar refineries, iron works, or dry docks. What happened? First, competing ports offered services at lower cost. Next, railroads, trucks, and airlines took on traffic that once went by water. And from the 1950s on, containerization came in, requiring more space than the port of New York could offer, so that a lot of business went to the vast facilities of the port of Newark. After that, much of the waterfront fell into decay, until the current movement to restore it and use it for recreation. Once dirty and cluttered and busy, now it is clean and green. I walk there often, see not a trace of the busy, noisy port of the past. Clean and green are fine, but bustle is a sign of life.

Chapter 35
Legendary Hotels

Nineteenth-Century New York saw the construction of a series of luxurious hotels—the Astor House, the St. Nicholas, the Fifth Avenue, the Waldorf Astoria—each one larger and more luxurious than its predecessors. Democratic America was determined to make available to ordinary citizens (albeit for a price) luxuries supposedly enjoyed only by the wealthy and privileged few in Europe. The result was the palace hotel, soon followed by the palace steamboat and the palace railway car. But in fact it was the New World's palace hotels that inspired the well-traveled British impresario Richard D'Oyly Carte to build London's first luxury hotel, the Savoy, which opened in 1889, with Swiss-born César Ritz as general manager. Fired for committing larceny and fraud at the Savoy, Ritz went on to give his name to luxury hotels in Paris, London, and Madrid, and to ninety-one more in the Ritz-Carlton chain, as well as to the adjective "ritzy."

Such are the forerunners, both homegrown and international, of the New York hotels in this chapter, all of which are, or have been, legendary.

In their heyday they had an aura of distinction and prestige that made them known to New Yorkers and visitors alike, whether they ever stayed there or not. They were, in other words, ritzy.

The Plaza Hotel at 59th Street and Fifth Avenue, at the southeastern corner of Central Park and overlooking Grand Army Plaza, is a massive 20-story French Renaissance chateau-style edifice built in 1907 and a National Historic Landmark since 1986. Kings, presidents, ambassadors, celebrities, CEOs, and world travelers have stayed there over the years, not to mention the Duke and Duchess of Windsor, and the Beatles on their first trip to the U.S. in February 1964, this last so unsettling, given the pandemonium caused by fans outside, that the Plaza never hosted them again.

When I came to New York I often heard mention of "the Oak Room at the Plaza." Finally, prompted by my friend Kevin (who else?), I went with him to this storied restaurant and adjoining bar, which had been serving men-only lunches since the hotel's opening, until Betty Friedan and the National Organization for Women staged a protest there in 1969. The Oak Room was a grand, opulent, and elegant space frequented by the rich and famous, even though Kevin and I managed to get in. I vaguely recall it as having a rather warm and woody atmosphere, supremely stylish and tasteful, with a high ceiling and an ornate chandelier worthy of the Phantom of the Opera. So it's dismaying to learn that it was closed in 2011, because the brunch parties staged there had become noisy and rowdy, annoying the Plaza's long-term guests. The participants in these orgies were said to indulge in drugs and loud music and Lady Gaga, while spraying each other with champagne. Lady Gaga's flamboyant presence, wearing a wild blonde wig, fishnet tights, and a dress made of honey-colored hair, would be enough to demolish instantly the aura of taste and elegance of any once legendary hostelry. A sad comedown, perhaps, for a once elegant locale, and a reminder that in a city like New York things can change, and not always for the better.

The Plaza has had a series of owners, including (briefly) Donald Trump, and is now owned by Katara Hospitality, the hotel division of the state-owned Qatar Investment Authority of Qatar. But the fabled Oak Room is open only for private events. Though the Plaza today claims to strike a balance between a storied past and a limitless future, one wonders if its glory days aren't long since past. But there's hope: It claims to be the first hotel in the world to offer iPads for all guests, allowing them, with the touch of a screen, to order in-room meals, communicate with the Concierge, request wake-up calls, and check airline schedules and print boarding passes.

Only one other New York hotel enjoys the status of National Historic Landmark: the Waldorf Astoria. I first heard of it, albeit indirectly, in my childhood, when my mother served her version of the Waldorf salad, the creation of the old Waldorf's maître d' in 1896. This hardly prepared me for today's looming 47-story Waldorf, the second of that name, occupying the entire block between Lexington and Park Avenues and between 49th and 50th Streets, a massive limestone structure in "restrained Art Deco style" that opened in 1931. With twin towers topped by bronze-clad cupolas rising above the twenty floors of the main building, its great mass has a majesty all its own; it overwhelms. The 1,413 guest rooms include 181 in the Waldorf Towers, a hotel within a hotel occupying floors 27 through 42, and of those 181 there are 121 luxury suites often named for eminent guests who once resided there, as for example the Presidential Suite and the Elizabeth Taylor Suite. Those guests have included ex-president Herbert Hoover, who lived there for over thirty years, Cole Porter, Douglas MacArthur, Prince Rainier and Princess Grace of Monaco, society hostess and party-giver Elsa Maxwell (who got a rent-free suite, in hopes she would lure the affluent), and Bugsy Siegel and Lucky Luciano.

Bugsy Siegel and Lucky Luciano, two notorious mobsters, at the Waldorf? Treading the same corridors as an ex-president and the Duke and Duchess of Windsor? Is this conceivable? Yes, it is. Thanks to prohibition and America's craving for liquor, Bugsy Siegel by 1927, at the tender age of twenty-one, was awash in cash and, to flaunt it, bought an apartment at the Waldorf. We'd like to assume that management didn't know who they were dealing with, and of course his money was good. The same goes for Charles "Lucky" Luciano, who in the early 1930s lived in room 39D in the Waldorf Towers under the name Charles Ross, and looked very much the affluent businessman, wearing custom-made suits and riding about in a chauffeur-driven limousine. He held meetings of the mob in his suite and was even photographed there with some of his cohorts. When the feds came for him in 1936, a desk clerk tipped him off and Luciano decamped for Hot Springs, Arkansas, a favorite mobster resort at the time. There his luck ran out when another agent recognized him and had him apprehended. When Luciano was tried for operating a massive prostitution ring, the testimony of Waldorf employees was devastating to his defense and helped bring about his conviction.

Another eminent guest was General Douglas MacArthur who, returning to this country in 1951, was lodged with his second wife and their only child in a suite in the Waldorf Towers. So it was from this exclusive address that young Arthur MacArthur issued daily to attend classes at Columbia College, where he was in the second-year French class that I was teaching in 1957.

A sensitive nineteen-year-old, he had an excellent accent in French that must have been acquired through private tutoring. Young Arthur had the distinction of being the only resident of the exclusive Waldorf Towers that I ever met. His parents resided at the Waldorf from 1952 until 1964, the year of the General's death, and his mother continued there until her own demise.

Lavish dinners, business conferences, and fund-raising galas have been held at the Waldorf. Prominent among them was the annual April in Paris Ball (later moved to October), which, in the words of an organizer, catered to "very, very high-class people" and raffled off prizes like a chinchilla coat, a Ford Thunderbird car, twenty-five cases of expensive French wines, a pedigree poodle, and other goodies, with earnings going to French and American charities. Unique among hotels, it also became involved in world affairs, hosting international conferences and secret meetings of statesmen and other figures of prominence, and receiving controversial foreign leaders requiring the highest level of security.

An international event of somewhat less significance was the stay there of the British rock band The Who in 1968, when a dispute with the hotel staff led to their being denied access to their room. What prompted the Waldorf to receive a band known for rowdy behavior and trashing hotel rooms is unclear, but the band's response was forthright and immediate. They blew the locked door off its hinges with a cherry bomb and retrieved their luggage. As a result they were banned from the hotel for life—a ban later revoked when The Who were inducted into the Rock and Roll Hall of Fame in a ceremony held at the Waldorf in 1990.

Though not a "very high-class people," back in my freelance editing days I used to obtrude my plebeian presence on this storied edifice. Coming back from a publisher on Third Avenue, I would enter the Waldorf on Lexington Avenue and walk the length of the arcade, lined with pricey boutiques, to reach the elegant Park Avenue lobby. There I would usually linger for a few moments, enjoying the music from the plucked strings of a harp on a mezzanine above. Most of the people traversing the lobby seemed totally unaware of the music and hurried on, but I and a few others savored it, grateful for the surprising presence of the woman harpist who sent these gentle sounds wafting down to us below. A harpist lodged above a hotel lobby: Once again, the Waldorf was unique.

And who owns the Waldorf today? From 1972 on, Conrad Hilton, but as of October 2014, the Anbang Insurance Group of China, who acquired it for $1.95 billion, then the highest price ever paid for a hotel. Anbang closed the hotel in 2017 for conversion of 350 of its apartments to condos, the first of them to go on sale in 2019. The hotel is to reopen when renovations are completed. But the Chinese government took Anbang over in 2017, to investigate charges of fraud. Under pressure to raise cash, Anbang has started selling other U.S. properties, rendering the Waldorf's future uncertain. Ah, how the mighty have fallen!

Legendary in another way is the smaller Algonquin Hotel at 59 West 44th Street, between Fifth and Sixth Avenues. Built in 1902 with a red brick and limestone façade and named for the native peoples who once lived in this area, it has a mere 181 rooms, small indeed compared to the Plaza and the Waldorf. But Frank Case, its longtime manager and owner, was fascinated by actors and writers and therefore welcomed them to his hotel and extended them credit. Among the habitués he snagged over the years were Douglas Fairbanks, Sr., John Barrymore, Sinclair Lewis, and William Faulkner, but he was a bit ahead of his time in welcoming women as well, including Gertrude Stein, Helen Hayes, and later Simone de Beauvoir. But what made the Algonquin famous was the Algonquin Round Table.

Initiated in 1919, the Round Table was a select group of journalists, authors, critics, and actors who met daily for lunch in the main dining room, where they had their own table and waiter and exchanged opinions, witticisms, and gossip. Prominent among them were humorist Robert Benchley, playwright and director George S. Kaufman, writer and critic Dorothy Parker, *New Yorker* editor Harold Ross, playwright Robert E. Sherwood, and critic Alexander Woollcott. Others who were in the group at times included actress Tallulah Bankhead, novelist Edna Ferber, and comedian Harpo Marx, always mute in his films but who in this select company presumably permitted himself to speak.

Besides exchanging chitchat, the Round Table members acquired a reputation as wits when their quips and doings were reported widely in the press. But those quips could be mordant, and not for nothing had they named themselves "the Vicious Circle." Critic H. L. Mencken, admired by them but emphatically not a part of the group, asserted that "their ideals were those of a vaudeville actor, one who is extremely 'in the know' and trashy." And Groucho Marx observed, "The price of admission is a serpent's tongue and a half-concealed stiletto." More proficient in wisecracks than in meaningful insights, they promoted themselves shamelessly, but for the most part were not consistently and profoundly creative.

The Round Table flourished through the 1920s but then flaked away, it isn't quite clear why. Novelist Edna Ferber knew the game was up when she arrived for lunch one day and found the group's table occupied by a family from Kansas. But the group survived in the collective memory and ultimately helped win the Algonquin New York City Historic Landmark status in 1987.

It is hard to recreate the atmosphere of the Round Table, but here are a few quotes:

+ Alexander Woollcott: "All the things I like to do are either immoral, illegal, or fattening."

+ Robert Benchley: "Behind every argument is someone's ignorance."

+ George S. Kaufman: "Epitaph for a dead waiter—God finally caught his eye."

+ Dorothy Parker: "If you want to know what God thinks of money, just look at the people he gave it to."

+ Dorothy Parker again: "I don't care what is written about me so long as it isn't true."

Today the Algonquin promotes itself as a luxury hotel near the Theater District and just a block from the lights of Times Square, a boutique hotel rich in history and hospitality, with 37-inch TVs, backlit mirrors, and an iPod docking station in all the rooms.

A unique hotel—unique for many reasons—is the New York Palace Hotel (that word again: palace!), formerly the Helmsley Palace Hotel, at 455 Madison Avenue, in the very heart of midtown. It incorporates two very different structures that are linked by a two-story marble lobby: the landmark Italian Renaissance-style Villard Mansion, built by railroad magnate Henry Villard in 1884, and right smack against it, a 55-story tower built by real estate magnate Henry Helmsley in the 1970s. The resulting mishmash—or ingenious blend, if you prefer—opened as a luxury hotel in 1981.

When you talk about the Waldorf Astoria, you end up discussing celebrities and leaders of international renown. When you talk about the Algonquin, you end up discussing wit and witty people. And when you talk about the Helmsley Palace Hotel, you end up discussing Helmsley's wife Leona, who managed the hotel from 1981 to 1992. I remember ads for the hotel showing Leona as the queen, radiant and imperious, inspecting her staff, who stood rigidly at attention. Her hot anger and readiness to humiliate her employees earned her the title Queen of Mean, but her reign was interrupted in 1989, when the federal government convicted her of conspiracy, mail fraud, and tax evasion. What doomed her was testimony by her former housekeeper, who quoted her as saying, "Only the little people pay taxes." She served in prison from 1992 to 1994, when she was released with 750 hours of community service to perform, some of which she assigned to her servants, thus earning her another 150 hours of service. When Leona died in 2007, she left $12 million to her beloved Maltese dog Trouble, who thus became the richest dog in the world. The hotel, now rechristened the New York Palace Hotel, still flourishes, with rooms starting at $525 a night, and suites at $1,100. I'm sure they're comfortable.

More flashy-modern than legendary is the Marriott Marquis Hotel at Broadway and 45th Street, where it soars above the hurly-burly of Times Square. It was born in controversy, for five historic theaters were demolished to make room for it—a demolition dubbed "the Great Theater Massacre of 1982." Yet it has also been hailed as the first major project in the revitalization of Times Square, which, contaminated by nearby 42nd Street, was then undeniably seedy, with an abundance of go-go bars and "adult" theaters. If the Marriott, opening in 1985, turned its back on Times Square, focusing attention inward on its soaring atrium, it's because it wanted no part of that seediness.

Two features especially distinguish this state-of-the-art structure, and I have experienced both. The glass-enclosed "scenic elevators" crawl up the sides of a central column in the building's atrium like big bugs, giving views of its soaring inner space. Visitors are said to flock from miles away and stand in line to access them, but when I rode in one years ago there was no wait at all. But even though I have no abnormal fear of heights, I was distinctly uncomfortable, having the feeling that this creeping creature with glass walls had no support under it and could easily plunge. When I got off and felt a solid floor beneath me, I was vastly relieved. On the other hand, the famous revolving bar and restaurant on the 48th floor is a unique and wondrous rooftop experience, slowly making a complete turn each hour while giving breathtaking views of the city. I was once there with visiting relatives at night, and the views of the lights of Times Square were unforgettable.

A less publicized fact about the Marriott Marquis is its popularity for suicides. Those planning it probably think they will plummet gracefully and land with a dramatic thump in the lobby. Not so. One jumper leaped from the 43rd floor, but his right arm and left leg were recovered on the 11th floor, his other two limbs on the 7th floor, and part of his skull in the elevator shaft. And another suicide, leaping from the 23rd floor, ended up with one leg on the 10th floor and his torso on the 9th. Why this dispersion of remains? Because the falling body bounces off a variety of obtruding structures, each breaking off a different part of the body. So would-be suicides should definitely keep away from the Marriott.

Chapter 36
The Next Big Thing

I t BUrsts Upon the sCene. Fans want to attend it, consumers want to buy it, investors want to invest in it before word gets out. It excites, it maddens, it intoxicates. Above all, it is something startlingly new, astonishingly different. And it can make the world better … or worse.

No, I don't mean the entrepreneur-led charitable foundation of that name that seeks to empower young entrepreneurs to take on the world, admirable a goal as that is. Nor do I mean any number of novels and high-tech gadgets and other stuff marketed online as "the next big thing." I mean a rich variety of breakthrough inventions, styles, fashions, and fads that swept New York and the nation, if not the world, changing, or seeming to change, the way we live. New York seems to be a magnet for the new, the startling, and the revolutionary. Let's have a look at some of the Next Big Things of the past.

Fulton's steamboat, 1807

In 1807 Robert Fulton's pioneer *North River Steamboat,* later rechristened the *Clermont,* made the round trip on the Hudson River from

New York to Albany and back in an amazing thirty-two hours. Amazing because, prior to this, the Hudson River sloops, sailing upstream against the current and often against wind and tide as well, took as much as three days to get to Albany. Steamboats revolutionized traffic on the waterways of America and the world, bringing distant places closer together. In New York State they let New York City legislators get to the state capital expeditiously, so they could pursue their legislative schemes and stratagems, and try to keep upstate lawmakers, whom they termed "hayseeds," from neglecting or abusing their beloved Babylon on the Hudson. Fulton's steamboat was the beginning of a revolution in travel.

Jenny Lind, 1850

Promoted shrewdly and outrageously by P.T. Barnum, the master of humbug, the Swedish coloratura became a sensation in America. Citizens who knew little or nothing about coloratura sopranos suddenly felt an intense need to hear the Swedish Nightingale warble her magical notes. Thousands thronged the piers to witness her arrival on September 1, some of them suffering bruises and bloody noses in the process; a fatal crush was narrowly avoided. To get her through the crowd, Barnum's coachman had to clear the way with his whip. As for her first performance on September 11 at Castle Garden on the Battery, she astonished the packed audience with her vocal feats. All tickets having been sold already at auction, some people without tickets hired rowboats and rowed out into the harbor to hear her from there, faintly but distinctly. Never before had a singer so entranced the public. But then, never before had a singer had P.T. Barnum as a promoter.

The Hoopskirt, 1856

When news reached these shores that Eugénie, the Empress of the French, had adopted a new style of dress, the hoopskirt, averaging some three yards in width, the fashionable women of New York and the nation simply had to add this marvel of technology to their wardrobe. The factories of New York bustled and hummed accordingly, turning out up to four thousand a day. For the next ten years or so, the ladies labored to maneuver through narrow doorways and to sit gently and comfortably in these cagelike monstrosities of fashion. Then word came that the Empress of the French now favored quite another style, the bustle, which spelled the end of the hoopskirt. Why the empress embraced the hoopskirt has been variously explained. One version says that she had bad legs and wanted to hide them. Another says that, being pregnant with the Prince Imperial, the son and presumed heir of Emperor Napoleon III, she wanted to conceal the swelling and appear svelte and elegant.

The Black Crook, 1866

It opened on September 12 at Niblo's Garden, a huge theater on Broadway, and ran for a record 474 performances. A heady brew of a melodrama with a hodgepodge of a plot, it featured a scheming villain who contracted to sell souls to the devil in exchange for magical powers. There was a kidnapped heroine to be rescued by a hero; a fairy queen who appeared as a dove and was rescued from a serpent; a grotto with swans, nymphs, and sea gods that rose magically out of the floor; a devil appearing and disappearing in bursts of red light; fairies lolling on silver couches in a silver rain; angels dropping from the clouds in gilded chariots; a "baby ballet" with children; a fife and drum corps; and the raucous explosion of a cancan with two hundred shapely legs kicking high and exposing their frothy underthings and gauze-clad derrieres. When, at the end of the five-hour spectacle, the cast took their curtain calls before a wildly applauding audience, they were cheered by leering old men in the three front rows who pelted them with roses.

Denounced from pulpits as "devilish heathen orgies" and "sins of Babylon," *The Black Crook* was a smashing success, revived often on Broadway and touring the country for years. Some see it as the origin of both the Broadway musical and burlesque.

Edison's incandescent light, 1882

At 3:00 p.m. on September 4, 1882, Thomas Edison flicked a switch at his Pearl Street power plant in downtown Manhattan. Illuminated suddenly were the Stock Exchange, the offices of the nation's largest newspapers, and certain private residences, including that of financial mogul J.P. Morgan. "I have accomplished all that I promised," announced the Wizard of Menlo Park.

The miracle of lighting by electricity had been demonstrated in New York, but throughout the nation the public held back, having heard reports of horses being shocked and workmen electrocuted. Insisting that electric light was clean, healthy, and efficient, not requiring the sprawling, foul-smelling facilities needed to provide gas for gas lighting, Edison staged an Electric Torch Light Parade where 4,000 men marched through Manhattan, their heads adorned with illuminated light bulbs connected to a horse-drawn, steam-powered generator. The marchers weren't electrocuted, proving that electricity was safe, and the public was slowly won over. Hotels, shops, restaurants, and brothels soon became radiant with light.

First U.S. auto fatality, 1899

On September 13, 1899, Henry Hale Bliss, a real estate dealer, was struck by an electric-powered taxi while getting off a streetcar at West 74th Street and Central Park West, and knocked to the ground. Rushed to a hospital, he died the following morning, the first such fatality in the nation. The taxi driver was arrested and charged with manslaughter, but was acquitted on the grounds of having exhibited no malice or negligence. All of which is a reminder that the Next Big Thing can bring perils as well as benefits. Installed on the centennial of the accident, a plaque commemorating his death now marks the spot.

The Armory Show, 1913

The International Exhibition of Modern Art, held at the 69th Regiment Armory on Lexington Avenue between 25th and 26th Streets, introduced avant-garde European art to Americans, who were mostly used to realism. The show shocked visitors with a heavy dose of Fauvism, Cubism, and Futurism. Especially jolting to their eyeballs was Marcel Duchamp's *Nude Descending a Staircase, No. 2,* which expressed motion through a succession of superimposed images not of human limbs, but of conical and cylindrical abstractions in brown, a double blast of Cubism and Futurism. Organized by the Association of American Painters and Sculptors, this assemblage of 1,300 works, including a fair number of nudes, was more than some could take. Accusations of quackery, insanity, immorality, and anarchy multiplied, parodies and cartoons mocked the show, and former president Theodore Roosevelt declared, "That's not art!" But the civil authorities declined to close the exhibition down, and Americans began adjusting to the startling, radical, nerve-jolting, and precedent-shattering phenomenon known as modern art.

The Charleston, 1923

It burst upon the nation when a tune called "The Charleston" ended the first act of the Broadway show *Runnin' Wild,* and the all-black cast did an exuberant, fast-stepping dance that grabbed the audience, the city, and the nation, and then went on, some say, to become the most popular dance of all time. (I demur: what about the waltz?) The song's African American composer, James P. Johnson, had first seen the then-unnamed dance danced in 1913 in a New York cellar dive frequented by blacks from Charleston,

South Carolina, who danced and screamed all night. Inspired, Johnson then composed several numbers for the dance, including the one made popular by the musical. But the dance itself, which made the tango seem tame and the waltz antiquated, has been traced back to the Ashanti tribe of the African Gold Coast. The dance was brought to this country by slaves, and after emancipation African Americans seeking jobs in the North brought it to Chicago and New York, where Johnson discovered it.

The dance spread like fever. Dance halls and hotels featured Charleston contests, and ads in New York papers seeking a black cook, maid, waiter, or gardener insisted, "Must be able to do the Charleston," so they could teach their employers the dance. Hospitals throughout the country began admitting patients complaining of "Charleston knee." An evangelist in Oregon called it "the first step toward hell." When three floors above a dance club in Boston collapsed, killing fifty patrons, it was blamed on the vibrations of Charleston dancers, causing the mayor to ban the dance from all public dance halls. But the more the dance was censured or banned, the more popular it became; the whole nation was "Charleston mad." (Ragtime, then jazz, then the Charleston: the African-American contribution to American pop culture has been phenomenal.)

And now, a personal note. I discovered the Charleston when I saw *The Boyfriend,* a frothy 1954 Broadway musical that recreated and spoofed the musicals of the 1920s, while vaulting Julie Andrews into stardom. Ever since, having been raised on the waltz and the foxtrot, I've wanted to do the Charleston, but never found anyone to teach me. Finally, thanks to two charming young teachers on You Tube, I learned a basic step or two, which I have done wildly in my apartment, swinging my arms and humming to myself some jazzy music probably snatched from *The Boyfriend.* I urge anyone in the mood for a bit of craziness to learn, at least a little bit, this wild and crazy dance. It banishes tedium, relieves depression, and incites joy.

New York World's Fair, 1939-1940

Covering 1,200 acres in Flushing Meadows Park in Queens, it exposed 44 million visitors to "the World of Tomorrow," as embodied in the Trylon, a soaring 610-foot spire, and the Perisphere, a huge sphere housing a diorama depicting a utopian city of the future. The fair's modernistic vision of the future was meant to lift the spirits of the country, which was just barely emerging from the Great Depression; also it would bring business to New York. (Little did the optimistic planners realize that the world was about to be convulsed by World War II.)

Exhibits included the Westinghouse Time Capsule, a tube buried on the fair's site and containing writings by Albert Einstein and Thomas Mann, copies of *Life Magazine,* a Mickey Mouse watch, a Kewpie doll, a pack of Camel cigarettes, and other goodies meant to convey the essence of twentieth-century American culture. A Book of Record deposited with the Smithsonian Institution in Washington contained instructions for locating the buried capsule, the text of which was to be translated into future languages with the passage of time. One indeed wonders what future generations will think of us when, if all goes as planned, they locate and open the buried capsule a few thousand years from now and find a Kewpie doll.

Also featured at the fair was Westinghouse's Electro the Moto-Man, a 7-foot robot that talked and even smoked cigarettes, and an appearance by Superman, or whoever was impersonating him. A General Motors pavilion housed an astonishing Futurama exhibit of the U.S. of tomorrow, showing a fourteen-lane interstate highway with divided lanes crossing various terrains, farms for artificially produced crops, rooftop platforms for flying machines, and pedestrian zones in cities. Other attractions included an IBM pavilion with electric typewriters and a fantastic "electric calculator," a Billy Rose Aquacade with synchronized swimmers, and a Salvador Dalí pavilion with scantily clad performers posing as statues.

The Dalí exhibit and some neighboring girlie shows prompted complaints, and the New York Vice Squad on occasion raided the Amusement Area, but these tributes to the world of today were never quite shut down. As for the World of Tomorrow, some of it, such as robots and computers, has come to pass, but a lot has not, showing once again the near impossibility of accurately predicting the future.

The Beatles, 1964

On February 7, 1964, the now legendary foursome, then newly popular in Great Britain, arrived at New York's Kennedy Airport. There, to their astonishment, they were greeted by 4,000 fans held back by police barriers, and 200 journalists. Intensifying anticipation of their arrival were five million posters distributed throughout the nation to announce their coming, and the phenomenal success of their song "I Want to Hold Your Hand," which had sold a million and a half copies in just three weeks. Grinning and waving cheerily, the lads from Liverpool were immediately subjected to a chaotic press conference where they played the journalists for straight men.

"What do you think of Beethoven?" one reporter asked.

"Great," replied Ringo Starr. "Especially his poems."

After an hour of this banter they were put into limousines, one per Beatle, and driven into the city to the sumptuous Plaza Hotel at Fifth Avenue and Central Park South, where a ten-room suite on the 12th floor had been reserved for "four English gentlemen." The sedate Plaza didn't know what had hit it, as Beatles fans—mostly hysterical young women—ran against traffic to the hotel, eager to get even the barest glimpse of the Fab Four in their collarless sleek mod suits, their young faces topped by pudding-bowl haircuts that provoked much comment, not all of it positive, from the press. BEATLES 4 EVER proclaimed an outsized sign that the fans held aloft, as they chanted "We want the Beatles" and screamed and wept, and sometimes fainted from excitement. Their idols reveled in the hotel's luxury but felt besieged, their suite guarded by round-the-clock guards. Two large cartons addressed to the Beatles arrived at the hotel, but each one proved to contain a female fan who, being detected, never reached her goal. A mob of sixty fans got as far as the 12th-floor stairwell before being caught and expelled.

Briefly eluding their fans, the boys were soon riding in Central Park in a horse-drawn carriage, staring in wonder at the city. Their first U.S. TV appearance on the Ed Sullivan show on February 9 was watched by an estimated 73 million viewers, this author among them, though their music was barely heard over the screams of the teenage girls in the audience. Continuing their ten-day tour, on February 11 they gave a concert at the huge Coliseum in Washington attended by 20,000 fans, then the next day two back-to-back performances at Carnegie Hall in New York, where fan hysteria caused the police to close off the surrounding streets. After more concerts, on February 22 they flew back to England, allowing a semblance of normality to return to this city and the whole East Coast.

Meanwhile their singles and albums were selling millions of records, and their first feature-length film, *A Hard Day's Night*, was released in August 1964, a gentle spoof of the whole scene that this author much enjoyed. And later that month the four-some returned for a second tour and played to sold-out houses across the country. Some critics scoffed and quibbled at their music, but it hardly mattered; the foursome now had the young audience firmly in their grip. The renowned conductor Leopold

Stokowski, commenting to an audience of his own at Carnegie Hall, complained that the Beatles' music, which he happened to like, was drowned out by the teen audience's screaming. "If you can't hear them," he asked, "why are they so great?" The answer came at once from a redheaded girl in the audience: "Because they're cuties!" As for the older set, they were probably relieved, in that age of youthful rebellion, to encounter four likable twenty-somethings who didn't threaten anyone. And the twenty-somethings raked in millions.

So what today will be the Next Big Thing? Driverless cars? Robot-operated factories? A cure for cancer? Life on Mars? Your guess is as good as mine. But sooner or later it will come, and when it does, it will astonish, madden, and excite.

Source Notes

MUCh oF the inFormation in this book I gleaned from various online sources, too numerous to mention here. Some of it comes from personal experience. Only the major online or printed sources are cited here.

Information on witches in New York comes in part from Sanam Yar's article "Witchcraft in the #Me Too Era," in the Metropolitan section of the *New York Times* of August 19, 2018.

Cited in "The Rich," the *Forbes* lists of the 400 richest people for 2015 and 2018 are available online. How TV shows try to convey the lives of the ultrawealthy is described in Alexis Soloski's article "In Pursuit of That Billionaire Look," in the Arts & Leisure section of the *New York Times* of Sunday, March 17, 2019.

For information on Evan Blum's collection of artifacts in "Construction and Destruction," I am indebted to Corey Kilgannon's article "A Haven for New York Relics Saved from the Trash Heap. In Connecticut," in the *New York Times* of June 14, 2016.

In "Dying," the article mentioned on dying alone is "The Lonely Death of George Bell," by N.R. Kleinfeld, on the front page of the Sunday edition of the *New York Times* of October 17, 2015. It is memorable.

In the section "Our Thoroughfares," much of the nineteenth-century information comes from original sources that I consulted when doing background research for my biographies on Daniel Drew and Madame Restell.

In "Broadway," information on Upper Broadway comes from an article by Sam Roberts entitled "Broadway Time Machine" in the Weekend Arts II section of the *New York Times* of June 15, 2018.

In "Wall Street," the article on Wall Street trading is "For the Love of Money," by Sam Polk, in the *New York Times* of January 19, 2014.

In the chapter "Lady Liberty," for information on Emma Lazarus and the building of the Statue of Liberty I am especially indebted to Tyler Anbinder, *City of Dreams: The 400-Year Epic History of Immigrant New York* (Houghton Mifflin Harcourt, 2016), an impressive and masterful account of the role of immigrants in the history of New York City.

In "Cemetery Wars," the article quoting Richard Moylan is "Green-Wood Is the Brooklyn Cemetery with a Velvet Rope," by Gina Bellafante, in the *New York Times* of October 30, 2015.

"Along the Docks in the 1870s" is based on the article "A Day on the Docks" in *Scribner's Monthly* of May 1879, which I read on microfilm.

About the Author

CLIFFORD BROWDER is a longtime resident of New York, living in the West Village high above the Magnolia Bakery of "Sex and the City" fame. He has published two biographies; two nonfiction titles about New York and New Yorkers; and four historical novels in his ongoing Metropolis series of historical fiction set in nineteenth-century New York. *New Yorkers* is his third nonfiction work inspired by posts from his blog, "No Place for Normal: New York." His blog and all his fiction and nonfiction deal with the wild, crazy, and profoundly creative city of New York. His poetry has appeared in numerous small reviews, both online and in print. He has never owned a car, a television, or a cell phone, never kills spiders, and is fascinated by slime molds and the mushroom known as Destroying Angel. Mostly vegan, he eats garlic for its culinary and medicinal values, and its reputed ability to keep off vampires. (So far, it seems to be working.)

Acknowledgments

For making this book happen, I am deeply grateful to my design team at 1106 Design, who throughout the process were wonderfully diligent, knowledgeable, and patient. From them, I learned a lot.

I hope you enjoyed this book.
Would you do me a favor?

Like all authors, I rely on online reviews to encourage future sales. Your opinion is invaluable. Would you take a few moments now to share your assessment of my book at the review site of your choice? Be honest, and remember that a review can be a paragraph long, or one or two or three sentences, or even just one word.

Many thanks.